Spirit of Desire

Personal Explorations of Sacred Kink

EDITED BY LEE HARRINGTON

MYSTIC
PRODUCTIONS LLC

Notice

Spirit of Desire: Personal Journeys in Sacred Kink
© 2016 – Second Printing – Mystic Productions Press
© 2010 – First Edition – Lee Harrington – www.PassionAndSoul.com

Published in the United States by Mystic Productions Press, LLC
603 W. Tudor Road Anchorage, AK 99503
www.MysticProductionsPress.com

All authors have retained their original copyright, with permission granted to Mystic Productions LLC for inclusion in this project.

Cover Art by Circle 23
www.Circle23.com

Interior and Exterior Layout by Rob River
www.RobRiver.com

Pictures of Lee Harrington by Darrell Lynn
www.KiltedPhotography.daportfolio.com

ISBN 978-1-942733-80-5
Ebooks: MOBI - 978-1-942733-95-9
ePub - 978-1-942733-96-6
PDF - 978-1-942733-94-2

Previously printed as ISBN 978-0-557-99241-6 – 2010
Spiral-bound edition available upon request from Mystic Productions.

For all the Explorers who came before us;
and for all the Explorers who will find
new paths we have yet to dream into being.

Table of Contents

Into the Spirit of Desire

By Lee Harrington

It came to me in a dream. *Let the tales be told*, a voice whispered across the veil, through the lines, echoing through my flesh. *Let the tales be told*, it said, half in dream and half in the world beyond. *Let the tales be told*.

My book, *Sacred Kink: The Eightfold Paths of BDSM and Beyond*, had just escaped out into the world, carrying my own thoughts on the interactions between the erotic and the profound. After a multi-year labor of love and research, I thought I was done for now. I was wrong. This, this thing, this line between faith and passion… it will not let me go.

So the voice came in the night. *Let the tales be told*, it called out to me, and pulled me into its web. *Let the tales be told*, it moaned and sighed, and I felt its lips fall upon mine in the shadow, in the light. *Let the tales be told*.

And here they are. As is the case with many anthologies, the call went out into the world on stacks of paper, streams of wire and fiber optics. I knew the tales were out there, waiting and hungry to be told. I knew I was not the only one who had had my BDSM, sex, or sensual journeys affect my magic, affect my connection with the divine. But the flood that opened up, I was not ready

for. I held on for dear life as the waves of passion hit against the levy. Until I let go. Until I swam. Until I dove.

I dove into the depths of what came and was astounded. Slices of autobiography filled me with hope. Glimpses of glamour from lives hard-lived shook me to tears. Dreams of desires painted their way across my brow and I felt myself renewed with possibility. And along the way, I got turned on, confounded, shocked, tantalized, and delighted.

Here is the child I have brought forth from the shadows. Here is the collection that I have gathered in the light. Some may sit easier with you, while others may shake you up. Listen to the parts that are uncomfortable – there is wisdom there. Listen to the pieces that resonate within you – there is wisdom there.

There is not a single path to or through Sacred Kink, and through sharing their personal life experiences and true tales, the authors in this anthology prove this to be true once again. There are more routes to the top of the mountain than our mortal minds can imagine, and herein are thirty-three of those winding routes to a vista that has been lived. These are not pinnacles, not things to be mimicked and mirrored, unless the path calls you as well. But they are sign posts, road maps, treasures along the path.

We begin by journeying into yoga as a route towards being present in sexuality, then struggle through faith and relationship identity with leather and boots as our guide. A psychic vampire lifts the veil on the line between energy and lust, while two pagan women weave a spell of ownership into flesh and astral form. Genderfucking and the roles of sex and gender come to the forefront, and tricksters dance into our consciousness to prod struggling supplicants on their sojourn of hooks and blood.

Disability is examined through context, through sexual exploration and personal ordeal, and priestesses discover their voice with a tab on their tongue and wrists pinned overhead. Sacred whores share the worst of their days and their struggle with the red light, before we turn the page and find the priest for a sacred journey caught up in his own revelation. We are asked what kind of mindfuck scene God(dess) is doing with us anyway, then slink into back alley ways to walk alongside a human animal on the prowl.

Love and kink find eloquence between lines of poetry, and then the beast comes out to roam, looking for destruction and rending flesh. We lift our eyes to the monkey king Hanuman, then struggle through the emotional aftermath of nailing someone to a cross. Sorrow pours out through moans at a Beltane fire, while enlightenment is found on the long, slow path of erotic slavery.

Online desires turn to magic through keys and blades, while across the country fists find messages from the messiah of self-awareness. A professional dominatrix from Mexico reveals the clues for being the guide along our path, while a devotee of Roman and Celtic divinities examines the academic and deeply personal arguments around consent and our relationships with deity. Race and humanity are painfully explored and forgiven, and in the shadow, many souls living in one body journey into service and surrender.

Travel to Malaysia and back to the Bay Area to dance with bells and hooks, then into the middle of the United States to bear witness to what helped one woman come to peace with her identity as a good Christian. Caring for the predators amongst us is looked at with humor and compassion, and heartache leads to two years of self-exploration and coming to a new kink identity. A long passage to an ordeal leads to personal growth and the removal of masks, a lifelong fascination with a dark Goddess creates a trail of orgasms and passion.

A Master finds faith in love again. Humiliation leads to revelation. We find safety in the arms of a service top, who will hold our fear for us as they walk with us side by side.

Walk with us, side by side. Hold our hands, you are not alone. Whether you have climbed your own mountain, or have never considered leaving the safety of home, you are not alone. *Let the tales be told*, the whispers said in the dark. *Let the tales be told*, the voices cried from the light. And here they are. Thirty-three journeys into Spirit. Into Desire. Into Sacred Kink.

Yours in Passion and Soul,

Lee Harrington
www.PassionAndSoul.com
October 2010
Phoenix, Arizona, USA

And Right Now:
Giving In Through Yogic Expansion

By Galeogirl

My yoga practice began when I was still a teenager, studying ballet and modern dance. Yoga helped me unknot painful muscles and enhanced my ability to strike mind-boggling dance poses. It was a way to exercise and, for many years, that was its sole place in my life. I used yoga as gentle self-care after I strained myself with dancing and all of the other punishing pursuits I undertook.

I drifted away from yoga for several years until I was called back to the mat in the aftermath of severe chronic pain brought on by my overly athletic antics of youth along with a series of injuries to my hips and spine that left me barely able to walk. My body had gained a lot of weight and I hated how I looked. An eight-year relationship had gone up in flames, and I found myself overweight, depressed, and wondering if I was going to be able to walk unassisted by age 40. I once again turned to yoga, my gentle self-care tool, to alleviate my pain and regain my mobility.

It was during this time that I also started noticing the more subtle changes that yoga had wrought in me. I realized that on the nights when I practiced yoga, depression's claws could not sink so deeply into me. Anxiety could be calmed with my breath. My mind was focused and alert without feeling the terrible self-induced pressure of my life-long tendency toward perfectionism. Most importantly, I found myself living more and more in the present moment, spending less time sifting through the past or pining for the future. Without being truly aware of the exact moment of its occurrence, I had made the transition from yoga as exercise to yoga as a lifestyle.

I had no idea how far-reaching these internal changes would be until one night in scene, when I found myself standing with my hands planted on the bench behind me, bracing myself, my legs spread wide as his single-tail left fiery lines of pain on my breasts, cunt, and inner thighs. I was sweating and shaking, near tears, held in place only by a desire to please my partner, but hating the stinging sensation, struggling with the pain. My tight muscles wouldn't let my chest open up and breathe, so I was panting, trying to endure. I was mere seconds away from safewording.

"I could just give in," I thought, chiding myself silently for my inability to submit like we both wanted me to. My mind latched onto the words "give in" as some sort of lifeline. I started to breathe the words, chanting them quietly as a mantra in my mind as his whip came down again, and again, and again. I steadied my breathing around those words, "give in," repeating them with each inhalation and exhalation. Finally, surrender flooded over me like a cleansing wave, calming my fears. It let me breathe, giving my body a chance to release the endorphins that it needed to deal with the intensity of the whipping so that I could ride the energy all the way through to the end.

There was nothing in the world but he and I and the energy we were sharing. *Give in.* The pain that I had struggled with transformed and became a sensation that made me purr with ecstasy. *Give in.* I found myself arching up to the whip, opening my legs further for it, until I ended up having a body- and soul-shaking orgasm. *Give in.* I came screaming as the wicked tongue of his whip snaked against my panty-clad cunt, the tip snapping sharply against my clit several times in rapid succession. *Give in.* It hurt and felt so good all at the same time. *Give in.* I came so hard that I felt my juices running down my thighs and he never laid a hand on me. *Give in.*

As I was basking in the afterglow, I thought to myself, "How did I do that? How do I do it again?"

My post-scene contemplation made me aware that I had subconsciously taken some of my yogic disciplines – rhythmic breathing and chanting – and used them to transform my sexual experience from something challenging and negative to a scene that still plays out in some of my hottest masturbation fantasies. Yoga had entered my sex life and I liked it. A lot.

I wanted to learn how to make that level of presence and openness a part of every sexual experience, so I went to the library and picked up some yoga books; not the books of poses – those catalogs of human flexibility – but the books on yoga philosophy and spirituality. It was in one of these tomes that I discovered the term "the here-now mind," which is when you are living in the moment without thinking unnecessarily about the past or the future, without applying expectations, history, or internal monologues, just accepting the moment as it is. This was revelatory for me. It was exactly what I had been longing for from my sexual experiences, that elusive place of focus that I had sometimes touched but not been able to sustain, those moments when I was so deeply in my body that my mind was quiet and I was just feeling and being. Sweet, delicious surrender.

I started consciously applying yogic breathing (*pranayama*) and my "here-now mind" to my sex life after I began studying the mental aspects of yoga and meditation. At first the level of intimacy that comes from being truly present, in BDSM play in particular, was terrifying. How could I be this present, this in tune with my experience? However, I persisted, wanting to come to a place where being present in the here and now was a constant in my sex life. Instead of going inside and disassociating myself from pain to endure it, I was learning to breathe into pain, embracing it and all of its sensations and emotions, even the uncomfortable ones.

I began inviting the whole experience of my sexual journey, opening myself to it. Once I got past the initial, vulnerable "oh fuck, what am I doing?" feeling, I realized that I was not only okay, I was wonderful! The play was raw and juicy, wild, intimate, hot. I had had a great sex life before, but now I'm having better sex than I ever thought possible. Even with partners I don't fuck, I end up feeling pretty thoroughly fucked when I play because my openness and presence increases my already prodigious ability to experience so much pleasure. Repeat orgasms, including non-genital orgasms through breathing, erogenous zone stimulation, and sharing energy with others now causes a wonderful, shared whole-body catharsis that leaves my partners and I glowing at the end of a scene.

My every sensual act now is born out of a place of love, happiness, and thoughtful attention. Delving deeper into my practice has brought me to a place of radical self-acceptance, freeing me from so many of the anxieties and stressors that used to prevent me from living in the moment, connecting wholly to my partners and my desires. Yoga has transformed me from the outside in, and I am no longer the woman I was when I first started this journey. I have a strong, pain-free body; a calm, quiet mind; a hotter, wetter, more intimate sex life; and fuller, richer emotional connections than I have ever experienced before. I have never been happier or more confident than I am right now. *And right now.* And right now.

Namaste.

Soul Stitching

By Sassafras Lowrey

I am the street-worn boot tread walked away by travels, by running away from my fears and then later striding steadily towards them. Each intentional step brings me closer to something I still cannot yet define. In his hands I glow with the same shine I bring to his boots. I am not dress boot or titleholder finest; I am lived-in boots that have walked through the elements. I am layers in scuffs, gouges marring the surface in need of being worked out.

I've searched for spirituality and I have no answers other than the thick and sour taste of boot polish, and the scraping of bristles against my tongue leaving smears across my nose. Leather is the closest to religion that I've ever gotten. Boots are the one place where my service does not tremble. Here I'm able to turn off my mind, push past the anxiety, let kneecaps sink into floorboards. Pain melts together with memory, mixing with surrender, deeper than the memory of my birth parents' tarnished faith.

I finger boot laces the way my grandmother clutches her rosary beads. Begging the boot, its wearer, our mutual owner to deliver me to self. When he found me shivering within my outer angry, crusty punk boi exterior, he read me picture books, tied me up, bought me Playdough, pushed me to my limits. It was through his care that I was able to reach a place of centeredness. When he found me, my gender was boi. Through the years that has shifted, but no matter what gender I've called home, even as a high femme I've always been, always will be his boy. As his boy I've been taught that power can be safe, that it/he can cradle, caress, tear me down and build up my shine so high that for the first time, I can see myself truly reflecting.

Through my submission I found myself able to begin searching for spirituality. I could not in earnest begin that journey until I was his boy. I could not begin a calm search until I had a Daddy to guide me. I need stability in order to do this kind of searching. I needed containment, and centering. I need to know that I will not be allowed to set my own course towards destruction. Containment means that I am not journeying on my own, that there is always someone holding my hand and keeping me from spiraling out on fear masquerading as spiritual practice. I am little and need to know that I am always safe.

I have a fraught relationship with spirituality. I've longed for something I could truly believe in since childhood. As I grew my searching would pause, as I would find a belief system that would momentarily pique my interest, meet my immediate needs. Religion and I don't have good histories together. I have, as much as I try to deny it, inherited my mother's addictive personality. It's the root of why I don't drink, why I've never been high. Religion became my acceptable form of addiction.

Spirituality has also not treated me well. Early on it justified my parents' abuse, fed my insecurities, and enforced my self-deprecation. I was unaware of the power I surrendered, submerging my submissive heart into my religion of the moment and watching my body and mind falter. I was never good enough for salvation. I would spend hours on my knees in tears over the smallest of infractions I believed would be displeasing to my higher power. As I experimented with new faiths I remained hyper-aware of my sins or transgressions. In my mind, there was no atonement possible.

I don't trust myself with religion. Though I am not my stepfather using total devotion to wield the larger power of violence against my family, the memory is still there. We don't share blood, but I was his child, and I've used religion as a weapon turned inward to convince myself that I am not worthy. I strove towards perfection and failed. Collapsing into shame, I felt that I would never be worthy of being loved, of being cared for.

I went religiously sober. I had to no choice. Like any addict I was incapable of recreational exploration, unable to set limits, I couldn't be safe with it. I chose to lock away my yearnings for spirituality in the name of self-preservation. It was not a journey I was fit to take unchaperoned.

I finally found that possibility with leather, carefully beginning the journey from a fresh perspective. Leather is what keeps me safe. It is the connection with my Daddy that grants me the freedom to search by defining the parameters of that journeying. He is, most of all, protecting me from myself. He does not give me permission to step into my susceptibility towards destruction in the name of salvation.

My seeking does not come in books. I do not step into churches or temples. It is those sorts of places that would make it far too easy for me to slide backwards into a journey based on self-destruction. Working on his boots is the place where I wander. As my fingers work polish into hide I find silence, I push my mind past the triggers that quiet brings. This is the closest I've gotten to what others call peace, what I imagine meditation must feel like for those who can in more traditional settings shut out the noise that permeates our minds.

Surrendering self to the quiet and calm pulls every one of my triggers. Letting knees press through floorboards, I force myself to remain present, focused on the task at hand. As my fingers stroke leather, my tongue gritty, I begin to understand myself, to tentatively search for spirituality within the safety of the world he sculpts for me. This time the journey carries no hidden agendas of self-destruction. It is safe because I know he would never allow me to lose his property.

I've been hunting for religion for as long as I can remember, searching for something I can do more than pretend to believe in. That doesn't make me feel hokey, that doesn't leave my actions seeming forced. On some level I crave spirituality with a similar depth of longing as I had for leather from my earliest memories of desire. This is the kind of longing that wraps your heart in intricate bondage, from which there is no escape. Both, perhaps, are connected to my core fears of abandonment and my strong desire to be cared for, but I believe it goes back to a far deeper, less damaged place than that. So far I haven't found the answers, but I know that leather is bringing me closer. Service and surrender has been the path that let me flirt with the edges. Leather is the only place where I truly surrender, where I trust — something I shy away from in nearly all other contexts.

This is a journey that I could not undertake alone. It's only possible because someone with whom I am deeply connected and who has the capacity to guide me is holding my hand. My Daddy loves and cares for even my most damaged places. Slowly I've come to understand that it is the journey, not the destination that may, in fact, be most transformative for me. I am his cherished possession. He's spent years building back my shine, and stitching my soul back together, replacing the torn stitched lacing, pulling tight my worn tread and scuffed leather.

Hungry for You

By Michelle Belanger

I step behind her and seize her by the hair, pulling her head back against my shoulder to expose the smooth line of her neck. With one powerful arm, I crush her to me, making it very clear that there is no escape. I can see the flutter of her pulse and it races a little faster as I bend my lips close, barely brushing the edge of her skin.

I do not have to bite her to get what I want, but still I place my mouth around that pulse, drinking the sensation in. She shivers and arches into me as I bear down with my teeth – hard enough to be felt, but never hard enough to crush or rend her flesh. The bite is a nod to the archetype I embody, but it is also a reminder that I am the predator here. I am the one that takes. She is the one that yields.

With that contact, I feel so much more than simply the rhythm of her blood as it rushes beneath her skin: I feel the electric jolt of her life-force. Like lightning, it lances through me, making every point of contact between our two bodies thrum with a warm promise of something deeper than flesh. I become profoundly aware of the aching, yearning sensation in the center of my chest, just beneath my ribs. It yawns like a hunger, yet it is so much more profound than the hunger of the body, for I can feel this to the very center of my soul. For a moment, the intensity of it makes me weak in the knees, but I ride out the sensation, and as I do so, I grip my donor more tightly to me.

I am a vampire, and while I do not need her blood to survive, I need the essence of her life. For the next little while, she and I will be bound in a dance of energy and flesh, emotion and sensation that runs harsh and sensual by turns. We may never lose a single article of clothing, and yet the eroticism of the exchange is inescapable, for I must penetrate to the very core of her energy in order to sate that trembling hunger within me. And when I am finished, echoes of her thoughts and feelings will linger in my mind for days, connecting us in a numinous bond that cannot be adequately described to those who live in the prosaic world of the mainstream...

The inherent eroticism of feeding is the dirty little secret of the vampire subculture. When modern vampires were just beginning to coalesce into a community, one of the most strident criticisms of our hungers was that vampirism was nothing more than a simple sexual kink. This sexual element was seen to invalidate the legitimacy of vampirism as both a condition and an identity. In the eyes of its detractors, vampirism was nothing more than a delusion rooted in the flesh. There were no mystical or supernatural elements to the activity, and people like myself who chose to call themselves vampires were seen to be sorely misguided perverts and just short of psychotic.

As a reaction to this criticism, many modern vampires (myself included) strove to draw a clear line between vampiric feeding and sexual kink, stressing instead the non-physical and numinous aspects of the vampiric act – the psychic connection, the energetic exchange (and for blood drinkers, the mystic qualities of the blood). For a time, the New York-based vampire network known as the Sanguinarium went so far as to describe vampiric feeding in overtly religious terms, calling the exchange between vampire and donor "Communion."

And yet, the lines between body and energy remained blurry – at least behind closed doors. It's no coincidence that the vast majority of vampire clubs in major urban centers such as Los Angeles and New York also shared strong ties with BDSM and kink events. Power exchange and energy exchange go hand in hand.

And yet, how can one explain what is really going on to someone who has never experienced the potency of the act of vampirism firsthand? If a person's perception and understanding is limited to what happens merely between the

physical bodies of the participants, then the vampiric exchange looks mainly like two people touching — sometimes chastely, sometimes not so chastely. But this perception is superficial at best. In order to fully understand the layers of sensation and meaning, one has to at least accept the reality of energy — a subtle essence that courses within and beyond the flesh, an essence that not only can be sensed but can be touched, manipulated, caressed, and consumed. If you can accept that energy is real, that certain activities enhance it, and that some individuals have a profound hunger for it, then and only then can a real understanding of vampirism begin.

I am a vampire. I need to feed, to take the energy of other people. When I fail to meet my need for energy, my health suffers. I grow irritable and lethargic, and eventually I get sick. For those first coming to understand vampirism, this symptomatic paradigm — vampirism as an illness or health condition — is often the easiest to grasp. Physical symptoms provide a clear motivation for a vampire's need to feed. No one likes to suffer, so a vampire's feeding seems justified, if perhaps a bit mysterious. Yet the drive to drink the energy of others is so much more than a need for mere physical maintenance. It's not just that my heart starts to flutter and beat irregularly in my chest when I go too long without feeding; it's that some part of my soul, the essence of what I perceive as my Self, begins to suffer. There is a deep and restless yearning to touch something more than flesh, the reach deeply into another being and kiss the fire smoldering at the core of their soul.

I don't use language like that often, because to an ordinary person, it so easily sounds like self-aggrandizing hyperbole. More often than not, I find myself trying to explain myself — and all other psychic vampires by proxy — to "ordinary" people who hardly understand energy, let alone vampirism. But this means that these people only ever get an incomplete picture of what my vampirism means to me. In the interest of promoting understanding, I can boil it down to material essentials, but there are whole realms of sensation and experience that are lost in translation.

If you've never touched another human being past the limits of their flesh, then try to imagine what it is like. Every person burns around you like a lambent flame, with heat and light radiating past the lamp of their skin. You may not be able to see this literally, but you can sense it on a profound and undeniable level. They all burn with inner fire, and you are a moth, drawn inexorably to that flame. Only, unlike a moth, this fire doesn't burn you. The closer you get to it, and the deeper you are able to kiss it, the more it invigorates you, enriching your very perception of that level of reality. In some respects, you are that fire, and by touching it in others, you burn more brightly still.

A lover who is unaware of this aspect of existence or who, for some reason, is unable to perceive it, is inevitably a disappointment. I can touch flesh, and there is nothing inherently wrong with the flesh of the body. But so much of me lives *beyond* that flesh — my senses, my experiences, my own desires — that to be limited to simply interacting on a physical level is like cutting off my arms and my legs. It is such a severe limitation of what comes naturally to me that it's painful. People ask me, "Why call yourself a psychic vampire and not something else?" This is one of the reasons. The ability to perceive on that level beyond the flesh is what most people mean by the word "psychic," and I have never met anyone who shares my hungers who isn't intensely, profoundly psychic, and psychic to the point where they *need* to be able to connect on that numinous level with others. We hunger for the connection as much as we hunger for the life.

There is no way to adequately express the vampiric exchange without involving that psychic aspect of perception. Flesh is a part of it, but only because the flesh is a vessel for the otherworldly fire which courses through the subtle pathways alongside nerves and veins. Sex can be a part of it as well, but again, sex is not the ultimate end of the process. Sensual contact as well as sexual contact are both gateways to the inner realm of that fire. They serve to connect and tune the energy, so the boundaries can dissolve and one person may more easily flow into the other. They are stepping stones to that amazing state of union where the sense of flesh and self and separateness melt away and there is just the touching of souls, each to each.

The real magick of the vampiric exchange is that it often takes very little to surpass those barriers. A touch here, the rasp of nails on flesh there, a firm tug on the hair at the nape of the neck, hot lips pressed harsh against the pulse in

the throat… There is penetration and consummation, but on a level beyond the body. The bodies can be swept up and carried away by the sensation as well – and often are, regardless of any direct stimulation of specifically sexual organs. In vampiric exchange, there is no need for such limitations, and why bother with them when the resulting connection results in tides of ecstasy that course through every fiber in wave after crashing wave?

The hunger I experience as a vampire is not merely for the base sustenance of people's life-force. That's a part of it, of course, and it's a part that must be satisfied. I can subsist on little sips of vital energy skimmed from the surface of others. I can drink in the ambient energy of a room full of people, and this will meet my needs for subsistence. But it won't – and can't – satisfy. There is a deeper need.

The real drive is to stick my energetic tongue into the very heart of another person, not only to drink their life, but to feel their core essence wash over me. My need is not only to take some of their vitality to support myself, but to work my way under their skin until I can feel what they feel, hear their thoughts, and have portions of their memories echo in my mind. There is no way in which this is not mystical and transformational for both parties involved. In order to steal this sacred fire, a part of me must penetrate deeply into them, and inevitably, traces of my own energy are left behind.

There is a dynamic of dominance and submission in this energetic exchange that translates directly into the BDSM paradigm of power exchange. In BDSM, one person often yields power to another through consensual activities of rough sex, bondage, pain, or humiliation. The various activities serve as gateways to open the yielding partner to the power exchange. Used by a skilled vampire, these activities can help a donor break down their own internal barriers, leading to an incandescent release of intense and profoundly satisfying energy. It is a shamanic use of sensation to throw wide the gates of flesh.

The prize I carry away from deep feeding brings with it a powerful *gnosis* of the other person. The connection thus forged links us in mind and spirit for days and even weeks afterward. In my own personal belief system, when the exchange is profound enough, it can forge a bond that carries over lifetimes. It is not uncommon for me to dream of the other person, and for them to feel my presence in their dreams. Accurate information can be gleaned from these dreamwalks, and it's not unusual for further energetic exchanges to occur in the dreamspace. Telepathic and empathic content is exchanged long after our physical bodies have separated, and it often takes an effort to prevent such psychic spillage.

This is what never makes it past the white-washed image of psychic vampirism that the majority of us feel comfortable sharing with the rest of the world. I can say that a vampire is a person who needs to regularly and actively take human vital energy in order to maintain their own health and well-being. But that is only a small part of the need. The real hunger has very little to do with the physical body, and its impact on physical health is merely a side effect of something much more profound. Psychic vampirism is deeply entwined with the concept of the soul, for as vampires, we not only can sense this subtle aspect of another person, we are driven to touch it, to know it, and to make a part of it ourselves.

Is it any wonder then that vampirism can be expressed so comfortably within the kink community? Energy exchange and power exchange operate on extremely similar principles – and in many cases, they are one and the same. In the early years of the vampire community, one of the safest places to express and fulfill vampiric hungers (both psychic and sanguine) was within the context of the BDSM community. That community provided a culture of tolerance that encouraged individuals to explore, embrace, and celebrate the many different ways of connecting to others physically and emotionally – as well as energetically.

That culture of tolerance still exists, and it comes with a built-in ethos and etiquette to help manage the complex interactions between consenting adults that often defy mainstream culture's rather simplistic definitions of "relationships." This makes the kink community an ideal arena for ethical psychic vampires to express and fulfill their hungers with willing donors in a positive and guilt-free manner. In BDSM, there is no shame in desire, no original sin lurking in the seeds of our flesh. The only shame exists in not exploring that desire, confronting it, learning its origins, its dirty little secrets, and, in the end, integrating it constructively into the Self. Every vampire should undertake this journey with regards to his or her vampirism. It is one of the better ways to evolve away from stigmatized and symptomatic schemas of vampirism that encourage the vampires to feel ashamed of their hungers. Instead, it can help us to view our vampirism as an empowering quality, a refined and numinous way in which to touch, taste, and know another living being.

And what better place to undertake such a journey than with other people who recognize its transformational power – and who are willing to surrender themselves in body and spirit to help along each stage of growth?

I have swallowed your heart, your sacred fire
I feel you burning deep inside.
Shining, rising, you and I,
twined together in light and wings.

Locked Over My Heart

By layla tromble

Though I am well aware magic cannot happen without intention, I think this spell surprised us both. It is evidence that the universe can sometimes understand one's purpose in ways the individual does not. It came, I think, from my desire to give and her need to take and met in the middle in a place neither of us expected. It sounds so strangely analytical to write about it at all, and yet I feel a certain compulsion to record it, to express the wonder, to somehow make it real in the documentation.

As she began touching my neck lightly with her fingers, tracing the lines where a collar would lay, sweet and heavy against my skin, I could feel it. I can feel it now as I write these words. The weight rests around my throat as solid and real as any metal or leather, the heart-shaped lock we both can see resting against my chest. It is connected to the very energy that runs my body. The simple act of placing it there has hardwired it into me, inextricably bound it to me just as it binds me to her.

Her touch was light against my skin as we created each link in the chain that she would leave around my throat. My devotion, my dedication, my submission to her was evident in my eyes. I opened them and left my most vulnerable self unguarded for her to see. She accepted what I gave and she took that part of me, made it hers, and made me proud to have it. Her power and protection became mine just as my surrender was hers. There was no battle of wills, no war to fight or to win. Dominance was granted with peace and blissful joy at the brushing of her fingertips.

Her touch traveled lightly, leaving bits of herself along my skin until the trail of energy joined in the hollow of my throat. Shared awareness passed between us before either of us spoke. Any words were superfluous, unnecessary as her hand rested near my heart and our eyes met. The sound of the lock sliding into place was just on the edge of audible in the quiet room that had only been filled with the sounds of our breathing.

From that moment I have felt the beauty of her within me each day as I wake. I embrace the joy of her possession. What I give is mine and yet hers, always. Her ownership has shown me the gift of myself. It seems paradoxical, but giving myself to her has allowed me to realize that my power belongs solely to me. She sees my submission as a gift that only I can grant, and through her eyes I have seen it, too. Our combined energies created the collar that lies around my neck, evidence that her dominance would be meaningless without my submission. We could not create the divine beauty of magic without the power we each possess.

When we are together, what we have created becomes something other than simple sexual connection… Her gaze is like a physical touch, her energy presses into my body, into my spirit. The physical touch of her hand goes beyond skin on skin, and there is bliss in the pain and pressure of it, and freedom in my submission, and joy in her dominance. I have been both overwhelmed by and held safe in the knowledge that I belong to her.

I have often heard it said that the submissive has all the power in a D/s dynamic, and yet it seems to me that this cliché is just lip service to a deeper truth. The power of being a submissive is not solely found in the capacity to voice a safeword, but in the act of submitting itself. When I surrender my will to her it is with absolute freedom. My will is mine to give, and in so doing I feel the strength of that choice. Before my collar was around my throat, I struggled to see the value of my spirit, my being. Seeing my precious nature reflected in her eyes allowed me to truly embrace my worth for the first time. Knowing that the collar I wear could not exist without as much commitment and power from me as her has opened my heart and body to the energy I possess.

The sense memory of the moment we created my collar is still concrete for me each time her fingers in their momentary gentleness have brushed softly over the skin of my neck. That simple touch reminds my body of the connection we created, and I respond to that touch in a way that feels like instinct, something baser than consciousness. Electricity never fails to rush over my flesh and it's as though I feel her deep within, her fingers buried in my instantly wet cunt. My breath catches, my heart races, and my knees go weak. Though I feel filled with her, the sensation only makes me hungry for her touch, to prove myself worthy of her.

Whenever her fingers trace the outline of the lock that sits atop and has become a part of my flesh, my body quivers in a soul deep place. This response in me causes her hand to grow more insistent, marking my skin pink with pinches and scratches, trying to leave the message of magic's existence for all to see. As she does so my body responds, and I feel slick wetness between my thighs and make no effort to control the moans and whimpers that are produced by the sensation. She tugs at the energy there, pulling the collar tight around my throat. My body grows perplexed at the pressure that is so clear but does not constrict my breathing.

The power and strength of her touch always inspires an equal response within me, and I feel pressure and passion building inside. She pulls my head up to look into her eyes and no words are necessary. She wants to consume me. She needs my energy, my orgasm, as much as I do. She will take everything that I give, and with that single look I give it all. There is no means of holding back as I feel pleasure rocket through my body. All that I have I give willingly without reservation, my body opens and my energy pours into her.

We exist together in this place, equal in strength and determination if not in position. From the outside it may seem that I simply kneel before her, but kneeling has become my strength and standing was always hers. Neither would hold meaning without the other, and the magic would fade to nothingness without the fuel we both provide to the fires of our spirit. There seems to be no way to describe what has happened between us without waxing poetic, and yet it is as it is. I attempt the expression in sentence and paragraph structure and somehow the words become slippery and incomplete.

She has pointed out to me that it is for just these reasons that poetry was invented and I smile softly and know that in many ways she is correct. And yet, somehow poetry feels like cheating, like only with these words can I see magic's face. I long to hold up the mirror to the true wonder of our joining without flowery appeal. My collar locked in place over my heart, I wish only to express the simple unadorned power of it.

The Godhood of Genderfucking

By Jaki Grier

God for me isn't as much a deity as it is a goal of maintaining an intimate relationship with the universe. Godhood is an attainable feat that requires learning to balance the push and pull of ashe (energy) that everything in the universe holds. In my life, that push and pull of ashe is gendered, and it changes the way I view my body, my sex, and my interactions with the world.

God is a series of connections and dichotomies. God is the gray area of nature as well as the stark contrasts of its natural categories. God created man and woman but first created person who was split into two halves with different types of ashe that swirls inside. A genderfuck is a person who attempts to achieve that original balance that God naturally embodies. Genderfucking is my personal expression of the divine genderless energy that lives inside me. Genderfucking is my ability to open my pussy like a flower and penetrate my lover.

It starts with my outward appearance. I sit in a chair and my partner's eyes wander over my body. There are shiny red pumps that hold my feet tight like a lover's grip. Then my calves, unshaven and muscled, lead up to wide, smooth thighs. All this is hidden under pleated suit pants, and my stance is so wide that my cock can point forward, reaching out while my pussy sirens you into me. My breasts are soft to bring you in and my arms enfold, crushing your breath. My lips are full and glossy with color but my beard tickles your face.

In order to be with me, you have to embrace it all because my confusion is a part of my humanity. I have always felt that confusion is the first step towards understanding. The moment in a person's life where they completely surrender to the idea that they will not fully understand is when a new type of knowledge forms. This knowledge encompasses facts and also allows room for doubt. This is knowledge that allows us as people to be contradictory while still allowing us to become fully realized beings, which is the innate purpose of our humanity. Allowing ourselves to not understand gives us clarity of the mind while grounding ourselves with the reality of our true existence. Genderfucking is about touching my partner with a piece of the problematic parts of my soul. Genderfucking requires me to walk in the fullness of the human experience in an attempt to gain insight into Godliness. My life as a genderfuck embodies this.

To be born a woman and to grow into a neutral being of power was a slow revelation. We are taught by our culture that neutrality means empty or without power. However, being in the middle of opposing forces can place you in great danger or create perfect clarity. Learning the true balance of yourself in the whirlwind is an act that should not be diminished. For me, my journey into myself lead me away from the Christianity of my youth and I was without any context to address my gender identity. Religion was the language I had learned to describe what I am, and without it, I had to start over from the beginning.

In the beginning, I had a vagina and it was good. Then I had a pussy, a cunt, a hole, a snatch. Then I found my clit, lost in the folds of myself, and realized it was just a very, very tiny dick. It isn't much of a leap. Science teaches us that the space between male and female isn't as concrete as we are taught to believe. Much of what we know about biological development teaches us that very few differences set humans into these categories. The thought of my clit as a budding potential cock intrigued me, and I began to think of it as such.

I stepped into a new puberty where I discovered how to use this new body that no one taught me existed.

I stroked my cock. I felt it harden with arousal. I parted my legs as it swelled inside my pants because my cock felt larger than it looked. My pussy would water and my cock would react. That became part of my balance and I began to treat it the way it felt to my mind. I went shopping for a toy cock to sit atop it and that felt closer to what I wanted. I would center my mind as I stepped through the tangled loops of my hardness and pulled my strap-on tight to my body. My cock would mash against the silicone, pushing forward into it and setting off mind-blowing orgasms. As I was exploring my newfound cock energy, I was unknowingly anointing my toy phallus with my own fluids. I claimed it as an extension of my energy, charging it with intent I had no language to express.

It was about two years later that I was introduced to energy work during a class on Spiritual BDSM. I have always had a close relationship with my strap-on, and I began to understand why it was painful to remove my cock after orgasm. It felt disrespectful when my cock was treated like a prop instead of an object of worship. Learning about energy work validated me because it made me realize that other people would understand my personal discovery. I might be crazy but I was no longer alone. In exploring energy work, Soul stopped being a word that meant "my passive conscience that will be judged" and was transformed into a pliable, active aspect of my daily existence. I was using my silicone cock as a container to embrace my true cock energy. For me, the energy of my cock and the energy of my pussy together created an ambiguity that helps me find my place in the universe.

When I play with someone and they see God in me, it is based on a bridge of commonality where our different life experiences weave us together to create a cohesive whole. Genderfuckery for me is about the beauty of change. I think of myself as a woman with a cock and a man with a pussy. I am an adaptation of the rules, and a small universe unto myself, joining together to give birth to the idea of both and neither. The absurdity of my Truth only solidifies it for me.

My cock is as real as my love, my thoughts, and all the parts of myself that I can't see that affect me. Once I discovered the power of my cock, I began to experiment with my partner. To be a living extension of God is to use ashe to create connections with all its aspects. Aspects of God might be the wind through the trees or the person lying next to you that unfolds to revel a landscape with valleys to be explored. Now when I penetrate my partner, I feel the warm flesh of our connection and my understanding of our Divinity increases.

Our push and pull teaches me to embrace my confusion. In that exploration, I found the differences between us were in our minds. My partner wishes to be kissed and touched in universal ways. They wish to press moist areas or lightly graze over sensitive skin. The Godhood of genderfucking involves pressing pass the names for these body parts and our related societal connotations, and using a seemingly subversive act to discover the simplicity of nature when words are stripped away.

The Sacred Role of the Provoker: There's a Coyote Within the Dance

By Master Dennis

The drumming beat fills the room,
Primal and hypnotic,
Heated sweating bodies flow aimlessly,
Eyes glazed and far sighted,
The piercings of bells or shiny roped hooks
Bounce, jingle, and sway,
The coyote glides betwixt the souls,
Breathing deeply the energies held at bay.

A chant arises primordial, guttural, and raw,
Not words, yet psychic, telekinetic,
The chant is taken up, refrain after refrain fills the space,
As souls are touched and reunited,
Bells tug and hooks pull the flesh beyond pain,
As the ego flees, the spirit holds the day,
The chanting Coyote glides betwixt the souls,
Looking for spirits, who wish to play.
–Master Dennis

I must give a disclaimer. I heal nothing and no one. I am not a doctor, nor do I play one on TV, though I have been known to play one at home or in a scene. I have no magical mojo, I am but a man. I am simply a man who has somehow learned to fill my spirit with love and power, to fill it with good intention. In this, my shamanic state, I can release my ego. As much as I would love to say that I am egoless, I would be lying and more than likely it would be a paradox. Any healing, real or perceived, would be on the part of the individual that I stood witness for or provoked into seeing what they needed to see or feeling what they needed to feel without any conscious knowledge or agenda on my part. For those moments I am not Master Dennis, I am a sacred provoker.

For the last couple of years I and my Dragon Clan, an extended mix of BDSM and leather family (currently around 55 members nationwide), assist an organization called Butchmann's in many capacities, such as running logistics, cooking, and being staff for the Butchmann's Experience weekends, to volunteering behind the scenes of the annual Southwest Leather Conference.

The Butchmann's Experience weekends are in-depth, intensive group and self examinations of the heart and spirit of who we are, using the model of Master and Slave dynamics as the baseline. This experience may be many things for the participants, but it will be their experience. These experiences have made me look at and continue to examine my life and my role in it. Butchmann's is where I learned the importance of egoless gifting of Love and Power.

The Southwest Leather Conference is held in Phoenix, AZ in January each year, and it is a gathering of about 500 leather, BDSM, and likeminded people. Here is a blurb from the website: *With its emphasis on education and the interpersonal and spiritual dynamics of D/s relationships and SM practices, SWLC provides its attendees with opportunities for a profoundly deeper experience of BDSM, irrespective of sexual orientation, gender identity, age, nationality, or religious/spiritual affiliation. SWLC also provides a vehicle for regional leather clubs, organizations and individuals to gather and celebrate the leather tribe of which we are all a part.*

Then there is the "Dance of Souls." This is a modern primal cerebration of temporary piercings, live drumming, chanting, and dancing. It is during this primal chaos that the dancers seek to reach an ecstatic state of being. It is a two hour-plus event. This event was inspired by the work of Fakir Musafar, who is known as the father of the modern primitives. It is here that my role as Sacred Provoker is fully manifested.

I hate needles and hooks… YIKES! Yet for the dance of souls, I have recently added to my Coyote state temporary weighted piercings, and for the last two years I have had hooks pierce my flesh simultaneously. I do not need them to act as I do, though I have found being pierced facilitates the focus of my intent as a sacred provoker. It adds an underlying rapport between me and the communal experience within the space.

Now a little bit more of the history of the dance in my life. I met Fakir Musafar and Cleo Dubois at my first ball dance held at APEX (Arizona Power Exchange) in 1999. I went to see and witness the ecstatic dance of people pierced and weighted with limes and bells, feathers and fetishes. My spirituality was at that time floundering on the rocks of clinical observation and the occasional bouts of dogma fights. (My dogma can beat your dogma stuff.) Yet here was something that tugged and pulled me in ways not even the pomp and grandeur of a Christmas High Mass in Latin had ever done. Not even when I was in a room of Holy Rollers have I felt this pulling; the emotional static of a coven or pagan ritual was not as compelling as this event unfolding before me. There is nothing wrong with the aforementioned practices; I have seen what they mean to others, and that is their path. This dance, however, called me as no other has ever done. I normally at spiritual happenings would stand aside and observe as a clinical anthropologist would watch a rite from the deepest jungles of Brazil.

Yet somehow I was called to step away from the witness role and join the dancers, but not as another dancer. I moved throughout the dance and found dancers who seemed to be struggling. I would dance in front of them, matching movements, building rapport, and staring into their eyes even if they were not looking at me. Once eye contact was established something would happen, a deep instant connection and the spirit within them would awake and dance, cry, sing, yell, laugh, howl, or dance in slow or frenzied sensual movements, or even in primal ritualistic combat.

I went from one dancer to another, to another, to another, to a young woman who laughed with tears rolling down her face to a young man in a homemade Aztecan feather headdress. To my friends, to strangers, it mattered not because I danced with spirits which glowed and shone in my mind's eye. At the end of the dance we lay breathing and basking in the energies and pheromones of a moment in time like no other I had ever experienced.

I was both drained and infused, I was tired and invigorated, but more than anything else I was stunned and confused. Why had I done that; why did I leave the pristine safety of the observer and jump into the maelstrom of chaotic joy? What possessed me to stand before friends and strangers and evoke within us such rapport and incite such releases of pure animal outpouring or truly humanistic visions of the others' core beings?

Fakir and Cleo both came to me and talked for awhile and named me with a moniker that I had no understanding of. It was strange to see their reaction to me. It was not bad, just a very strange look as if something had surprised them. The name they gave to me was Ka-Seek-ka. I had not the foggiest of what it was so I did some research and found an interview that Fakir held and his definition of the word is: "– a Kaseeka. That's a Mandan word used to describe an elder, an initiate, a medicine man in some cases, who has been on the trip before, who has used some kind of technique to get from ordinary states of consciousness to a shamanic state of consciousness. When young men were initiated, usually each one had a Kaseeka."

I was and will always be honored by that moment, even before I knew what the term meant. It was that day I really started on my shamanic path. This was a day I saw my search for the sacred integrated with my Coyote, my Loki, and My Provoker.

Historically a sacred provoker has been called many things. A radical thinker can be a sacred provoker, and many of history's greatest sacred provokers pissed off a lot of their peers or their perceived bosses. Gandhi, Mother Teresa, and Pharaoh Akhenaten (who believed in one sole god… ended badly, though), Plato, Aristotle… Now, I do not believe to be amongst their ranks. One does not need to be. I found that you just need to provoke thought, provoke change, and provoke action in a sacred manner, with good intent. I too can be a sacred provoker in my own neck of the woods, on a small scale that is tribal, local, and where it is needed.

Native Americans call their sacred provokers Coyotes or Heyoka. In Norse Mythos it is Loki (though his intent was not always good); Carl Jung calls this archetype the Trickster. All of these are one and the same. If the intent is bad then they can be a deceiver, who takes pleasure in misleading and upsetting others. Yet if the intent is good they can be a helper or messenger from the divine, can help one see an alternative to the straight and narrow path. This is my calling.

A lot of what occurs is difficult to explain. Using words to express the tidal tempest of the event is trying to describe the sacred world with the profane clinical filtration of language belonging to the far removed human from their humanity. Yet I shall strive to.

I go to three places:

1. The **spirit veil**, this is where I see the spirit within each individual soul present. I do not see auras (wish I could). I do not see guardians or angels. What I do see in these moments are fleeting and nondescript defiantly nonverbal expressions of the spirit within the flesh. I sense the spirit riding the razor's edge of release. The silent cry for catharsis, not the clinical meaning but the purely animalistic-human need to let something go that the rational (funny, that) brain holds dearly to. We like our stories and will hold them tight and close no matter the damage they do or their validity. Voices: of our parents, peers, bosses and losses, the fears of our failures and of our success. So much for a rational mind, eh? More like rationale for fears. When I was trying to understand it, I found that reading *The Four Agreements* by Don Miguel Ruiz was incredibly helpful.

2. The **holder of the sacred space**, the mover of my own chi with the ebbs and tides of the space, a holder not in the sense of anchoring, but of tidal flows and both the eye of the storm and the progenitor of the tempest.

3. And finally, I am **cognizant of the real world**, the true here and now as the Shamanic OSHA safety officer. Aware of the drums and when the spirit is flagging and when it needs to slow down or speed up, the chanting of non-language emotion-filled verbal outcries. This is a shared consciousness role between the Shamanic side and the Coyote. I do not go into a head space or become lost in the spirit world; I part a veil and hold each spirit I encounter with love and power.

I have always found myself in situations where I felt I was more the synonym of the provoker. I was the *irritator*! I was the one who knew instinctively what buttons to push and where to probe and prod. Not to be mean, but to see what was behind the doors of the person's eyes or to just make life less serious. I did not know of the sacred, nor what the Coyote or Loki spirit meant. It just was what I did.

Whether it was to frustrate a teacher to allow me to do what I wanted to do, or drive a force to break and abolish a dress code in school. It was a useful skill to diffuse tensions in potential altercations or between feuding friends.

Unfortunately, it was a skill set that the military felt was useful for other things. It was there that I started to see the difference between the sacred and the profane. It was at that point I started seeking a compatible and congruent understanding of sacred that had nothing to do with organized religion (I was a recovering Catholic, who served a very small stint as an alter boy) or one that was not attached to some stigmatic dogma.

So I searched and questioned and found that I really did not care about or resonate with organized religions. I searched them all, from Judaism to Islam, Christianity to Paganism. I searched Wicca, the occult, the five magics. I searched all the ways between as well, including some way points that were way out there, too. I found that all claimed to be the one true way. For me they were not. Do not get me wrong, my way is not your way, and that is the way of it. How one searches for the reason they exist, the way that allows them to come close or to touch the divine is individual. If it works for you then as far as I am concerned, for you that is the one true way.

Yet as I searched for the way for me, I found that all had a commonality in reaching their purpose. **Intent!** As Doctors, those priests of the technocratic, symptomatic healers (yes, healers of symptoms, relievers of dis-ease) have found in their experiments to prove or disprove the power of the divine through prayer, that prayer seemed to work, and those who were true scientists studied other forms of prayer beside Judeo-Christian. They found that the prayers worked for pagans and even people who were not of organized religions.

The main thing I found in my search was basically backed up by this and other experiments. **Intent!** It does not need thirteen witches to cast a spell. It does not need a temple full of parishioners paying their tithes. It takes focused good intent. This is why Shamans throughout history stayed Shamans, by the power of intent. Intent is where I found the sacred. If my intent is good and healing in nature, I am in a sacred place. The trick now is to visit it as often as I can. Not easy, but I feel a worthwhile goal.

Now as far as the Coyote, the Trickster, the Loki spirit minus the dark juju (Yes, the Breaker of Worlds has a role in life.), I have found that when I place myself in what I feel is a sacred place for me. With good and healing intent, a state of love and power, I can let my ego float away; it is not needed. I can then open up and let the Trickster out with the understanding that it is to be filled with the love and power intent. Yet it is also tasked to seek out those who need its skills the most. Not to heal or fix anything, but to share what it is and allow the other soul to use as it needs, even if that means just to enjoy its presence.

Now my sacred provoker is called to join with the Kaseeka side as I teach and talk with many about what we do and how my journey of BDSM has gone, like many, from sexual to spiritual. I speak to anyone from leather conferences to college classes of young media misinformed and wide-eyed future therapists or clinicians. To those who serve me, I am that damn provoker when I ask them, are they serving in joy? My sacred provoker also challenges those within my community about what is a leather family? Who and what are we? What are and how to deal with Littles? This world of, as some call it, kink, is my world. I do not considered it kink nor off center. I consider it the basis of the human condition that we have forgotten. Oh, I will still flog, single tail, spank, and what have you. Yet I will always do so with love and power, good intent.

Though, I will always ask people what their intent on this event is, whether it be play, work, or a scene. Is it a need for growth or release of pent-up pressures or fears? When the answer stirs and awakens within me, then my conduit to the divine awakens my sacred provoker. Then the Coyote silently joins the dance.

The Coyote looks within your eyes,
Called the windows of the soul,
Tantric breathing, rapport sealed with sighs,
The Coyote guides your spirit to its goal.

Fear not the Coyote's intent,
Take from its power and love,
Embrace the transformative bent,
Set your spirit to the sky above.

Dance yourself in freedom,
Laugh yourself to tears,
Scream where your soul is from,
Sleep anew without fears.
There is a Coyote within the dance!
–Master Dennis

My Love and blessing to all of my fellow Sacred Provokers, and to the community Shamans both known or soon to be self-discovered, to you I offer this:

"How boundless and free is the sky of Awareness!
How bright the full moon of wisdom!
Truly, is anything missing now?
Nirvana is right here, before our eyes; this very place is the Lotus Land; this very body, the Buddha."
–Hakuin Zenji, "Song of Zazen"

To find out more about Butchmann's Experience, please visit:
www.butchmanns-experience.org

To learn about SW Leather Conference, visit:
www.southwestleather.org

For more information on prayer that worked, see:
www.wired.com/wired/archive/10.12/prayer_pr.html

It Hurts All The Time: Fibromyalgia as an Ordeal Path

By Margo Eve

Imagine for a moment that you are into BDSM (Which, if you are reading this anthology, I imagine you might be). Imagine you enjoy bottoming in a masochistic way. You like impact. You like pain.

Imagine that slowly you find you can't take it anymore. A deer skin flogger is like a baseball bat. A caning of rattan is more like a Singapore infraction. Even a well-meaning massage from a friend is a torture worthy of Torquemada.

Fibromyalgia. One word. Five syllables. A diagnosis debated in the medical community that basically means this: Pain.

All. The. Time.

The best way I know how to describe it is the body ache you get when you have the flu.

All. The. Time.

That's a good day.

This is my tale about me and Fibromyalgia, its impact on my kink and sex life. It is not the typical tale for one with my disability. I call it a disease; I believe somewhere out there a cure exists. I refuse to believe otherwise. Further, because though it is at times, disabl*ing*, I will not let it disable *me*. It is perhaps that stubbornness that makes this disease part of my ordeal path...

I was finally diagnosed with Fibromyalgia – "Fibro" for short, or as I would call it, "Fibro-ick" if I was feeling particularly snarly – during my first year of grad school. I'm not so narcissistic to think that when Lee Harrington discusses Academics as Ordeal in his book *Sacred Kink* that he had me in mind, but I did laugh when I read that section. This essay isn't about an academic ordeal, but that is part of my overarching tale as well. I'm not sure I can convey the despair of being in an academic program that thought I entered it in error as my legs were physically rebelling with every step as I walked to class. Telling me to lie down. Stop walking. Give up.

Then there was the mental haze of trying to focus through this disease. People with Fibromyalgia often experience a fuzzy-minded state of confusion and forgetfulness that is commonly referred to as "Fibro Fog." Add this in The Scene and you have a recipe for social faux pas out the wazoo. Forgetting names. Not picking up on social cues. Missing that you just walked into the beginning of a scene. Name it. The potential for cluelessness is unlimited when your brain chemistry is in a haze – and that's without medication that contributes to the haze.

Let's talk about the medication for a moment. At the time, treatment options were basically pain management. Muscle relaxants. Vicodin as needed, but limiting that because of a fear of addiction. Oh, and this non-narcotic called Tramadol.

That they didn't tell me was a synthetic opiate. Splitting hairs on the non-narcotic part really, it was still physically addictive. Unlike most narcotics, which have a physical withdrawal of 3 days, Tramadol has a withdrawal of 5-7 days.

I was on it for 7 years. This is not a medication you are meant to stay on for 7 years.

But I am getting ahead of myself... I'm telling you my end. Or, the end of one cycle. There is still much more to the middle. See, Fibro Fog. Where was I?

Here I had a chronic illness where pain was my constant companion, and I was, *am*, a sexual sadomasochist. The irony of this became so delicious I could choke on it. How does one eroticize pain when it is a constant companion? The lover's bites that I once enjoyed were now an actual torment. The gentle touch became sandpaper. The warm-up never came because pain was instantaneous. The happy endorphins were never triggered.

There's a joke that there is a difference between the pain of S&M and the pain of stubbing one's toe or slamming one's finger in a car door. Not with Fibro. Here is a condition that, on some days, I needed pain medication just to put clothes on because my skin was so sensitive to the fabric.

Humans need touch. We thrive on touch. Our society is increasingly touch deprived. Imagine having to purposely shun touch. Touch you crave because it causes agony.

Humans need interaction. Yet imagine your mind being in such a fog, that you cannot trust that interaction to be genuine. You cannot trust your own words and so do not trust others. You are afraid of that which you need to thrive.

So you go untouched and isolated. And you deal.

I dealt. For 7 years.

Some people don't deal. When I first went looking for support I found boards where people were talking about getting on disability because the fog was too much to work. Getting wheelchairs because their legs hurt too much to walk. And getting morphine pumps installed because the pain is just too much to live with. To me, it seemed like getting to that point, getting to the point that people get when they are dying of cancer, would be giving up. Because this is a disease you don't die from.

There are just times you wish it would kill you.

There are times I wanted to die.

But when I first FINALLY got a diagnosis. FINALLY got a doctor to say "No, eating less and exercising more will NOT help this. You aren't insane. This is a real disease." There was hope.

And treatment. In the form of drugs. Pain management.

"We're going to avoid narcotics. Here's Flexaril and Tramadol."

I did mention earlier that Tramadol was a synthetic opiate. This means that even if I felt better, I would go through withdrawal if I stopped taking it. It got to the point that I did not know the difference between a Fibro-flare and withdrawal.

Welcome to a cycle of hell.

Now I try to live my life, with a partner, the scene, an academic program, and a job.

Something had to give. What gave was my kink, my sexuality, and my sense of self.

To understand this, you have to know a bit about me. I am someone who started reading about sexuality in pre-teen years. I prided myself on my sexual prowess. If I chose to play with someone, it was because they deserved me and I could command that moment, even if I were to bottom. My erotic energy was linked to my confidence. Without it, I was nothing.

And pride goeth before a fall.

In my struggle to keep walking, to not give up as others had, I was stripped of all that made me desirable. I had no energy to play. So many nights I sent my life partner, Elkor, out on his own while I lamented a lack of energy to do the

things that were necessary as well as that which I wanted. That put a strain on our relationship too. I could not give him what he needed and felt the guilt of this weigh on me. I could not get what I needed and felt the resentment of this eat at me. I missed the sexual being I once was. I missed being touched. I missed those moments of endorphin-filled ecstasy. I missed giving as good as I got. I missed the energy to do more.

It was the ordeal of a half-life. A constant struggle to exist.

Existing is not living, and simply existing was not acceptable. I had to LIVE with this disease. There was no other choice. It had to change.

The change started slow.

With water.

Water is the element of cleansing, of emotions, and of creativity. In this case I started literally with coconut water. An acquaintance named Holly Fogelboch suggested that coconut water was good for Fibro, and that since drinking it she had been asymptomatic. Given everything that I had tried, why not?

Turned out, she was right. It worked for me. I noticed a difference within a week at my pain levels. And other things too, like my skin being softer and hurting less and my nails being less brittle. I could also focus better. Turns out coconut water has a lot of potassium, a mineral I lacked because of an allergy to bananas and citrus. It cleansed and replenished me.

Along with the element of water is emotions. I had to become okay with mine. This is an ongoing process. At its most basic level, it meant learning to recognize what my body was telling me about a situation and separating that from the stories in my head. For example, I had to learn to recognize the difference between a sinking feeling in the pit of my stomach when my I was too weak to finish a task and me telling myself that I was a failure for not finishing that task. I had to own my emotions.

With air.

The element of intellect, communication, and literally, the breath of life. A class on erotic breathwork by Barbara Carrellas, the author or *Urban Tantra*, taught me the power of oxygen on the cells of my body. That I could breathe with intent and change pain into pleasure. Had I known what I could accomplish with intentional breathing, I may never have picked up those damned pills to begin with.

We learned two breaths. First was "bottom breath," a way of grounding and centering energy. The other, the most amazing one for me, was the "Firebreath Orgasm." This charged my whole body with oxygen and made every cell come alive. By the end of the class, my skin was sensitized to the point that all my darling partner had to do was brush it and I would cum. It was such a change, to have my skin not over sensitized with pain, but with pleasure instead, I laughed with the pure joy of it.

I found I could use this to get through my worst pain days as well as my kinky play. Later, this breathing would assist me in transforming how I framed my Fibro pain. Now, in everything that I do, I try to incorporate breathing.

With fire.

The element of passion, of cleansing, and of primal energy. I had, in the course of this disease, Godmother of Fun, learned to fire dance. Poi spinning, dancing with fire on the wicks at the end of chains, was the one activity that did not trigger flares. My own journey with fire could fill another essay entirely, but I will tell you that I used to be terrified of fire and fire play due to an accident that happened to a close relative, where they suffered 3rd degree burns. Learning to spin fire around my body, to be in the center of a roaring fire rushing past my ears, and dance with a semblance of grace, became a holy communion with the flame. I don't simply dance with fire, I spar with my fear every time I light up. I battle the voice in my head that says, "You cannot do this. You will burn."

Along my journey with fire, with the help of 3 wonderful fire play experts,

Pyromancer, Brian Pyro-Sadist, and Elkor, I also learned that the moist heat of fireplay acted therapeutically on my muscles. In order to get relief from much of my muscle pain, I would have to confront the terror of having fire actually touch my skin. I would have to breathe through my anxiety and trust in others not to burn me.

In doing this, surrendering to those who were essentially priests of the flame along with learning to dance with fire, it would cleans me and invigorate me. I could move as I could not before.

With earth.

The element of material things, the physical realm, and of the body. Of course this would be the element I have always been the least adept in. Dealing with the physical realm, I had to get into the core of my body to deal with Fibro if I had any chance of living with it. What did I miss? Playing. Connection. Endorphins. I could not get to them through slow means of the rhythmic flogging or impact. I needed to learn other things. Fast things. Sting. Scratch. Needles. These would be my new allies in my quest: the stinging thorn rather than the steady tree-like thud.

In finding other ways to get into my body I asked myself the following question: What if I could use my constant pain to my advantage? What if those classic Fibro points could be used to stimulate endorphins fast if pushed on harder than normal? What if I could eroticize this? Make my disease work FOR me?

With breath as my ally, I sought to get into my body. Each painful trigger point was a nodule of pain, an impenetrable rock sitting in me. With each inhalation, I dove into myself, creating roots around each boulder, finding chinks within them, making them mine, not the disease's. Reframing them to make them a source of energy rather than agony. Now, when touch is done *with intent*, I can work my way through this root system of my own making, dive past the initial pain, drive past the initial discomfort, past the emotions of "can't," to the source of endorphins. Now I can enjoy my trigger points and eroticize them, just as I once enjoyed deep tissue bruising, but without the thuddy sensation.

I turned the source of my pain into a source of pleasure.

With spirit.

The final element: the aether, the self, the soul. With the changes I had made in how I looked at this disease, and with the final element, I looked at the medications I was on and found they might not be serving me as well as I thought. I realized I did not know my baseline for pain anymore. Upon discovering 7 years later that Tramadol was a synthetic opiate, I put myself through a deliberate ordeal. Withdrawal.

It seemed fitting. Most narcotics are 3 days of withdrawal. After weaning down to the lowest possible dosage, after being on the drug for over 7 years, it took 7 days to withdraw.

Seven days of agony. Sweats. Chills. Aches. Diarrhea. Vomit. Wanting to die as I had in the beginning of all this. Seven days to recreate myself. Seven days to rebuild a soul crushed by a drug.

And at the end of those seven days?

On the last day of withdrawal I made the trek to a kink event at a spiritual place, Ramblewood. Such events in and of themselves allow for exploration of self in a way that the mundane world does not. They provide education and exploration space for desires that are often not spoken about in the outside world, and so naturally many come out of such events changed. Couple an event of this kind with the sacred space of Ramblewood, a campground dedicated to creating safe space for various groups to explore what they need, and you get a temple space for transformation. It was here that I was able to shed the last of the drug sickness.

In a moment of complete serendipity, shortly after my arrival, a spectacular thunderstorm rolled in. Such violent storms are often a natural agent of change, washing away the old debris to make room for new growth and harvest. There I danced in that storm, which in turn caused a blackout at the campsite. With no electrical power, I was able to dance to the drum beat of an old friend, and was baptized. Washed clean of the last of the hold that drug held on me.

Thus, I found my baseline. And in that weekend I found through a moment of bliss, with all my elements in play, that I could live with this baseline, narcotic pain med-free.

Free.

I was free.
I had come through an ordeal and been reborn.
My play had changed.
My life had changed.
I had changed.

Now, lest you with Fibromyalgia out there get false hope, I still have Fibromyalgia. I am still on other medication, including one for migraines, which *may* have influenced some of this. I still get flare-ups that leave me low. Just not AS low as they did before. This is my path, and I cannot expect anyone else to walk it.

That being said, I did walk it. Every agonizing step. Not with a morphine pump. Not in a wheelchair. On my *own* legs.

Fibromyalgia took me away from what I desire, but it doesn't need to keep holding that role in my life. It forces me to rethink my desires. To reform those desires and to transcend them, because I have the capacity to rise above this challenge. I have proved it dancing in a thunderstorm. I have come out changed.

My ordeal is but one path. There are many. If someone is out there reading this, in the dark despair of one of these chronic illnesses, I hope they can take something from my tale. That they can make their illness, their *ordeal*, into their triumph. To make it work for their spirit of desire rather than against it, then, perhaps the Universe had some reason for it all.

Of course, you reading this might not put much faith in the will of the

Universe. After all, I just might have been that stubborn. So I ask if you can find the will in yourself? I ask, if you are in that dark place, how strong is *your* spirit of desire?

What *ordeal* are you willing to face to feed it?

Namaste.

Priestess Birth

By Kaye Buckley

The story of how I chose this sado-erotic journey – or perhaps how it chose me and became sacred – begins as many stories do: before birth, and I think, partly in my DNA. In discovering the source of my calling. Tribal connections, clitoral orgasm, and everything that emanated from it. Not atypically, my Bitch-Muse would only let me write this while laying her whip across my back. And drawing blood.

When I was six, I discovered reading and began devouring books. Wildlife fascinated me. In the depths of one black night, I dreamed about a pig drinking from a stream in a primordial forest while an alligator stalked it from behind. The closer the alligator crept, the more my excitement grew. An exquisite tension was building. The pig, oblivious, kept drinking as water gently rippled downstream. Suddenly, in an acrobatic feat, the alligator lashed its tail out, batted the pig into its mouth and clamped its jaws down. The frenzied rush of feelings almost smothered me as I came, tasting blood. This became my archetype for the creative dynamic within life, primal intimacy between predator and prey, top and bottom, Domme and sub. I had experienced myself as both simultaneously. It was profound.

And then I forgot how to do it. The orgasm, I mean.

I began my life named _Sylvia_, from a song mentioned in Shakespeare's work, containing these words: _Who is Sylvia, what is she, that all the swains commend her...?_ Never intrigued enough to learn more, the question presented a karmic riddle that would haunt (and taunt) me: Who _was_ I?

The darker, more pagan root _Sylvan_, meaning "of the woods," lay below the name. I didn't know that growing up, and am sure my parents wouldn't have taken that route had they known. At least not consciously. Perhaps the Ancients whispered it, and by design they heard, pulling it out of the air while over the years, new names and identities would emerge. _One of which is Kaye Buckley._

In any case, the die was cast, the journey begun.

In truth, the real inspiration was the music by Schubert. Both classical musicians, my mother played cello, my dad the violin. He was also a demon writer, laying down words that tore up a page with their intensity. As an adult, I found letters that finally told me more about the interior of their relationship.

Their shared passion, music, was also their profession, and out of this milieu I was born. That and the war. However, their passion for each other burned out shortly after my birth. At twenty-one I remember seeing my father twice. His sin became one of omission. A woman scorned at _any_ age is a force to be reckoned with. Three of us, my mother, grandmother and myself, shared a household. Three cats in a bag.

My mother was afraid of everything. She was also the enraged one, the artistic one, the crazy one, the wounded one, her projection part Victorian, part whore. At age five, I called her _Spider_. Stomping around like an angry stripper, her eruptions were gothic; red hair flaming, voice issuing in blasts while my grandmother, mostly stoic but outraged, muttered under her breath. The color was from a bottle, but she kept a braid in her hope chest, a memento of her teenage self, and it was deeply, truly auburn, a mythic clue.

Then there was the ghost.

I never met my grandfather in life. But he was there in parentheses. The only corporeal evidence were the clothes still in my grandmother's narrow closet along with her black granny shoes. No photos, no stories explaining why he was still so enigmatically dominating the household. I saw him in my mother's furious face, heard him in wind stirring high oak boughs, my grandmother's muttering, the fact of my absentee father.

I knew only bare bones. From England, loving gardens and roses, he built the house my mother, then I, grew up in. When I got old enough to ask salient questions, answers were always the same, incomplete. Most important was what happened between my mother and my father; the question of why did she have the nervous breakdown that led to electric shock treatments that led to hospitalization for six months before I was a year old. *Would it happen to me?* The Sword of Damocles hovered. We became the family outcasts, stuck in our third chakra life.

And my grandfather was the one who still had any power.

At nine, I vowed never to marry. How could I? Stark, eloquent beauty of Bach's Unaccompanied Cello Suites filtered out to the garden, the same passage repeated over and over. Getting older, I fantasized about what else my mother wanted between her legs besides her cello. Down the street neighbors heard the shouts she and I hurled, anger being the default tone. Rage and its twin, shame, burned deep while in public I carried the secret, never the troublemaker.

When I was twelve, I fell in love with black music: R & B, the rougher, earthier, the better — poetry of rampant desires, dangerous edge. In black toreador pants and tight sweaters, my self-image was a cross between beatnik and prostitute. Boys in souped-up cars cruised the main drag wolf-whistling at me and my girlfriends while in the shadows lurked a temperamental man who beat me if I didn't live up to my potential.

Around that time, I dreamed of two spools attached by the same cord turning in black space. As they spiraled, in grief I held scissors up and cut the cord, realizing I was ending my mother's life thereby freeing myself.

The next morning I looked into the garden. Breasts and hips mounding, vaginal lips growing longer, ruddier, asymmetrical, I had begun to bleed, not as a girl anymore. I felt upended, filled with new complexities. Suddenly faint movement caught my eye: a parrot perched in the distant fig tree. The jungle bird straight from Eden seemed a revelation, heralding my incipient womanhood. Like a ripe fig laid open.

Then I was fifteen, hair bleached platinum, black tights, red sheath dress. Though I lived in a wealthy suburb, my house was on the wrong side of the tracks. I found high school a sprawling wasteland. I didn't belong, didn't want to. I began drifting, languishing.

Happy Valley School probably saved my life. Comparing notes with other public school dropouts, that was something we all agreed on. Nobody twisted my arm — the first day of junior year I said, —I'm not going back. Within a week I was living in a dorm in Ojai Valley just outside Santa Barbara. My roommate was daughter to the Greek artist, Jean Varda. HVS, founded in 1946 by Aldous Huxley and J. Krishnamurti, was ahead of its time. I fit in and my fetish for small, intimate communities was formed there. Before classes, the student body gathered in the Main Room where we listened to classical music, then meditated. The ritual was mandatory, part of the curriculum.

Against the lavender-green of the Topa Topa Bluffs, I began to draw breath. I wrote poetry, danced, began my first foray into teenage sexuality with Dyon, a quintessential boy-girl with turquoise eyes and short chestnut hair. Learning to color outside conventional lines, as I looked into her eyes, the throbbing in my genitals stunned me. When we broke up, I rubbed poison oak all over my face. She didn't notice. The headmaster, a strict Viennese man with surprising empathy, counseled me to help salvage my equilibrium. It worked. Senior year, I got stoned on marijuana, played conga drums on the beach with a new paramour — a boy this time. Then I met my future husband.

Swain was older, more experienced than anyone I'd met; full of stories, fantastic and plausible. He'd lived with his family in the jungles of Peru and Venezuela. As he began pursuing me I felt sexually attracted, yet my overall response to him was more complex.

After graduation he lived in Alaska for six months before an earthquake that registered 9.2 hit and sent him hurtling full boar to California. En route, he stopped at my mother's house. I returned to find him on the top step staring fixedly into the distant trees. The presence of destiny lay heavy, one I wasn't sure I wanted, but had little choice in.

He proposed. The day he left, I challenged him. He picked me up, threw me over his shoulder. In a couple of hours I was watching the ocean pass on the way to his house in Capistrano Beach where the sex became a *fait accompli*.

Our new relationship was launched, but something was missing for me: connecting pleasure with sex. Though it was about what the sex *meant* that mattered more and was a driving force for what I did next.

I wanted Swain to prove he was strong enough to take me out of that house. But sex and his seeming devotion alone wasn't enough. I took charge by upping the ante and getting pregnant. It was my ticket out. We were married in Carmel when I was four-and-a-half months along by his grandfather, a Mormon minister drunk off his ass who couldn't pronounce my name.

The baby was stillborn. We grieved, and afterwards I think something broke in Swain. I continued to work the procreative part of the equation, conceiving again. If I couldn't have the pleasure, I needed to prove I could successfully create and bring forth a living being. Immersing myself in homemaking, I couldn't get my body to respond to Swain's advances and we reached an uneasy stalemate. Identity, self-esteem, resistance, independence all tied together were at war. His own esteem must have suffered. If he couldn't reach me, what did that say about his sexual prowess? In a couple of years, the power dynamic shifted. He became the swan, replete with red beard, a future Don Juan of the Sausalito Houseboat Community.

Marinship Corporation was a shipbuilding company created by the government in 1942 in support of the war effort. Against the backdrop of Mount Tam it lay across a stretch of the Waldo Point mud flats. Built by workers in shifts around the clock over three frenetic months, the keel of the first of fifteen Liberty ships was laid.

By war's end, the waterfront lay quiet, the ghostly hulks of LCVP's and other vessels beached – testaments to the end and beginning of a new era. Alongside wartime vessels were assorted others steeped in history, among them ferryboats, grande dames of the bay. By the late 1940s Donlon Arques, long-time boat builder and rebel millionaire, owned much of the waterfront. He believed those with the capacity to build something should be provided with space to fulfill their visions. It was he who dragged the ferryboats, scow schooners, and barges onto his mud flats so people could live in them.

To say this didn't sit well with the Hill people and county supervisors would be an understatement. It culminated in a war fought on the water in a series of police raids. Local police and coast guard cut houseboats from their moorings, while boat owners defended their homes. A movie, *The Last Free Ride*, was subsequently made about it.

During the late 50s and early 60s the waterfront community burgeoned. The infamous Juanita's Galley became a fixture, while Alan Watts and Jean Varda lived respectively in the bow and stern of the ferryboat *Vallejo*. Otis Redding, John Cipollina, Shel Silverstein, and others also dropped anchor, some for a short time, some permanently.

On the peristaltic movement of the hippie wave Swain and I rolled in, charged with the fire of youth and two young sons in tow. In true pirate spirit, Swain began resurrecting one of the beached crafts. The boat, an Oyster Lugger built in 1901, was fifty feet long, and originally had a huge cat-rigged sail and centerboard. She was later converted into a tugboat. While digging three feet of mud saturated with fuel oil out of the hold, he decided she was haunted, and asked me to sing the ghost away. It must have worked because it took him only a matter of months to raise her up, patch her hull, anchor her out, and move myself and our sons aboard. Then another ten years to rebuild her, sister her ribs, steam-bend her planks and re-rig the boat á la Jack London.

Our boys had virtually grown up on her. She was *The Governor MBM* and there is still a photo of her in the Maritime Museum in San Francisco.

By the end of the ten years, they would all sail to Hawaii. But before that, I jumped ship.

If Swain was living his vision of hippie-pirate-lover, my life was somewhat curtailed. From the outside it looked pretty good, depending on *who* was doing the looking. Anchored out just off Strawberry Point, I was mothering our boys, cooking on a wood burning stove, pumping the boat, rowing in for supplies, to do laundry and feel solid ground. I ground flour, baked bread. Evenings were spent playing music with our neighbors; our boat a local hangout.

One afternoon Swain dropped a bombshell. —I've been balling Mona, he said. I was outraged, but strangely charged. Surrounded by water something broke loose in me and I started dancing over the decks.

—Go ahead. You can do it too, he said. Ball other guys. It's OK with me.

What could I do? I agreed, partly because I didn't want to feel more left out than I already did. What marriage and children couldn't fix, maybe free love could. Besides, I was outnumbered. It seemed to be happening all around me

With our agreement in the open I experimented, but except for the freedom of balling someone new nothing changed. One experience was like another, a disappointing lack of fireworks. Not to mention I was taking care of two small sons so there wasn't parity.

Something seemed out of whack. It was the men who were *running the fuck*.

Over time, Swain spent the night elsewhere more and the distance between us grew. I missed him less. My interest in being sexual with him continued to wane. I became glad other women were taking care of his needs.

I began to look elsewhere.

When *The Governor MBM* was dragged onto the ways, Swain moved us onto a houseboat in Gate 6. Perched on a couple of steel drums cut in half, we dubbed it *Ramshacklia on the Half Shell*. Searching for a new identity, I channeled my latent frustrations into music and performing venues.

The Gates was rife with performers. Thep Redlegs were the neighborhood rock 'n' roll band. They were incredible: Ike and Tina Turner-good, Rolling Stones-good. Long into the night I'd lie awake burning to shockwave after shockwave. *I'm blue-ooo-blue-du-be-du-be-du-be-du...gong, gong, gong, gong, gong, go-go-gong, gong, yeah...I'm blue...ooo-ooo...*

Their female lead singer with a voice like a siren made my nipples hard.

I started my own band. We practiced on the stern of the *Charles Van Damme*, the ferry where Juanita's Galley once existed. I was also part of a small theatre group that sang sea shanties and, as the Waldo Point Wenches, danced the can-can. One of my characters was the handsome cabin boy, after a shanty in which a girl poses as a boy to crew on a sailing ship. Performing at small events, we once sailed to the Hyde Street pier, dropping anchor and rowing to shore; quite the entrance.

Parties raged, raucous, sometimes going on over several days. More children were born. The community was tight; everyone knew everyone. We started a *School Without Walls*, an alternative to the Marin City school system. I was sleeping with a sixteen-year-old boy just breaking into manhood. But around the outskirts of this potpourri of energy ranged a different culture. The second wave of women's liberation was reaching the Waldo Point shores, a quieter one I was not very familiar with, but was beginning to open my ears and eyes to.

Tantric workshops were held in *The Yes Center* at the end of Gate 5 road, in what had been the old Schooner Restaurant. Betty Dodsen with her unisex haircut sometimes passed through. Trying to throw off the karma of my Sylvia identity, I changed my name and got a job as a topless dancer. I was learning the mud puddle didn't contain the world.

Around that time a family from Esalen moved into the neighborhood. J and

A lived on *The Oakland*, a potato barge across from the *Ramshacklia* with their two girls, whom they were raising as young witches in a pagan household. They'd taught workshops in love, sex, and intimacy at Esalen, were creating their own Tarot deck made from lino-blocks. I once asked why women figured in so prominently. J said the female power perspective had been missing too long. The equation needed to be balanced.

John Horler was the artist, J, with his photographic memory, put in seven years of research. A had veto power. If something didn't look right, John simply nodded, tore up the artwork and started again. Her-story vs. His-story. They called it *The New Tarot Deck* and rubbed shoulders with the likes of Joseph Campbell who once visited.

Their home was an architectural oasis in the surrounding chaos. They had an open relationship and compared to ours, theirs seemed more… open. Though friendly, they kept themselves a bit apart. They had a hot tub. She was a professional masseuse and they developed this full body awareness at Esalen. When they made the choice to open their sexual relationship to include others, they did it together. Monogamy went out the window.

The Gates people didn't quite know how to respond to them. I could only speak for myself. Highly attracted, I wanted to know more. I found reasons to visit. The cards were a good one. I flirted with J, but when he responded I didn't know what to do and skittered away. Their nine-year-old daughter joined our act, the youngest of the Waldo Point Wenches can-can dancers.

That fall, J and I exchanged a Tarot reading for a leather pouch. It was my first reading, and the cards told a different story from the one I presented. During that reading, something shifted in me. I found myself stuck. I couldn't move forward; couldn't move back. I was finally beginning to unravel.

Indian summer settled over the water bringing out shifting colors: pewter, lavender, gold. The fragrant stench of mud flats rose in the warmth. One card appearing in that reading was the Ten of Wands, a naked woman with wrists bound over her head, faggots at her feet ready to be ignited. I had posed for the card and I *was* her. Sexual energy burning me at the stake.

My struggle intensified. One evening J hung out naked in the wheelhouse overlooking the bay. I had dragged someone new into my bed that morning, fucking his brains out. A few hours later I found a long-time admirer who was happy to help me search for the missing release. Nothing. In desperation I made my way to the lion's den, climbing the ladder and barging in. I ranted. He listened. I seduced. Nothing. I... all but begged. He... listened, waiting for a modicum of sanity. I didn't know how to do that. I finally pulled him down on me and approximated having my way with him.

Mildly startled, he straightened up.

–Well, you not only got me hard, you got me to come. I was surprised to hear what came out of my mouth next.

–I want to take an acid trip. I've never taken it before.

–Who do you want to take it with? He asked.

–You, I said.

Intrigued, he smiled. He had gotten hard again. Immediately.

The next week, I procured the acid. A was at her massage booth at the Renaissance Faire over the weekend; a friend staying with my sons. I learned that J really liked acid. He and A had tried it together, but she and acid didn't mix well. Sometime later he told me the other thing he tried and liked was SM. Again, not her thing. But that didn't figure in his decision to take acid with me; it wasn't even on the radar.

I spent a solitary night before the trip wrestling with my old nemesis: anxiety, the fire-breathing dragon. My mind cycled, a maniacal Ferris wheel drowning out sleep. Seeming to belong to no time and all time, it only dissolved at daybreak. I hung on. If I bled to death, I wanted to bleed as a woman, not a pre-orgasmic girl.

That morning I went over to *The Oakland*.

—I don't think I can go through with this, I began.

Looking at me in my rock-and-a-hard-place he spoke without resentment.

—I've cleared my weekend, made the preparations. I'm really looking forward to doing this with you. He told me how he had set an altar up with three cards for clarity of intention: The Lovers, The Priestess, and The Magician. Flanking them were red and green candles: port and starboard running lights.

—To guide us on our journey; a point of departure and return, he explained.

In turmoil I stood debating. Then, out of nowhere, it felt like he reached into my mind and just like that, I surrendered. We toasted each other, dropped the acid, made the accent to the wheelhouse. There began an enchantment of the first order.

Undulation comes to mind to describe what I felt when the acid was coming on. That and electrical charge heightening my senses. The visuals began, and they weren't garish, dark, or scary. No wheels. No *spiders*. No… mother. I didn't go crazy. The acid was *White Light*, and everything I smelled, saw, heard, felt, seemed infused with it. Our flesh looked like clay, glowing with subtle tones of peach, lavender, blue. When I closed my eyes pinpoints of stars appeared so white they held the sum of all colors. They rained down from a black expanse with no limit, striking my skin with static electricity.

We were naked. He began introducing me to smell. Essence oils — sharp, sweet, smoky, earthy, musky — passed under my nostrils. I closed my eyes, inhaled as each formed visual patterns. Hearing was underscored by music. The Beatles. Janis Joplin. I finally began to feel the erotic connection to music I didn't know existed. Bass tones reverberated in my lower chakras; lyrics and harmonies stirred my upper, letting me in on their secrets.

He sat cross-legged on the bed, meditatively moving his hands and arms. When I asked him what he was doing, he said, —Teaching you about energy. Like a dance, the energy was moving him as well. I could *see* the interaction; intangible becoming tangible, the oneness of it all.

Throwing myself into the fire I spread myself over the bed. He moved his hands closer, still without touching me. They hovered over my body, and I felt sparks, a density of energy between us. I had as powerful a response to that motion as if he were touching me. The undulations grew stronger.

Then he put his hands on my body. I felt them gliding over me like water. Nipples hardening to points, wetness seeping between my legs. We were listening to Janis Joplin. *Trust in me, Baby, Give me time, Give me time, oooohhh, just a little more time...*

I melted under her voice.

—She has a voice like liquid velvet. He said. —Like the inside of a cunt...

He began pleasuring me, trying a little bit of a lot, introducing me not just to fucking or to oral sex, but to a huge spectrum. The way I pleasured him was through my responsive participation. He was a sexual magician introducing me to sex **magic**.

Enthralled, I heard myself say, —I'm... in... *love*...

I meant *inside* love rather than outside looking in.

Layers kept falling away. But still I waited for the bottom line, the throes, the release of clitoral orgasm that eluded me. Pushed up hard against an edge the mantra chanted, —Are you gonna do it? Do it? Are you gonna...? No, I wasn't. The coiled knot in my solar plexus kept me bound.

So I asked *him*, —Are you going to give me an orgasm?

Resting his hand on my lower belly he answered, —No, that's not mine to give. That's yours. In fact, it's not just yours; it's the energy of the universe. It will move through you if you allow it to.

Behind closed eyelids he seemed to be watching something, offering me a way to get at that energy, through the energy currents flowing between us. The

core part was still missing, though I was beginning to discover it in *myself*.

We sat up. In surreal twilight, we were coming down a notch. Raising his eyebrows, he invited conversation. Bewilderment spilling over, I began to talk about the absurdity of how I was supposed to come while being fucked by a man, humiliated that someone else should be in charge of my orgasm. Enraged, resistance held me captive. I didn't wonder where my power was. Fucking alone wasn't doing it. Neither was pitching the woo.

—You're good at doing it for the man, but not good at giving it to yourself, was his comment.

Suddenly, he farted. I froze, mortified. He farted again. I reacted as though shot.

—Got her! He chortled.

He did it a third time.

—Got her again!

Though still red faced, I began to see the humor.

We began looking at my dilemma from another angle. He stood up, lighting more candles around the room. Reaching for my hand, he led me to the mirror as I pondered,

—If my orgasm was my *own*, how was I going to give it to myself? Candlelight flickered, licking our bodies. Gazing into the mirror next to him, my reflection peered back, eyes dark pools. I began to fall into them against the silvery backdrop of the mirror. Trembling slightly, I felt vulnerable, exposed, fragile.

Suddenly as we watched, the flash of a young woman in brown and green darting through a forest emerged. Afternoon sun filtered through trees as, startled, she stopped. Caught in the mirror she looked back at me.

He made a noise that sounded like it came from deep in his throat.

What we were witnessing looked like another time, another place; the time was the 1600s, the place England; past and present converging in another dimension. In that instant, our relationship changed in ways none of us could ever have foreseen.

—Tell her. Look into her eyes. Tell her, 'Give me back my body'. I repeated the phrase.

—Louder, he said. Overwhelmed, in awe, I said it louder.

We moved from the mirror to the bed.

—What do you think she'll ask for in return? I didn't know. Gesturing to one of the candles he said, —Let's see if you can come up with the answer by the time this candle burns down.

For roughly forty-five minutes, I contemplated what trade I might offer this otherworldly being. Anything I came up with sounded shabby, like pot-metal currency. I was on trial. Whatever I could think up, there was no parity. He suggested I look into the heart of the flame for a clue. The center burned so white-hot. I felt part of it, holding the difference between living and reflected light.

Then there was half an inch left. The dying flame grew taller, longer, somehow more menacing. Black smoke rose from its tip.

I began to despair.

—Come back over to the mirror, he said. Feeling profoundly isolated, I lifted my head.

—Tell her, 'I love you'.

It was an offer I couldn't refuse. More naked than ever, I looked into my own face holding past, present, and future.

I said it.

—I love you. Again, he said. —I love you.

As we turned away from the mirror I lay down on the bed, stunned. I felt a new presence making herself known somewhere behind my breastbone. Warmth spread into my limbs. She began to settle in as I tentatively welcomed this missing part of my soul.

He spoke once again.

—Now that you've said it to yourself, I can say it to you as well: I love you.

The last thing he said in the morning was, —Thank you for trusting me. I made my way over connecting walkways, home to my sons. My friend and I looked at each other.

—How was it? She asked.

—I'm a thousand years old. Time doesn't move in a straight line; it's like rock strata, layering upon itself. Right now, this time… it's all time that's ever existed… ever will exist. All time is now.

A couple of weeks later I dreamed again. My mother stood, her back facing me. She turned slowly, smiled, and my orgasm began. Afterwards I discovered vibrators. I was finally making the connection and learning to *run the fuck*, Betty Dodson-style.

Pieces assembled, some quicker than others. Conversations began that would include relationship renegotiations, mine, theirs. Their relationship hadn't included falling in love with others. Suddenly it was on the table.

I started saying *Yes* to everything J suggested. I took a tantra class, explored my newfound sexuality. I got rolfed. I had orgasms, some deeply profound. J was trying to find a way for A and me to connect with each other sexually.

Between the two of us he was going to be very busy.

When they invited me into their bed it was my first experience with more than one person at a time. I had a lot to learn. She and I were on different wavelengths, only knowing each other socially. But she was willing to open up and give it a try, because it mattered to him. What an extraordinary woman to allow me, an interloper sixteen years her junior, into her nineteen-year marriage. After the relationships coalesced, someone once asked how she did it. With typical directness she replied, —Sometimes with difficulty.

One difference was that she was able to raise, hold and exchange energy in ways I wasn't. Another involved a perverse streak of resistance in me; that and my active fantasy life. Between J and me SM reared its beguiling head. We experimented by holding down my wrists while fucking. And spanking. Pain play. Cutting fantasies. Blood lust. Our rampant desires had us going for the jugular. But J knew we couldn't learn in a closet. We needed the support and experience of a community.

I didn't just walk away from my marriage and my sons. J encouraged me to try to work things out with Swain. But our paths had already diverged. Over time and different steps, Jay, Kaye, and Amber emerged into the community as a triad. Through Cynthia Slater, we discovered San Francisco leather, land of sexual warriors. We went to mixed play parties at *The Catacombs*. An outreach of Janus, we created the first women's SM support group, Cardea, after the Roman goddess. To quote Ovid: *Her power is to open what is shut; to shut what is open.*

From beneath my ancestral shadow to the mythic, in past life regression Jay and I discovered more about the woman we'd seen in the mirror. Pieces emerged, hidden parts of my family legacy and personal spiritual heritage. I was descended from a line of priestesses submerging themselves to avoid persecution when Christianity overtook the Old Religion. From Celtic tradition, my descendants made up a guild of sacred prostitutes. I discovered a core truth: for me sexuality and spirituality were linked.

Making my dedication to the goddess, I immersed myself in the sacred and

profane, becoming a practitioner of these arts. I recognized my calling as a sex worker in the erotic power play arena. To honor a practice and profession overtaken by religious vandals that was stigmatized and pathologized in their wake. As both a private and pro-player, my first experience on acid and subsequent trips formed that basis. I learned to build energy. Journey safely, becoming a guide myself. Exploring the realm of sex work, learning as much as I could, I knew if I was a whore, I was the *goddess's* whore, no longer a figment of patriarchy gone mad.

One regret I have is that I didn't find strength enough to be a fiercer mother. I missed out on my sons. Sailing to and settling on The Big Island, they claimed the musical heritage passed down. They started their own band as adolescents continuing to play, write music, and perform as adults, offering the torch to their children.

Seven years later in Japan, I dropped acid for the last time. Goddess of the East, *Benzaiten*, called and I responded. And as for today, in the here and now, I've written this and in so doing looked into the mirror once again.

Mein Kleiner Tod

By Xochiquetzal Duti

Le petit mort. The little death. Orgasm, or so they used to describe it as such. I, however, believe it. That moment, inexplicable, intangible, surprising. Yes, it is death.

When I signed up for this gig, my life's work, the idea of being a whore was unappealing. The hours, long, sometimes tedious; unsatisfying, I thought. The urge to call it quits in the middle of a blowjob, so strong. The ubiquitous image of the working girl with the bored look on her face as yet another client described his ultimate fantasy, knowing full-well he was describing the previous client's? Yes, that was what I thought of when the g*ds said it was who I was to become. That was then.

I traipsed into pagan spirituality quite by accident, a momentous occasion that greeted me with bleeding everywhere, cramping to the point of an inability to walk, to move, to function. I remember being laid out in a hotel room far from home, where no one knew me. It wasn't until later on that I realized that if it hadn't been for one close friend/lover, I would probably have shattered physically and mentally trying to deal with knowing what I had become, with being this thing the g*ds have made of me.

I had been expressly kinky for a while, and despite knowing that rhythmic flogging, needle play, and a new found favorite, body punching, put me into quiet states of mind, I never put the two together. In my head, what I did to get my rocks off did not in any way connect to what I did with my spirit. Catholic guilt was so deeply ingrained, that the idea of calling out to g*d in the middle of sex was blasphemy, but I would do it anyway. It felt good, it made the sex feel great, I felt energetic and filled (hah!), but never stopped and considered why.

Fast forward through my training and I hit a crossroads. I was presented with an option; a rarity in my path, but it was there. To one side lay the path of holding onto the attachments of Mother Church, continuing to try and live with expiating guilt for the world and for myself, likely to feel frustrated with not getting anywhere. On the other I could offer up my body, and all its processes, for the g*ds to use as they saw fit. To wallow, to be uplifted, to be able to use this vessel that housed my spirit for the coming together with Spirit. All I had to do was turn on a red light. Maybe, once in a while, put on a dress.

My g*ds, my holy pimps. My Malachis. They traveled a road of being in between everything, a part of and yet, apart from. Psychopomps, sexual beings, they used and lived in a world where the idea of sex and death mingled, coalesced. I was led to learn their attributed powers from the rituals of pain and pleasure. They blurred the lines between my world and theirs. They always asked me for a bigger orgasm, a longer trip through the emotions of pain; through the joy of the needle entering flesh to the fear at the feeling of tails stinging my flesh. In the beginning I went at the merest nod from them. I went where I felt I needed to be. I soaked in education and experience knowing my body was being used as the record for all that I put myself through.

Over time things got better, I was able to pick and choose the work, the clients, and the effort I put forth. But there were days when I could not look at myself in the mirror. When I saw that in order to do this work, of being their whore, that I had to become something else; something darker, brighter, heavier, lighter than my true form. I had to shift mentality, psychically, physically, in order to survive a few more minutes of this bondage, this fucking, this orgasm, to reach that state where it all falls away and it is just me, being used by the g*ds. The g*ds put me to my paces, they test me out with different scenarios, clients, even in established moments of privacy by drawing forth a new shape from me; can I endure this as a member of the Fae? How about as a shewolf? As a dark elf? As herself? What is she, past all this? When does she stop shifting? What is her limit? I hear these questions asked as I go through yet another ordeal. And boy, do they use me. I have bled profusely, cried my eyes out, come home battered, bruised, broken, destroyed. I start out each ritual clean, fresh-pressed as the saying goes, and at the end of it, I am a shell of myself. I get scooped out, emptied, eviscerated at their feet; their mouths insistent, hungry for flesh to taste, tear into, and rip apart. They cut and slice and spread me open, forcing me to strip away the external. Drawing out of me the base, the dark, the hidden depths I willingly wallow in for them.

That was the first inkling of wanting to turn off the light. Wanting it to shine less brightly, less red. Longing to be myself for myself – once again. I grew exhausted, drawn, and uncommunicative to them, I recoiled from all of it. Instead of giving my body and staying present I started drawing inward, hiding from what was going on, thinking that whatever was going on with me was happening to another body, another person, another self. I succeeded at this – more than I expected. I was pulling away, mentally and physically. They could not draw me out and unfortunately, those around me – lovers of my choosing, former clients, friends, covenmates, family – all suffered the effects. The clients did not care as long as I was willing to don the mask and play along. I would lie there, responding enough for it to be convincing, but feeling the deadening happening to me. The more I felt it, the more withdrawn I became.

Deepest crimson became candy apple became the palest pink as I withered from the red light. I could feel wounds that had been opened up by the process that I had let fester. World wounds, personal, impersonal, whatever the cuts and stabs had come from, I had not repaired them. I felt the bones that had been broken fused into wrong positions and wrong angles. I felt useless. To myself, to my clients, to them. I felt myself crouched down in this dark corner wanting to be ignored, to be cast aside, forgotten.

But, my g*ds, they never forgot me. They found me, wherever I would attempt to hide, and drag me out, kicking, flailing, screaming my lungs out. They would take the rags I had used to try and hide my nudity and shred them off me, their nails scratching flesh, snagging in my skin, pulling at scabs as their fingers found breasts, mouth, cunt, ass. I would go limp, tears rolling down my cheeks, as they moved me and positioned me as they needed for easiest access. Down on my knees with my head tilted up? No protest here. On my back, my legs spread open to the point of snapping my hips? Not a whimper. The tears poured down my chin, bounced off my skin, or continued their slide down my torso to mat into my pubic hair.

There finally came the day when I realized that some semblance of a balance had to be achieved. I had been working on being drawn back to them, I knew that despite the ordeals, despite the feeling of not owning my flesh, that I was never going to back away from the work. The day they dragged me in front of them, stood me there as they surveyed what they had made of me. They wanted to see, and I would show them. That day I flaunted for them. I had hooks inserted into my chest, and the tethers on the hooks were attached to a huge chain spider web. I was attached to its center, the lines drawn taut as I swayed and danced on the web. As I did this, I felt it. The instinct to spin a web of my own, to watch as I joined the web before me and how it became the web that joins the worlds. I had but a small part in it, but I could see where my lines lead: to lovers, to friends, to spirits, all towards the center. I climbed up onto the web, feeling no shift, just this human body of mine taking and placing my hands on the chain with reverence and awe at the power that flowed through me. I could feel the heat from my cunt, pulsing.

My clit was hardening at the sense of this; kundalini awake and moving, yet not being the focus, merely being strength I was drawing on. I stepped up onto the web, my left foot leading. I looked down, and saw so little blood coming from the hooks. I climbed up the rings of the web, each time coming into the center, closer and closer to the nexus, to Spirit. I watched as my spirit swirled around me, took in the feeling of those who were watching me and joining me in their own way, felt their energy swirl with mine. The maelstrom all around me and yet I wasn't being tossed around by it. I was cradled by it. I kept climbing, past the center of the web, reaching up, reaching the top of the web, stretching myself up higher. I called down, my one distinctly

human moment, I was still afraid. I heard a dear friend, one who has hit, cut, punched, flogged, slapped me all whilst knowing that she loved me and recognized my need to go through that for the sake of the path I walk, she called out to me, reminding me that the g*ds were on my side, that they would not abandon me now.

My humanity slipped away as those words wrapped me in truth. I stood up, let go of the frame, and reached for the divinity that embraces me. I reached up, alive and glorious in the eyes of entire pantheons, worlds that exist not on this plane; demons, dark elves, fairies, others? all watching in amazement at the surrender of myself. That moment brought me to the edge of my own sanity, took me past it, further than I had ever traveled the road of my own madness and showed me, myself. This thing of energy that could be harnessed and directed by their will but that could make manifest self-will as well as theirs, that I was not only a being apart, but that I was also a being a part of.

I climbed down, collapsed into the center, felt the way stars feel as they collapse and form new galaxies, new wonders, new worlds. I kept coming down, knowing that the cheering I heard wasn't just in the plane of experience but outside of it as well. I stepped off, I undid the hooks, I fell back onto the earth, felt it reach to me as a lover would. I felt the arms of my friend wrap around me and I shattered. I came and cried and laughed and came. I was orgasm made manifest at that moment. I came as the world, for the world, because of the world. I came in ways I had never before. I came for the violence against women to end, I came for the wars of the world to stop, I came as a dance of Spirit upon the earth. I saw the cremation grounds of Kali, the dust kicked up as she danced on her lands and I joined her in that dance.

This is what they made of me. This is my light, and oh, how bright it glows. How red and alive.

Over the Top:
An Ordeal Master's
Foray into the Numinous

By D. Christopher Dryer

"I want you to cut me."

Vesper stood in the kitchen, bathed in springtime sunshine that poured through an open window. She pronounced each word as if it were a personal manifesto, her silvery voice ringing with clarion certainty.

"I have been feeling for a while now like I wanted to do something," Vesper explained, "something to focus where I'm going, something to align my direction with the Universe."

I'd been sharing an evolving, eclectic spiritual practice with a handful of people, and Vesper was one of them. She'd been called to ministry as a spiritual healer and teacher, and, for the past few years, she and I had walked much of our religious path together. When Vesper had left me a message a few days earlier, letting me know she wanted to talk, I'd wondered what was up. Now I was starting to understand. She was planning the next step on her path. I felt grateful she wanted to share it with me.

"At first I didn't know what," she continued. "I sensed it would be something for my body, but I wasn't sure what exactly."

"Hmm. And then the 'something' found you?" I offered. A warm breeze moved through the room, like a spirit in our midst.

"Yes, definitely. One day from who knows where – snap! It came to me. Just like that, I got this image in my mind of an ampersand," she proclaimed, presenting her left hip, "here."

Vesper's lithe body snaked into a sinuous curve as her right hand gestured to where thigh meets hip, and hip meets buttock.

"You've heard of an ampersand, right?" she asked, her hand moving to the space between us and tracing an invisible line that curved and looped in the air. "One of those squiggly things?"

"Sure," I replied. "The hieroglyph for *and*. It used to be in the alphabet. Right on beyond z. I think ampersands are fascinating."

"Of course. I pretty much figured you would. And you get what I'm talking about, right? It's a way for me to set the course for who I'm supposed to be – or maybe to get help being who I already am. It's about both of those, at the same time. *Ampersand* just sums it all up. You know, like *AND!*"

I nodded. I did know. The word *and* had come to represent a spiritual path for her. *And* was about holding something as true without negating something else. It was about transcending paradox. It was about allowing both "this" and "that" to be beautiful, such that the appreciation of one would not devalue the other. Without question, an ampersand would serve as a fitting symbol for Vesper's creed.

"I can see its shape – I can *feel* it – in me already. This is a part of me, it's mine, and at the same time it's something I still need to receive. You know? So, I'd really like to have you and Starlight give it to me in ceremony."

Vesper, Starlight, and I knew one other well. Starlight was, in her words,

"several different kinds of witch," and she tapped into the Sacred Feminine like no one else I'd ever met.

Starlight and Vesper's devotions blended well with my soul's purpose: the Path of Ordeal Mastery. On this path, I worshiped the Divine through intentionally challenging rites, starting with the ordeal of self-mastery. As I mastered my craft, Starlight and Vesper were Path-walkers who sought my direction and offered their service. As Ordeal Master, I drew on liturgies of intense discipline, affect, and physical sensations to join them on explorations of uncertain realms.

The ordeal Vesper sought was scarification. Although different techniques are possible, I almost always use a sharp blade to scarify. More often than not, I go over the entire pattern twice. The first pass is shallow, and the second is deep, but not all the way through the dermis. Over time, a scar forms in the desired shape. Like tattoos, piercings, and other body modifications, a cutting need not be a form of worship; people pursue body modifications for many different reasons, such as aesthetics, self-expression, and as a sign of social affiliation.

Vesper laid bare her desire: "So, I'd love for you to put together a ritual for me and carve an ampersand into my skin."

She stood hand-on-hip, carefree in her tank-top-and-jeans-shorts attire. Through strands of blonde hair, Vesper's luminous eyes met mine, and for a moment nothing moved except gossamer drapes that danced on the slow, undulating zephyr. As I studied her in silence, the breadth and depth of her momentous entreaty continued to unfold.

"The radiant creature in front of me is inviting me to witness the next stage of her evolution," I mused. "Vesper wishes to surrender herself to me. With her body in my hands and under my will, in service to Spirit, I would sire something new. From her healing flesh would emerge a lifelong symbol of her chosen way of being."

Ceremonial scarification is not something to undertake lightly. Cutting can be rather more painful and bloody than, say, tattooing, and entails serious considerations, including those related to skin infections and universal precautions.

"Why me?" I wondered.

Vesper's eyes revealed the answers. Her view of me reflected the man I most aspire to be. "She trusts in me," I realized. "She sees the care and mastery I bring to officiating liturgies. She believes in the power of my love. She feels safe with me — body and soul."

I felt my blood surging to my chest as I basked in Vesper's esteem. "And why not?" I asked myself.

"I know that we journey together well and care for each other well. I don't doubt my experience with scarification. And I have yet to meet a Path-walker who is more ready than Vesper is.

"It's not about our strengths eliminating the chance we would make mistakes," I reminded myself. "It's about recommitting ourselves to what's sacred, again and again, in each moment so that when things don't go as planned, our rites can still support growth and healing. I believe we can do that."

"I'd really like it if you could give that to me. Will you do it?" Vesper asked. Without warning, her tone had shifted from dominance to deference.

In my mind's eye, the man I aspired to be, like a ravening predator, chased the woman Vesper intended to bring forth. My mouth watered in anticipation of plunging my fangs deep into her sweet-smelling flesh, marking her forever with my bite. My heart pummeled against my sternum, as I pounced at chance before me. Seizing my quarry, I took Vesper's hands into mine.

"Absolutely. I would be honored to make that happen with you."

Two white candles burned atop the wooden altar. Their flickering flames illuminated the sacramental tools that I had blessed for tonight's rite. Sharp blades of steel scalpels glittered on a resplendent blood-red altar cloth. Nearby, an ornate bronze censer held smoldering myrrh. Its smoke gyrated up into a languid musky-sweet cloud. A colorful multitude of pinpoint lights glimmered on ropes and strings throughout our temple. Starlight knelt in the center of our sanctuary, petitioning Gods and Goddesses, compassionate and ferocious, with devout prayers. Sensual, swaying trip-hop undulated from the sound system, while Vesper danced with Starlight's familiar — a living serpent — slithering around her hands.

Billowing incense pervaded my nostrils, and I tasted its spicy, ancient scent on my tongue. Tonight, I would be guiding Vesper's exploration and affirming her strength and dignity. By accepting Vesper's surrender to the journey, I took on pivotal responsibility to attend to all of our needs: physical, social, emotional, and spiritual. From the kink community perspective, I was the Top, the one doing the cutting and directing the flow, yet I also was bottoming to Divinity, the Top above us all.

My duties called me to guard my congregation from harm. I paced the perimeter of our temple, step by slow step. Deep in concentration, I visualized spiritual energy flowing through me and out the red-stained oak wand I held. The gleaming energy I'd laid down formed a circumscribing barrier around us. "I consecrate this sacred container," I chanted, "to hold everything that is needed for our rite and to keep out everything that might interfere with our success."

Still on her knees, Starlight had not moved since I fastened a collar around her neck. In accordance with my instructions, she was "holding center." By continuing the breath-work and meditation we'd started earlier, she was building a reservoir of spiritual energy that we could draw on when needed. At the same time, she served as an anchor for parts of the liturgy, such as being the center for the circle I'd cast. Anchoring the worship in this way brought focus to our intentions, attention to our needs, coordination to our collaborations, and spirit to our devotions.

In the role of co-officiator, Starlight's job was to support both Master and Journeyer, expanding the possibilities for each of us. She was a practiced Ordeal Path-walker, with experience both giving and receiving scarifications and a consummate talent for harmonizing energy with those around her. Her broad expertise allowed her to excel at bottoming and topping under me, bottoming to less experienced Path-walkers who were topping under me, and being Witness to all the players in a scene.

Vesper's soft fingertips rubbed holy oil onto Starlight's chakras while visualizing the unction driving out malevolent influences and imbuing a divine emanation. Meanwhile, I performed the Lesser Banishing Ritual of the Pentagram. I was clearing our temple of annoying spirits and everything else that might inhibit our purpose. "For about me flames the Pentagram," I incanted, "and in the Column stands the six-rayed Star."

Out of nowhere, I became aware of Starlight's magic. It felt like a warm caress that crossed from my skin into my body, where it added to my spiritual energy. Without seeing Starlight or knowing what she was up to, I could tell she was performing one of her special kinds of witchcraft. She sometimes would support my rituals by feeding my spiritual energy.

Once my banishing was complete, I thanked Starlight for her assistance and directed her to smudge Vesper. Starlight glided across the sanctum, her vestments flowing with her. She wore a long black open knit robe, one tie at the bust, cut away below. Once she had the sage stick burning in an abalone shell, Starlight used a feather to waft the smoke around Vesper's body, head to toe, front to back. The white smoke smelled green and woody and made my body feel unburdened.

I moved to the far end of the temple to start our ritual quarter calls. I was evoking spiritual support into the cleared space. "I call to the East!" I hailed, summoning the guardians with words, tools, gestures, and visualizations. "Goddesses and Gods! Ancestors and Angels! Spirits, Totems, and Elementals of Air! Of Truth, Discernment, and Imagination! Come to Us! Protect Us! And Support Our Work Tonight!" I called each direction in time, summoning each to guard, protect, and support our work.

I switched our liturgical music from the sexy beats of trip-hop to lush, euphoric house in preparation for the next phase of our liturgy. Moving to the middle of the sanctuary, I sat down with Starlight and Vesper. "I think we may be ready for the cutting. Is there anything else before we begin?" I asked.

"I'm ready to go, Sir," Vesper replied.

"All right. Me too," Starlight affirmed, joyful excitement shining brightly in her eyes. "We can start whenever you want, Sir."

"Sounds good. Our rite has begun," I stated.

Sitting in a triangle, we started raising our awareness. We brought attention to our breath and our bodies, resting in stillness. Expanding our awareness, we tuned into our energetic field, noticed the sensation of subtle energy flowing through our bodies, visualizing the unseen currents. We allowed ourselves to open to that flow, receiving it with gratitude, and revering the source of the energy as divine. Without hurrying, we began to interact with the energy. We channeled it in a gentle, respectful manner. I sensed serpentine vibrations rising along my spine.

Extending our energy out, we started to feel out ways to tune in to each other's field. I became aware of an ever-changing circuit of subtle energies running among the three of us. I found places where I could send energy out and receive the return. The more I explored, the more I found that I could maintain the exchange longer, and the more intense the body sensations became. I then took these energies to my Scalpel, connecting to His field with respect, like calling on a respected elder unannounced, and brought this entity into our circuit. Having raised our awareness of each other, our context, and ourselves, I directed our attention to the purpose of our ceremony.

"Vesper, if you would, tell us what your intention for the cutting is."

She collected her thoughts for a moment. "I want to express who I am in terms of the philosophy of *And*. *And* means living with respect for the possibility of choosing *both* instead of *one* or *the other*. That's what the symbol, the ampersand, means to me, and I want to make that a part of me. Sir."

"Very well. May we dedicate this rite of passage to the Divine and may our work tonight sanctify this intention. So say we all."

"So say we all!" answered Vesper and Starlight.

I brought over our ritual tools, including sterile gauze, bandages, rubbing alcohol, antibiotic ointment, a felt tip temporary tattoo pen, a sharps container, reusable scalpel handles, and single-use blades. To scarify skin, I use different shaped blades. The shape of the blade determines the kind of shape that can be cut and the kind of scar that forms.

Vesper was lying on her side, left hip up with her skin exposed. She wore long black fingerless gloves and a formfitting strapless black dress. Starlight had wrapped herself half around Vesper and cradled her in a sweet embrace. I kneeled beside them, resting for a moment with my hand on each of them.

I began to spread alcohol around the area I would soon cut. Its sharp odor stabbed the air. I knew that the quickly evaporating liquid felt chilly on Vesper's skin, and that the sting of it in her open wound would soon overpower the cooling sensation.

I placed a firm hand around Vesper's hip to hold her fast if necessary. Journeyers may not be able to avoid flinching, and quick movements are best avoided around surgical knives. Often, I use a temporary tattoo pen to draw the design. This time, however, my intuition told me to cut without a template.

Holding the shape in my mind's eye, with Vesper's words of power still echoing in my ears, I started carving the symbol into her flesh. I brought the blade down, perpendicular to the surface of her skin. Moving the edge slowly along her thigh, I pressed down until it pierced into her body. The steel scalpel glided shallowly through her pale, smooth form. In the blade's wake, a red, curving channel formed. Vesper's sensations flowed along an empathetic conduit into my body. Driven by the pain of the incision, we rode a precarious crest of intensity. Over the course of a dozen seconds, my inexorable knife curved bit by bit along a four inch-long arc before the first incision was complete. A long, low purr vibrated out from deep inside Vesper's body. Starlight's soft lips smiled and then kissed Vesper's cheek.

I was paying close attention to Vesper, gauging how she'd coped with the first cut. I've found that well-mixed cocktail of torment and comfort often distinguished the most successful ordeals. After a brief respite, I raised my blade for the next slice. Recalling the shape and meaning of the sigil, I willed that my actions would help bring Vesper's intention into reality. I first traced the design without touching her, my knife hovering first over the crimson slash I'd just made, then over the virginal skin I would penetrate next. Once my muscles had memorized the gesture, I brought the blade down and into her body. I moved the sharp edge through her skin, following the sacred shape that seemed a part of her already. Steel parted flesh. In the aftermath of my blade, Vesper's skin opened like a blossoming flower.

She seemed to welcome both the pleasure and the pain of her experience. Starlight's hands stroked Vesper's skin, and her love soothed Vesper's soul. Enjoying the powerful feeling of her inner being, I continued my carving once again. I chiseled in her body another long curve and another, which she received with poise.

"Your strength and your spirit are beautiful," Starlight whispered in Vesper's ear. "You are doing a really amazing job."

My slices had opened Vesper's skin into a single, twisting canyon, as thick as a stick of incense and half as deep. The initial scarifying of Vesper's sigil was complete. For the second, deeper incision, I switched to a different scalpel handle and blade, while Starlight lit more incense to re-consecrate the space. Centering ourselves once again, we reconnected with our own breath and energy and then with each other's. With our awareness raised, I charged the new knife.

I brought my blade to the design I had already sliced into Vesper. Placing the tip within the red furrow, I penetrated the gash at an oblique angle. I began tracing the exact same pattern, only this time I cut more deeply. Getting the optimal depth for a scarification is tricky. Too shallow, and a lasting scar may not form; too deep, and physical injury may occur. The precise depth depends on the individual's skin and the location of the incision.

The feeling of cutting deep into her was amazing. The skin on her thigh was silky and seemed delicate. Nonetheless, a mesh of tough connective fibers rested within the depths of her dermis. I could feel my blade rending apart the strands in her body, like a saw through a fishing net. The sensation was similar to unzipping a zipper. Each and every fiber tugged along the edge of my blade while Vesper's skin opened wider behind my knife.

That intense visceral sensation focused my consciousness like a laser beam onto the tip of my scalpel. Because I was going over the same design, I was cutting into a delicate sore spot – an existing wound. A compelling impulse to protect the wound from further injury would only be natural. Nonetheless, she welcomed me as I slid between her already parted flesh before pressing deeper still into her body.

Starlight cued a new playlist, and the adamant, techno-shamanic beats of ecstatic trance music vibrated throughout our souls. The wet, metallic scent of her open flesh tingled my nostrils. Across Vesper's body, a thin sheen of perspiration glistened. The sharp edge of my knife pressed deeper into her split flesh, puncturing through structure of her skin. Such rare intimacy bound my ardent emotions to her. Through this link, my own body experienced the sensations of Vesper's living meat being rent by merciless steel.

The agony of her pain uncloaked the strength and humanity of Vesper's heart. The ordeal transfigured my image of Vesper, her inner divinity radiating from her body with blinding brilliance. Oceanic swells of loving compassion submerged my heart. At the same time, the white-hot pain aroused sensual desires and fed lusty, gluttonous pleasures. I craved the feast of her torment.

"These desires are wrong," a part of me condemned. "How could I want to hurt someone for whom I feel such compassion and respect?"

All of a sudden, I experienced rapture. Where I had been Ordeal Master, holding flesh and soul in my loving control, now I surrendered to holy authority. The appearance of my surroundings became dreamlike, and I watched the veil between my world and the numinous dissolve. A force outside myself lifted my senses up to another plane. From this new vantage point, my vision of Vesper and myself changed.

Compassion and respect had allowed us to explore challenges together, to find pleasure in them, and to share that pleasure. The pain wasn't something I was doing to her; it was something that I was doing *with* her. The pleasure wasn't something I was feeling at her expense; it was something she shared with me. Without the compassion and respect, neither of us would have felt pleasure. My voracious feelings seemed loving rather than shameful.

Descending back into the sanctuary, I felt deep gratitude for all that is. The epiphany reverberated through my being as I became aware of the sigil I was helping to create: *And*. Finishing the final cuts, I felt its wisdom speak to me. The pain was something Vesper and I were doing together: *And*. The pleasure was something Vesper and I were feeling together: *And*. Experiencing pleasure from the pain required having compassion and respect: *And*.

When the last incision was complete, we all charged the symbol by meditating on its intention and its form. The sigil was done, its crimson line snaking through the tight twists and turns of an ampersand. Despite the moist, pink trough in her skin, Vesper did not bleed.

I had never seen anything like it. Always before, heavy trickles of blood would pour out from such a deep cut. Instead, only a tiny reservoir of blood pooled within the hollow of the incision. The skin around the wound stayed bloodless. The miracle astounded us all, and none could account for the mystery. Starlight pressed a cloth flat across the cutting, absorbing the contents of the trough to form a well-defined imprint of the sigil.

The rite of passage complete, we began to conclude our liturgy. I changed our music to the subdued spaciousness of relaxing ambient music. Starlight placed the cloth with its bloodstained stamp on the altar. Holding hands we offered thanks to the quarters for the blessings we had been given. For a final clearing, I performed the Lesser Banishing Ritual of the Pentagram a second time. I brought down our perimeter by reversing the actions I used to build it.

As we returned from our journey, I marveled at the beauty of Vesper's sigil and pondered my numinous encounter. Spirit held me rapt in Her mysteries: how is it that my experience as an Ordeal Master connected me so powerfully with the Divine?

"You have to see this," Vesper enjoined.

Several months had passed since the scarification ordeal, and, up to this point, life's vagaries had prevented me from seeing the final result. To remedy that, Vesper dropped her pants and clambered up onto the counter. A serendipitous encounter had landed us both back in the same fateful kitchen where she had first proposed the rite. She settled one foot on the countertop to offer me a better view of her unclad thigh.

I moved closer to behold the body art on display. The wounds had healed into a striking scar. Smooth lines of uniform width curved to form a perfect ampersand. The coral-pink scar contrasted with Vesper's honey-amber skin. My fingertips traced the twisting design, feeling its raised ridges beneath my soft stokes. Without a doubt, it was one of the best scarification results I'd ever seen.

"It's amazing," I said. "That's what I imagined it looking like, but it's also even better than I hoped."

"It is," Vesper agreed. "This is what I imagined there when I first talked with you about it."

"What's it like having it?" I asked. "You took your intention and put it in your body. How is that for you?"

"I love having it be a part of me. It is me. I see it. I feel it with my fingers. It's just who I am now."

"Has your relationship to *and* changed?" I wondered.

"You remember how I didn't really bleed when you cut me?"

"Oh, yeah," I replied. "Very much so."

"I think the reason I didn't bleed was that I was letting the pain happen and I was welcoming it. It wasn't like it didn't hurt. It just didn't have to matter. I could feel the pain a hundred percent and be a hundred percent okay. *And.* On some body level I think I just didn't register that anything was wrong, so my body never felt like bleeding."

"Uh-huh. You know what? I can understand that. Shortly before the cutting was complete," I reported, "I had two seemingly paradoxical feelings: I felt deep compassion for you, and I really was enjoying hurting you."

"Yep," Vesper responded. "I can see that."

"At first, I felt horrible that I was enjoying hurting you like that."

"I can see that for you, too!" she chuckled.

"But when I felt that, I had a vision. I saw clearly that the pain I gave you was coming from the same place of love that my compassion was. Seeing that allowed me to better love all of me, not just the parts that look like I expect them to look. And I want to love myself – all of myself."

"And you know what," I noted, "It's kind of like another piece of you and your ampersand. It's loving the easy parts *and* the rest of me: *And.*"

Vesper headed out soon after that. Even so, the image of her sigil lingered with me long after she was gone. It continued to exist for me as a history of the ordeal and my encounter with Divine Grace. By tracing its contours, I recounted the image of Vesper's figure while ridden with pain. I recalled the texture of my pleasure while I rode with her. The ampersand reminded me to look beyond the paradoxes in my everyday life. Her scar memorialized the shape of the experience. Just as paint on a canvas records a stroke of an artist's brush, the wounds had recorded the arc of my knife and the arc of my soul.

The Divine Scene

By Alexandra Entendre

The only Universal Truth is that there really is no Universal Truth. Believe it or not, dear reader, this seemingly trivial idea propelled me hopelessly towards connecting with existence. This was a connection born through chaos, through *not*-knowing, and through Eris, the Greek mythological Goddess of Chaos and Discord and the Discordian matron Goddess. She is the Divine Top of the Scene that we are all a part of, this Scene called existence. Given my upbringing and background grounded firmly within mathematics, logic, and strict ethnic culture, I need to explain how I came to my spiritual beliefs. I cannot really say if there is a definite starting point, but if I had to pick one, it would be during my sophomore year attending Rutgers University.

One night during the semester that I stayed at the ludicrously lascivious living quarters on campus, I happened to hang out with a crazy-yet-surprisingly-insightful woman named Lucy. Lucy and I have known each other for years now, but the experience to which I am referring was only our second encounter. Being a curious young math major, I brought up the subject of mathematics, which we began to discuss in earnest. Our conversation focused mostly on the view of mathematics as the language of the sciences. We spoke of some of the more advanced aspects of the subject; primarily complex analysis and chaos theory. Mathematicians make a distinction between society's common usage of the word chaos and its deeper function within mathematics. Gradually, after the discussion with Lucy began to wane, I began to form a crude awareness of certain patterns that pervade our existence. These patterns were similar, but only to themselves; the fractals apparent in trees and ferns, weather, society. Chaos is everywhere, I soon concluded, and from then on I was obsessed with discovering just how deep the relationship between mathematical chaos and existence delved. This fascination with fractal patterns and chaos soon brought me to the deliciously discordant, deluded Discordian dogma (or was that catma?), and to my own spiritual beliefs.

My worldview has always contained a certain modicum of spirituality. Ever since I was young, I have had the tendency to categorize things according to the classical Greek elements; air, earth, fire, and water. Though I did not realize it at the time, dear reader, my prior brush with Lucy added chaos as the fifth, unifying element. The Discordian system of ideas helped to further cement that, and would pave the way towards my first truly spiritual experience. Discordianism is the belief that the underlying nature of existence is chaos, and that order and disorder are just illusions imposed on Chaos. It is an absurdist approach to the Eastern ideologies of Zen and Tao. The matron deity for the Discordians is Eris, the aforementioned Goddess of Chaos and Discord. Prior to my initial spiritual encounter with Eris, I had been reading *Principia Discordia*, the principal text of Discordianism, at the suggestion of a friend. At the time, I recall thinking to myself, "Yeah, this stuff sort of makes sense, I guess it's in line with the connections that I've seen between mathematical chaos and the universe," but on some intuitive level, I did not really *believe* in it. I had always admired people with faith, seeing as I had none myself. When I was about sixteen, I came to the realization that I was not a Christian, despite being raised Armenian Apostolic. After that, I did not feel like an atheist, or an agnostic, or any of those other words that I had heard to describe people's beliefs. I just felt this sense of total emptiness, as if I was lacking something. That would all change, however, as I hurled myself headlong into filling that feeling of desolation with a love for everything in existence, for Eris, and thus also for you, dearest reader.

It all started on a spring night like any other, in the middle of 2010. A close friend and I were sharing an experience with Lucy, our topics of discussion mainly concerning Chaos and Discordianism. Eventually, we fell silent; my attention had been drawn towards a picture of Eris, scrounged from the depths of the Internet by my stalwart companion. Looking back now, I was essentially meditating upon this picture of this figure who was *supposed* to be my Goddess, as by that point I had decided that Discordianism was "pretty okay." As I stared on, *things* just sort of lined up, in a not-at-all sort of way. New clarity quickly pervaded my awareness, the sort of clarity that required my having a concept of just how little I really knew about how existence *worked*. It was as if the Discordian ideologies that I had absorbed fell into place, into a pattern resembling something out of a M.C. Escher painting. The crux of what I had absorbed from reading Discordian texts was that Eris represents the universe, Chaos, everything that exists.

See, my dearest, *dearest* reader, up until that point I had always consciously (or subconsciously) marked the distinction between *myself* and *the rest of the universe*. I am not separate from the rest of existence; I am a part of it, a part of this Chaos that we are all amidst. I am a part of Eris, and I love her with all of my being. With eyes still trained upon the image in front of me, the phrase "sometimes Goddess likes to fuck with your mind" echoed throughout my mind. There was an imposing feeling of being watched by something *more*. It felt like *She* was staring directly back at *me*, and the image of Goddess grinned. Now, dearest reader, this perception resounded and ripped through my reality; that is to say that my perceptions visually distorted and changed. I had never, *ever*, felt anything quite as intense as when She was looking at me. I suddenly started feeling a very powerful, passionate, pervasive love for this Goddess, for *my* Goddess! The only thing that I can relate to my experience with Goddess is the feeling that I get staring into the eyes of my Dominant as she gives me *that look*. The realizations that had brought me to the love that I feel for Eris were overbearing, crushing me under the weight of the nothing with which I formed a connection. Her presence is everywhere, Her divinity present within everything, topping existence.

My friend and I decided to take a stroll outside after dawn broke on the morning after my initial Erisian encounter. At the time, I was living on the outskirts of the college city New Brunswick in central New Jersey; my immediate surroundings upon exiting my apartment being run-down houses, garbage, and asphalt. Stepping outside just then, I was taken aback by how beautiful everything seemed. It struck me how that simple idea that "Goddess is everything" made the subjective reality around me more aesthetically pleasing, easier to bear, easier to *love*. As a somewhat submissive soul, I see Eris as the purest idea behind existence, the state of unknown that comes prior to understanding, the state of flux. Though the novelty of this has worn off, the effects still stay with me, reminding me of the underlying connection that all things share. In this way, Eris changed the very way that I see existence. Her effect on me is akin to a permanent mindfuck; my perception of the universe is altered. With Goddess, the only safewords and negotiation that we share are my own limits; how deep I am willing to let myself go is up to me, is up to Eris, since She is everything. Of the various altered states that I have experienced, connections with Eris take me somewhere akin to subspace, the weight of the realizations that She brings me to sending me careening into that space-sundering, sanguinely serene spell of a trip. The feeling of that connection to existence, that *power* comes before anything else now, Eris's presence dominating everything in my thoughts, in my reality.

From a simple conversation with a surprisingly insightful crazy woman to a bond forming with craziness divine, my spiritual path propelled me up and down, headlong into an understanding of kinky divinity. Everyone's path to making a spiritual connection is unique. The bonds that we make with spirits, with deities, with entities beyond, are not unlike the bonds we share with our Tops, with our bottoms, with our kinky partners. Our spiritual journeys are a Scene unto themselves, with us at the bottom and whatever we happen to connect with at the top. My personal experiences with Eris put her at the Top of my Divine Scene... What will be Topping yours?

Hunting Lions

By Scratch Hunter

"What's your name?" chuffs the slender male standing across from me in a dimly lit alley behind *The Mix*. Undoubtedly, faggots have sucked and grinded on one another here for decades. It is the Castro, after all. Although, tonight seems awfully tame for a Bay Area bar; I had romantically envisioned lots of back alley sex. *Expectations*.

"Scratch." I smile and extend my paw. These months of yoga are apparently paying off – he's cute.

He shakes my paw and stifles a laugh. "No, man... What's your real name?"

My real name? I think to myself. *My name is the one I give you.* "It's Scratch," I purred, my tail swishing behind me.

He searches my face, trying to understand. I persist wearing a wry smile, thinking it'd draw him in.

"Whatever," he says and slinks away into the flashing darkness of the club, a pedestrian Bud Lite in hand.

Hmm. Didn't he know he was caught? He must not know much about big cats like me. We're some of the most efficient hunters in the animal kingdom; we get what we want. When we pounce from our tree branch, the experience is over very quickly. It's the shape of our jaws. Our canine teeth sit in a deep recess in the mandible, which allows them to sink deep into the neck of our prey — animals sometimes as large as an elk. These teeth are like blades slipping between vertebrae, severing the spinal cord in fractions of a second, and then it's over, our quarry lying helpless in our jaws. Like Craig Childs wrote about us, "Why would evolution improve upon such an efficient design?" Indeed.

But this situation got me thinking: is this a mask or my genuine self? He probably thought I was a hustler or something. My guess is he's run into enough wacky types in such a big city that he's leery of anyone with an unusual name or persona. *Who knows?* Maybe he was once exploring identities too, but was done with the game. It's hard to tell these days. Queer identities are everywhere, shifting quicker than anyone can keep up with, especially if you've been reinventing yourself as often as I have.

I came out of the closet about six years ago, during an English-teaching gig in China. I was isolated and desperate for human contact, but since numerous sites were blocked by the Chinese government, all I had access to was an online community called "furries." Never heard of them before. Their artistic renderings of anthropomorphic animals got me hot, and I was masturbating feverishly as I pored over the digital menagerie: humanoid dogs with enormous cocks mounting one another, bears getting fucked by otters, African lions spurting buckets of cum onto the snouts of three hungry zebras kneeling before them, centaurs piling atop one another in a pastoral orgy, underage cubs in human clothing and settings exploring their sexuality and gender — behind closed doors, so mom and dad don't find out — a magical dragon with four enormous breasts devouring a tiny unicorn with twin cocks. Interspecies mating. Genderfuck. Age play. Gigantism. Vore. The realm of possibility suddenly became boundless. It was more human than human. But I continued to wrestle with my sexuality, struggling to maintain control of my animal urgings — the spirit was to be master of the flesh.

To assuage my Mormon guilt, I wrote a poem about the gay lifestyle, as I understood it. In it, I compared homos to a pack of ravenous lions that called to me from the depths of their cave, a rumbling chant that enticed me, my cock leading in the direction of my desire. Loathsome temptations I so desperately wanted to give in to. I was Daniel – thrust into the den, helplessly surrounded by sweaty, hungry cats, their manes brushing against my naked skin, their intoxicating musk filling my nostrils and saturating every pore. Permission was all I needed. I gave in. I surrendered. And instead of being devoured, I began transforming into something primal. Prophetic.

I'm not the kind of fursuit-wearing, convention-going, anime-obsessed nerd hidden away in his parents' unfinished basement, like some believe most furries to be (although I love them, biblically). I simply enjoyed the idea of portraying myself online as something other than human. *Me.* I started out identifying as a bunny. My affinity for rabbits turned into a justification to get my ass pounded as often as possible. Countless furry play partners seemed to enjoy my desire to be as much of an unabashed animal as I could be; but a few other furs didn't seem to like that I was proudly upholding the "shameful" stereotype portrayed by that episode of *CSI* – that furries are a community of mascot-costumed sex fiends. But, I kinda *liked* being a big furry sex fiend. I was proud of my shameless sexual persona. Having spent so much time ashamed of my sexuality, I pushed the pendulum the other way. Being the hare, I could justify away all my sexual proclivities, for after all, what are bunnies known for if not an insatiable libido? I didn't discriminate. God would see just how far down the rabbit hole I was willing to go. *I wanted cock.* I was prey. *The fluffy white tail just made it all the more attractive for a possible mate.* I loved to fuck. *Come get me.* I loved getting dick in my ass and I would whimper in ecstasy as a lion from the local furry group would mount me bare, thrusting deep into my bunny hole. As he *came inside me, breeding* me, he growled, snarled, clawed and called me by the name I chose for myself – Blue.

I was the color of his delight. But not his love.

Blue embraced her chaotic embodiment of transgression. There was a certain thrill in liminal dimensions; it kept everyone guessing, *including herself.* (Who am I?) No one could touch its heart. *It worked for a while.* (I'm so confused.) *Blue keeps getting hurt,* my eyes would say in the mirror. My tailhole was torn last night. *She'd spread her legs just to let someone touch her heart.* I needed to think of a way to protect myself. *So, she started with a new name, Cyanide Beijaflor.* (What am I?) "Cyan" is Greek for the color of the sea – sometimes tranquil and warm but often deep and tempestuous; and "Beijaflor," Portuguese for "hummingbird" – an unpredictable flit with a needle for a beak. Cyan was a beautiful creature in transformation. The name would warn others "I am venomous and will sting if I must," like many brightly-colored creatures in the animal kingdom.

In my last year of college, I met a human. His nineteen-year-old vitriol mixed well with mine, and I discovered that I was falling in love with a boy. Dylan had heard about furries before; he'd been around the internet. He didn't know what to make of me at first, but we quickly developed something that was beautifully dark and seductive. Despite my warnings that he would be jumping in to the deep end of the pool, the boy took the plunge anyway. Dylan was either just as self-destructive as I was or he really loved me for me. *Just couldn't trust.*

The relationship failed, *as did Cyan. The bunny got lost in her hole somewhere... somewhere deep in those tunnels, didn't you?* I'm not coming out. *Such a scared little bunny. She pulled her hair out as she rocked, sobbing on the kitchen floor, the X-acto knife safely removed from her paws.* "Why does he hate me?" *she wailed.* Didn't she know she was transforming? (I need help.)

"When the student is ready, the teacher will appear," goes the old Zen saying. I needed a guide to help me make this transition. That's how it's supposed to work, right? Bobcat to Wolf to Bear to Eagle Scout. And then... what? Grow up? Into what? Boy to man? (Whatever that means.) I was wandering in a desert, a wilderness of identity, trying to understand the changes I had been going through, reluctant to feel my way through the pain and to grieve. I was lost and meandering close to a precipice I couldn't see but could feel. There was a shrill, ghostly scream in the desert night – about as chilling as one could imagine when lying under little shelter. The native people of the Americas told many stories of the mountain screamer. Was this he? And is this a warning or a call?

The phone was ringing. I was nervous to talk to a professional dominatrix.

Ring. She specializes in behavior modification. Former military. Ring. Maybe Miss Raven Grey could help, but what would I say to her? What do I need? Ring. She answered and we set up a time to meet at her home that weekend. I breathed a sigh of relief for the first time in months. Perhaps I had finally found my mentor. Appropriate that she would come in the form of a raven, the carriers of new magic.

"If you're going to be my submissive, you need to understand that it's not about what you want – it's about what I want. And there are probably going to be days when I will not be your most favorite person in the world. We'll start with the basics." I belonged to Miss Raven Grey. *I was her big kitty.* And so her tutelage began:

"Go wash the dishes. I want the kitchen spotless."

Yes Ma'am.

"I want the floor vacuumed; I have a client coming over."

Certainly, Miss Grey.

"Make me some tea – and do it right this time."

Yes, Ma'am.

"I want you to learn massage, so read this anatomy book. Color the muscle groups and get familiar with it. You can practice on me."

My pleasure, Miss Grey.

"Time for yoga."

Yes, Ma'am. With a CB-3000 locked around my sex (which now belonged to her), I started my morning salutations with newfound devotion.

"Suryanamaskara 'A'... then 'B.' Keep your thumbs grounded and your toes pointed."

Yes, Miss Grey.

I pressed my paws into the royal blue mat, gripping the whole earth below me, digging my toes into the rubber like it was topsoil. Prana. Breath. Vinyasa. Flow. My blood was circulating through every muscle, each breath filling my lungs to capacity and more. I'd push myself because that's what She wanted. *And what I want.* Miss Grey is my Mistress because I submit to her. Or am I the master of myself? *Is there a separation?* Stop thinking. Ma'am does the thinking; I do the feeling. With yoga, crunches, pushups, gardening and housework, Miss Grey would work me to the point of exhaustion. I didn't have time to think. And then I'd collapse onto the mat.

"Now lay there still and let everything wash over you."

The intoxicating smell of our commingled sweat rose to my nostrils as I lay on her blue mat. The music playing from her laptop in the background reminded me of Dylan. Of Jordan. Of Faolan. Of Dad. Of Mom. Of Grandma's passing. Of my failures and broken relationships. Pain. Suffering. *Dukha*, as the Buddha called it.

I laid there exhausted, drained, weeping. "Keep breathing in through your nose, out through your mouth. That's how you feel through it. Don't waste energy dwelling on the past – be present. One moment at a time. One breath at a time. Feel it fully, breathe it into your being and then release it. Just let it go."

Out of the corner of my eye, I saw a little wooden carving of the weeping yogi sitting on the floor next to me. He was curled up into himself as he sat in full lotus, his face in his hands, feeling deeply the suffering of the world. The ceiling stared down at me, a blank slate reflecting nothing but the memories I projected upon it. Breathe it in, let it out. The Raven indeed brought new magic into my life. I didn't know I could feel and breathe at the same time.

"Go shower up. I need you to run some errands."

Yes Ma'am.

Those winter months last year were my proving grounds. The plate of candles upon my altar provided light and comfort in the dark season, and my yoga kept me warm. I spent many nights in contemplation, reflection, reviewing the ground I had covered throughout my journey, the progress I had made, and thinking back to my first negotiations with Miss Raven Grey:

"Are you scared that you won't recognize yourself when you've come to the end of our work? Trust me: you will look into the mirror and see an old friend looking back at you."

My posture had changed. I wasn't slouching as much as I used to. Muscles had become toned and defined. My limbs could move more freely from their joints and a power from within emanated from my core, outward to my strong, capable paws. Now, I wore an eagle's feather in my mohawk. I was as a warrior in the Raven's employ. I carried myself differently, walked differently, and interacted with others differently… as a lion in the Raven's service. My focus was returning, as was my desire to live and love.

I wanted more of this magic.

"You should come with me down to Phoenix for a leather conference," offered my friend Eric. "I'll pay for the hotel and the food; I just want you to accompany me." I couldn't, wouldn't say no. I needed to learn more about spiritual leather.

The convention schedule showed a hook-pull was to take place on the last night, and spiritual preparations were to be made the night before at an ecumenical service that welcomed everyone, no matter their spiritual path or master.

I sat next to Eric and brother-bear at the devotional. We held paws, listening to the songs and prose invoking spirits of all colors to inspire and embolden all participants. I was excited, nervous to participate as a witness for the tribe. *Miss Grey would be so proud of me!*

"Will the witnesses please come forward." I rose from my chair, a proud smile on my face.

My eyes welled up as I approached the elder, brimming with the honor and privilege of dancing alongside such magnificent creatures the following night. My body shook and my chin quivered as I was set apart as a witness for my tribe, to "be the clean mirror that honors and reflects the experience of all participants" at tomorrow's ritual. He anointed my forehead, my third eye, "that my vision might be clear." Those particular words released a flood of memories of my past life as a Mormon – of temple washing and anointing, being pronounced "clean" and passing through the veil, holding the hand of God and entering into His presence – and filled me with an ecstatic joy I hadn't felt in so very, very long. The tears streamed down my face. *Breathe in through your nose and out through your mouth. Let it in… and release.*

I confided to brother-bear that since coming out of the closet, I hadn't been invited into a circle as a spiritual equal and had forgotten how vitally it was for me to be included, no matter what shape I took, what name I chose for myself, or what path I had followed. We wept together at recognizing the divine within ourselves and one another.

I was ready.

It was long past sunset. Now was the hour. The drums' pulse, steady and inviting, drew me closer to the chamber where our altar stood. Every participant had transformed. I wasn't interacting with human beings anymore, but gods and goddesses. Tricksters, sages, and beasts grappled with hooks in their flesh, attached to one another by steel and rope, thrusting, lusting, and howling, clawing, and grunting with pulsating abandon, driven further, deeper by the pounding drums.

When I awoke the next morning, I felt different – as though my transformation was complete. Scratch had found a place where he could explore, expressing himself more fully. I stood in front of the mirror, admiring the changes my body had undergone, filled with gratitude, grounded and clear.

Dark Natasha, an anthropomorphic artist within the furry community, painted a beautiful image that I look upon regularly to remind myself of who I am. It depicts Cougar, standing regally in full Native American headdress, draped in blankets, overlooking the land. The mountains and fields lay out in front of him. He loves all that he sees in his view, wishing to nurture and protect. This image is now a mirror that asks me, "Do you follow Cougar?" Yes.

I am now a mentor, imparting what I have learned. My roleplay with Kimba as his older brother requires me to teach him how to hunt in our tribe. Papa and all the other elders celebrate one another's accomplishments with pleasure, and so I am to teach my younger brother the same. Yesterday, we compared our spoils: I caught seventeen fishes, and he caught a beautiful butterfly – magical metaphors for the accomplishments of our daily lives. He's getting stronger, too. Soon, as a reward for his growth and efforts, I will give him pleasure. It will be his first time in our respective roles as brothers. When I spill my seed inside of him, it will seal our bond as brothers and I will gently, lovingly whisper my devotion to him, to teach him what I've learned, to share the magic I've been given.

We hiked up the canyon the other day; he was so excited to show me what he had found. With walking sticks in hand, we climbed the rocky path, leaping from stone to stone, crossing over dry stream beds, breathing in the cool mountain air. Kimba asked me to look in the opposite direction for a few more meters, until he said, "Here's my surprise, brother!"

I looked up to see a sheer cliff rising above us. At the base sat a fire pit fashioned out of rocks, the cliff wall blackened by soot. I spat upon the charred wall and rubbed my paw into the blackness, making a paste. I painted three lines over my right eye, and then painted Kimba with a single line across his brow. We were overcome and kissed passionately below the high cliff wall. It was sacred space for us alone. With only the sounds of the crickets and the owls nearby, we stripped to let our naked bodies receive the cool mountain air. Kimba honored me and I fed him my seed, welcoming him as my brother. Lions together in nature as intended.

The time spent wandering through identities was coming to a close; I was becoming master of my own transformation. My furry identity started out as a means to relieve sexual repression, but with guidance and magic became something deeper, something that reached into the core of me and conjured a ferocious, majestic being. I am known by many names: panther, cougar, *puma concolor*, mountain screamer. I am prince of the desert, the catamount. Behind these whiskers is a singular creature to be loved, challenged and nurtured. I am Scratch Hunter, the mountain lion.

i love you perfect

by Crystal Gem

cosmic dust inside
your galaxy
i try to look away
from your bright light
even as it blinds me
my body dancing
to the rhythm
of your heart
my head spinning
in complete adoration
a whirling dervish
as you touch me
so deep within
it hurts

i love you perfect

Blood Run Down

By Raven Kaldera

In the beginning:

I walked into the room where the new boy was hanging, naked, waiting. The horned mask on my head limited my vision, but it telescoped my awareness to him and his pink flesh. My hand, black-gloved, reached out to run down his back, cupping his ass. Exploring the territory. Marks flickered on the inside of my eyes, like lightning across my vision, telling me what the unmarked skin would look like by the end of the evening. I cannot see the future in visions; that thought was not mine. It was the thought of other Presences who rode on my shoulder, sharing my eyes. They did not share my body, not yet, anyway; that would come later. For now, they shared just the eyes, and the desire.

He tried not to gasp when I touched him, but his breath was coming hard through his flared nostrils. I spoke words of power to him, words that made him bow his head. *This will change you. After this night, you will be different. How different, that will depend on you, and how willing you are to be open to this transformation.* By the time I was finished speaking, I knew that it wasn't me talking. There was a long pause, and then, Yes, sir. I began.

The first strike of the whip was a caress, making him acutely aware of his skin. The second strike cut like a blade into that sensitized awareness, leaving a blooming red mark on his left shoulder blade. I struck, I chanted – or I struck and *They* chanted – and the Power worked into him. I could see the welts slithering over him like snakes, burrowing into him, seeking out old pain. Pain in search of pain, living fire to draw out dead, charred bones. He threw his head back and cried. He'd begged to be gagged, but I'd vetoed it. This won't be an ordinary scene, I said. You need to hear yourself weep. The pain-snakes ran through his body as I worked, rooting out the buried layers of filth and purging them through his open mouth. Eventually, the crying became screaming. There would be no safeword for this scene, because it wasn't a scene. It was real. I broke skin, finally, and the blood ran down. I caught it in a cup and we gave it back to the earth. Afterwards, he said to me, "This is my religion."

The next day he would regret that statement and repent, returning desperately to the faith of his upbringing which had no place for such holy rites. He was my lover, and remained so for a year, but this issue was eventually what came between us, what broke us up. It was one thing to give oneself, vulnerable, to one's lover. It was quite another to give one's self willingly to something bigger that spoke through your lover's mouth, worked through their hands... and made you hurt in ways that your lover was not capable of, no matter how fine a top he might be.

Others before him, others after him, felt that dissonance between me-their-lover and the Something Elses that spoke through me and worked through me. It would drive most of them away. A handful, though, would stay. One in spite of what I was becoming. The others, because of it.

In the beginning, SM was something I did with my lovers, for myself. I went to play parties and hung them up on crosses, rejoiced publicly in an intimate communion with them – intimate in spite of the formality of the structure. There was distance between us, the distance of a flogger, or a signal whip, or a coin-hung scarf. I would cross that distance periodically to touch them and remind them that they were not alone with the pain. It was a formal dance where we each knew our various steps, and I was good at it – damn good. I was a performer, and I loved the audience. I was in control, and I loved the positive impact that I could make on these people that I cared about. I lived for it, back then, more than a decade ago. I couldn't wait for the next scene in our bedroom, the next chance to attend a play party.

The distance created by the structure of those scenes was useful in many ways. It created a space where I could get sexually turned on and never need to take off my pants – which, considering the acute level of my body dysphoria at the time was a great thing. It gave me a performance-oriented skillset that I could polish and hone, and get applause for, if only the shining eyes of the bottom while they lay wrapped in blankets and drinking cranberry juice. It created a filter through which I could push a carefully measured amount of intimacy, just enough to keep us both going but not enough to make me too raw and vulnerable.

It also put a nice layer of leather and steel between my inner predator and the outside world. My internal predator is not someone who can be allowed to drive my body. Given his head, he would rape and kill, slice through that unmarked flesh and cut it to ribbons, bathe in the showers of blood. He's the one who whispers those things to me when I run my hand over someone's flesh. The formality of "traditional" scene protocol made him safe. It used his passion and sadism and threw him occasional bones through his cage bars – never enough to satisfy him, because he is impossible to satisfy with activities that wouldn't leave me strapped down for lethal injection, but more than he'd ever been given before. Still, he was at best on the end of a tightly held chain leash, occasionally allowed to growl and nip but never sink his teeth into that tasty flesh. It was all still entirely safe.

The formality of the top-dance also lent itself well to ritual, and that was ironically the hole that let in the force of change. Somewhere along the line, I realized that the Gods I work with were pushing their way into my scenes with my lovers. It started small: I'd be stuck for a moment and wonder where to go, how to get them to where they needed to go and a Voice would whisper in my ear and tell me. Soon they were speaking louder, then borrowing my own voice, then borrowing my hands. I started calling these "special scenes," then "rituals." When They would come, my inner predator would be pushed aside, thrown back into his cage alone. My scenes were starting to become sacred space, and I was becoming a tool, and there was no place for selfishness on holy ground.

It was inevitable that people I didn't know would ask me to do SM rituals for them. I'd played with strangers before, but it was all for fun. This wasn't about fun. It was serious stuff — pulling them through their fears, guiding them down to the Underworld and back, helping them to find their way to a place of altered consciousness where change could occur and Spirit could be connected with. I found that I could rarely say no when they approached me with That Look in their eyes and asked, please, if I could help them. The more I did this Work with them, the more this Work ate everything about SM in my life. I apprenticed, I trained, and I learned skills I never thought I'd be studying — cutting with ashes, branding, suturing, designing ordeal rituals, learning from both human beings and spirits. Slowly, it all slipped over into that space of being a tool for the greater good of others. I became an Ordeal Master.

Other changes were happening in my life at the time, so this wasn't an isolated incident. I had an actual near-death experience that shifted and congealed my spiritual path, I got sex reassignment, I called myself a shaman for the first time. Vows and taboos came into my life that hedged it round with strictures and disciplines. I wasn't free any more; I was a god-slave, a bound servant of the Powers that had been whispering in my ear all this time. All the random threads of my life were being twisted together into one piece of cord... except for a few wisps that got left out. My personal SM desires were among those threads. The dance of the dungeon, of the whip and the cane and the St. Andrew's cross, went from being "rituals" to being Work. I didn't do Work with my lovers, or rather when I did it with them recreationally, it became Work. And the Work wasn't about my hard-on, so my hard-on tended to vacate the premises. I didn't need it to do the Work. It wasn't about me.

It was years before I found a place for my own desires again. My internal predator had gone into a state of sullen rage, robbed of his only outlet. I didn't play at parties or public dungeons anymore; the Work was too personal and private for that... for the client. For me it was far less personal, but it was the client's needs that ruled. I was aware of the hollow in me that was my predator's smoldering withdrawal, but I wrote it down to the inevitability of my transformation into a sacred tool. There are sacrifices for every destiny; personally fulfilling SM seemed that it would be one of those.

My personal desires, however, were not so easily set aside. Denied the outlet of "traditional" SM, they morphed into another shape and poured out through my sexual fantasies. I'd always had two kinds of fantasies: the ones that were impossible because they were too brutal to become reality, and the ones that were replaying of sexy things I'd actually done, or variations on how they might be next time. In my days of public play, the second sort usually fell into "traditional" formal SM scenes, but when the Work ate those, they changed. The fantasies that grew in me weren't distant floggings, but pantingly, growlingly personal. I wanted to beat the shit out of someone up close, with my hands, my fists, my nails, my booted feet. I didn't want them on a cross to be whipped, I wanted them on the ground to kick while they curled up like a fetus, whimpering. I wanted to slam bodies into walls with my own weight. I wanted to growl awful, abusive things at them while punching them in the gut. I wanted to shove them in filth and grind them into the dirt. I wanted to shove cock up a clenched asshole. Most of all, I wanted to not have to worry about how they were feeling. In other words, my predator wanted something that was just for him, only for him, as up close and personal as it was possible for him to get.

Obviously, bottoms who are sturdy enough – both physically and emotionally – and actually into this kind of play are few and far between. I'm also well aware that it's difficult to do scenes like that in public playspace. People get triggered, and even if the DMs are aware of it and willing to run interference, spectators can still come away with the idea that you're an asshole. It's also much more intimate for me – my internal predator has no interest in being put on display, really. He'd prefer the dark solitude of a back field in the woods, or a darkened basement, or an alley. On top of that, the general ambience of most dungeon spaces with all the people doing their formalized scenes tends to push me into Work mode, so it looks like public play is still not a personal choice for me. But that's a fair sacrifice to make for bringing SM back to my personal life.

Except… that isn't spiritual, is it? I bought that lie for a while, even though I ought to know better. Well, I bought it in the sense that while *all* sex is technically sacred, I felt that the "selfless" Ordeal Master service I was rendering was what was *really* sacred, while beating up a friend with a shinai while he rolled around on the ground, thinking only of my own hard-on, was only an "ordinary" sort of sacred. I should have known better, because I have spent my life attempting to integrate the sacred into the ordinary. But I had one major block: I wasn't proud of my selfish internal predator. Actually, I was the opposite of proud. He is, frankly, a pain in the ass. A scary, awful pain in the ass — and scary to me as well, as I'm the one who has to keep him constantly chained up and listen to his constant cursing from the depths of my psychic basement. I couldn't imagine the rough, brutal SM that I'm now drawn to in my current life as being anything but a sop for him, something to shut him up, something to shut up my perverse dick that wants so many inappropriate things.

It took a couple of Gods to tell me differently. I'm a polytheist, but most of the Gods I work with — including the one that I primarily belong to and call, affectionately, my dominatrix — interact with me around the Work, or keeping me in shape to do it. These two, however, are in my life solely for the purpose of helping me work through my own shit — the internal spiritual experience as opposed to the external one. As someone whose whole life revolves around the external spiritual experience (and the internal experiences of others), I sometimes forget that I need spiritual maintenance as well. I'm not perfect, and I have plenty of flaws. I even have a couple of unlovely self-loathings, and this was one of them.

It took Baphomet, the androgynous half-goat deity of rot and perversion, to point out that I was being a hypocritical idiot. I've certainly done many a ritual scene with clients around their unacceptable desires, and witnessed or ground-crewed many such others that were facilitated by fellow Ordeal Masters. I understood the sacredness of reclaiming something that you are ashamed of… I just had trouble applying it to myself. (These things are always harder when you're aiming the gun at yourself.) Baphomet took the time to explain to me, in terms that made my teeth rattle, how useless it is to hate a part of yourself when you're going to have to live with it anyway.

He started with lesser targets. People tend to assume that dominants are tops and submissives are bottoms and never the twain shall swap. While I have never been able to get the hang of submission to another human being for even a minute, once I had changed my body and accepted my shamanic calling, I ended up on the other side of the "activities" on a regular basis. Shamans have a long tradition of doing extreme things to their bodies in order to achieve altered states, and frankly most of the straight-up shamans I know who work the Ordeal Path are fairly dominant personalities. It confuses people who see those kinds of ordeals, in historical documents or in actual reality. Are they masochists? Not necessarily. Are they submitting to the technician who is doing the work to them? No, the technician is probably little more than a service top, doing what they're trained to do. Why, then? They're doing it because it works, because it's what they need to do in order to get the Work done smoothly.

Baphomet started out by having me write about my experiences of being anally fisted, and that act of sexual yoga being a spiritual opening. After I gritted my teeth and published that piece – and several others along the same lines, writings about acts that blurred the "traditional" lines of the BDSM scene – he said, "Now you're ready to go down to the basement. You know what's waiting for you." Clean up that last little bit of hypocrisy, he pointed out. Just as you have helped others, an Ordeal Master will come for you.

Baphomet is a scary fucker of a God, and anyone who has worked with him will tell you that. (Well, any deity is scary when they're in your face, but Baphomet is a special brand of scary.) However, on his heels came the call of another God, one that was even more terrifying. He was Fenris, the son of Loki the Trickster and Angrboda the Wolf Mother in Norse mythology. He is a god of destruction in the shape of an enormous wolf, and he lives only to destroy his Universe, as bloodily as possible. He was chained by the other Gods in a deep cave and waits there, sullen and wrathful, to be released like a nuclear warhead should the end of the world be imminent. Sound familiar? Yeah. If my inner predator has a God that he kneels before, it is Fenris.

And Fenris told me bluntly that when I feed that part of me, I feed him as well, through his connection to me. It is a devotional activity and one where

I don't have to sacrifice any part of my selfishness and brutality to make it into a devotional act. He understands, better than any other, the chains that require one to make those sacrifices for the greater good. He knows just how that feels, and while he might ask painful things of me for my own good, he won't restrict me for the good of others. He laughs, terrifyingly, at the very idea. *There's more than enough of that bullshit going around,* he says.

But the hard act that he asks of me is that I learn to love the part of me that would make most therapists visibly draw back in fear if I talked about it. I have had therapists react that way before. He doesn't ask that I try to change him – I am doomed to carry my Fenris nature to my grave; that's what I've been told by every God I've communed with – but simply that I love that part of myself with the same love I have for the rest of me. He is not simply a flaw, a burden, an error to be endured if it cannot be erased. He is part of me, and if he is made in the image of a God, then he has a connection to part of the Divine as well.

Fenris is my Ordeal Master in this process, which is still going on. I am working with painful slowness, but I can feel myself making progress. *Can you love me?* he asks. Yes, I can do that. I can stand before a God and love him, even terrifying as he is. *Then you can take a small part of that and love yourself,* he says. How? Where do I start? *Where you start with any lover,* he says. *You do things for them that show your love. You give them gifts; personal things meant only for them, that only they would understand. Mouthing the words doesn't count. Show that love by your actions, or shut the fuck up.*

Loving that part of me means finding ways to feed him, finding people to feed him with who desire what I desire, who can accept this with joy. Loving that part of me means removing the barrier that holds him back during sex – not the barrier between him and my partners, which must stay in place, but between him and the rest of me. That makes the sex painful and raw and frighteningly intimate, and "scene protocol" would recreate the distance that kept me safe from my own darkness. It's hands-on, up close, teeth and snarling and bruises that don't show off well after the fact. It's my own fear of me being rejected because of that part of me, a searing vulnerability in the midst of power. *Say that you want me, just as I am. Show me with your body, even*

as I show you who and what I am. There is no ritual here. This is all about me.

So you won't see me in dungeon space with the edgeplayers who occasionally feed my needs — and that of deeper Powers as well. You won't see me there with clients, either. Occasionally I wander through and look at that world; sometimes I'm a little nostalgic. But things are different now, and I'm learning to accept the difference. I'm learning where I fall with both external and internal spirituality, and how very different those can be for some of us. I'm learning, again, that thing which I should know bone-deep: that there is no sexuality which is not sacred, and perhaps not even any which is "less" sacred. I need to keep telling myself that, over and over again. Perhaps, eventually, it will be hammered into my bones.

He almost puked when my fist went into his gut, this new boy. He would almost puke again, when I would fuck his face so brutally that it was one long round of choking and gagging. He curled up around my fist when I hit him, exposed what was between his legs. I hit that, too. I smack his face until his ears ring. I yank his head over by the hair and sink my teeth into his throat. He makes small whimpering noises, paws the air, but does not push me away. He is prey, and he knows it. The sacrifice of prey can only be made sacred by the predator. My knife flashes, I break skin, and he will feed me, and more.

No, not for public consumption. Even here, I know some people will be upset when they read this. But now I know better than to hide what needs to be seen, to be ashamed of what needs to be reclaimed. "But how can you reclaim this?" you ask.

"It's all about love," I say.

Let the blood run down.

Hanuman as My Guide

By Shuphrique

You say I look familiar. You ask about my way of topping so you can tell if we are a good match. It is standard protocol these days in the dungeon, this checking of references, so to speak. What you like, what I like, what kind of scene you want, what I want. Let's talk before I put myself in your hands, you say.

Okay, let's talk.

What I like is a pleading gaze, an involuntary tug away from my whip strike. What I like is a cute long-haired boy crawling to the pointed tip of my shiny shoe, hands tied behind his back. What I like is hurting him, really hurting him, and seeing tears.

The kind of scene I want involves power and sex and high heels and you lacing up my corset just so. The scene I want includes needle play: molasses-slow insertion and eye-to-eye contact during removal. What I want is to whip you until I see you considering your safe word, then to fuck you with your cuffs still on and send you home. Maybe make you come back tomorrow and clean up, still in those cuffs.

But no... it rarely works out that way. Something else takes over and I go to another realm. There is a moment when I realize it's time to go with it; it doesn't work when I fight it, anyway.

When I truly allow myself to "go there" I feel inhabited by an archetypal being who hijacks the scene (with my willingness, but still) from one about sex and power to one about glorying in the roles of Service and Devotion.

That hijacking occurs as I prepare the scene. The process itself moves me into another persona. I lay out my shoes, my corset, my whips and needles.

As the high heels go onto my feet, the transformation begins in earnest. I sit more carefully and stand with more purpose. Then the corset. It strengthens me, it girds me in truth. This uniform covers and supports my heart and my feet, my connection to solid earth and my wings. It takes me out of the mundane world into the realm of archetype and angel.

Somehow I end up teaching my boys how to seduce other women with deep service. I end up explaining the service aspects of dominance and how both sides of the situation are spiritual processes. I end up making quite certain they understand how noble it is to crave dominance the way they do, how this alone can be their spiritual training course.

I do this because Hanuman is my guide, my yardstick for dominance and for submission.

Hanuman is not much known in this part of the world. He is the King of all the Monkeys and the General of Ram's (God's) army. He is therefore both ruler and ruled.

Ram's wife Sita is also Hanuman's ruler because she is the Lady of His Lord. He could have saved her from an evil demon, but instead he helped her husband to do it. He carried away a whole mountain rather than come back without the herb that grew there that would save someone beloved of his Lord.

He spent most of his life unaware of his True Nature and role. His greatest strengths are obedience, humility, and his deep devotion to Ram and Sita. He offers all he has in their service. He rules by serving and serves by ruling. For them, he has become the greatest warrior on earth.

Thus, Hanuman is also the yardstick against which I measure a sub. He is the quintessence of power in service, strength under control, total fitness, total humility, total reliability. Total hotness.

Hanuman is the yardstick by which I measure both dominance and submission.

It must be admitted that I do not achieve the mark I set for myself as dominant. But he is in my mind when I am in domination mode. At the best of times, he is in my heart too.

So... I might tell about a hunk of a man who was phobic about needles, but was willing to do anything I really, really wanted him to do. How I felt later when I found out that now he can take his medication and stay calm. I've heard he smiles sometimes.

I could tell about someone who rarely cried and needed to be whipped until he did. How he let go of his tension and relaxed and slept after so long without deep rest. How I felt watching him snore, knowing how long it had been.

I would tell a story of a tranny girl who never got over her painful youth and felt safe almost nowhere. She was never a boy and the other boys could tell before she did. She rarely feels safe enough to relax and enjoy being a girly girl.

I could tell a story of – well, any number of similar moments. The stories seem dry when I tell them, and simple. But not so the feelings.

There is a sensation borne of being a conduit to someone's healing. The feeling of doing something that few people would even recognize needs doing, and knowing how to do it well. The satisfaction of helping someone know to their physical core that their essential needs are valid and valued.

There is deep satisfaction in the leading of someone to a place they might not have known they needed to go. That place is always about awareness or self-acceptance or appreciation of service and its importance in the world. Our world (the U.S. and its culture) does not truly honor service and humility, so those who hold the need to serve can feel very wrong and embarrassed.

And it turns out that as much as I like the corsets and the high heels, they are just the signposts to something greater. Is this how they recognize me?

Do they realize, here is a woman who will whip me until I cannot stand anymore and then hold me tight against her until I stop sobbing and my heart's calluses melt.

Do they think, this one will push me past that point I have cringed at; she will show me how to experience the needle differently enough to hold myself in The Witness while it pierces me.

One of the most popular depictions of Hanuman shows him on one knee, pulling open his breast with both hands to show Ram and Sita inside his heart. This is the service I offer, with Hanuman in my breast.

Somehow they recognize me. We are in the Hands of the Gods.

On the Cross

By Master Malik

It was straightforward enough, a short scene, a crucifixion. A demonstration to examine the "Hidden Prejudices Against Extreme SM Plays." The message was "Acceptance and Tolerance," but it took everyone involved deeper than we expected.

Painboy was the bottom for the demonstration, for the journey, and I was honored, once again, to walk on a path of SM with him. The scourge, designed after the scourges of Romans, and made by Painboy himself, was vicious to say the least. It was designed to tear the flesh and it did its job well. Blood flowed and screams and suffering resonated through the room named Flame during Tribal Fire 2010. It earned its name, flames burning in our hearts so brightly.

A resounding NO echoed from my lips when he said he was ready to go to next step in the crucifixion. I saw and felt a fear in him at this point. He fell down almost to his knees after every blow of the thirsty scourge. I stopped when I felt like I was reaching a point of no return. Those dark recesses are enticing and inviting.

We, the sane practitioners of SM, are, in a very real sense, Beast Keepers. In the jungle of dark desires where serpents, scorpions, venomous spiders crawl among the sharp claws of predators of many kinds, the path is enticing and enveloping. The light, the flame, comes only from deep within from the source which could be faded in the surroundings. This is all intoxicating and addictive and we must, from time to time, turn to our sisters and brothers for guidance and strength and light. We, all of us, should be our sisters' and brothers' keepers to the extent they allow it.

The demo affected many. It affected me, perhaps the most. The flashbacks are not as strong as they were, but they are still there. The memory of the smell of fear, anticipation, fascination, and blood is all too fresh. Sufferings touch everyone. We all can relate to pain.

The nails went into the webbing of his hands, and cries of anguish and hot white pain were visible on his face. I have asked myself these questions before: Where was I? Who was the being hammering the nails into live flesh? How do repulsion and attraction meet and become one?

The answer came clear. I was with him. I too was suffering on that cross. I too was in the throes of pain and anguish. The invisible lines were binding and there was no escape. There was no attempt to escape.

Two women crawled towards the man on the cross. I saw shadows and forms. I do not know who they were. I know them, but I do not remember them. I felt tears and sobs and empathy from every corner of the place of sufferings. I sensed quietness in the room which was deafening and reflective.

I cleaned up the altar with mechanical motions. I was surrounded by many and I was alone. I suffered and I felt pain on a deeper level. My smile vanished inside and there was emptiness and the desert sun was hot and scorching. I was afraid because I wanted to do it again and again and again.

Beware, for this abyss can pull you in.

Please do not hold these thoughts against me. You have not been on the cross as I have, you have not felt the nails go in. You too might be called to go back if you had.

Fit for A God

By Otterdancing

Late that night, I went to the drummers and laid my head upon Abraham's knee. Abraham, drummer, priest, friend, and teacher, let me stay there as he played. There I felt safe and small and quiet. I let the rhythm of the drums soothe my aching heart and let the sacred fire warm my soul. I rested and remembered.

It was Beltane and I was Venus' priestess. A hundred or more people, friends and strangers alike, had come to the annual festival to celebrate this feast of fertility, observed through the ages with joyous joining in the fields to honor the earth and to receive the Goddess' blessings of abundance in return.

They had come here tonight for ritual, to Venus' Temple, to accept challenges, to seek enlightenment, and to offer their hopes and dreams and yearnings up to Her. Feeling powerful and blessed to be acting as one of the priestesses in that Temple, I hoped to offer a vision of grace and sensual exultation to those who approached. Surrounded by abundant love, integrity, and trust embodied in those who had offered this work, their vulnerable leadership gave permission and a pathway for those who would experience the Divinity present in the sacred space.

What few people knew was that, underneath that apparent joy, I was in deep grief. Hours before, this loving team had held me as I mourned. Earlier that day, my marriage had ended. There was no room for me in the relationship my husband had developed with his new lover. And while I was capable of surrendering to the duties of my role in the evening's ritual, when the two of them came to the sacred fire together, I could no longer contain my grief at the loss of my Beloved and our life together.

I found myself lost in my own emotions, and as a result, lost my composure. I felt like a fraud in the Temple of the Goddess of Love and Desire. My mate no longer desired me and our mythic love had failed. The only place now that offered solace was that place between drum and fire where I sat.

When I finally opened my eyes, a stunningly beautiful naked female form was inches from me. There in the sweet spot between drums and fire, she was boldly fucking the equally beautiful redheaded young woman beneath her with a strap-on. Bearing witness to their lovemaking was awesome and roused me from my stupor. The lady topping the redhead was a campmate and a new friend. I watched as she pleasured the squirming bottom. They were glowing in the wicked abandonment of this public act and the delight of experiencing this with such fierce accompaniment.

Her love, another of my campmates who was also a friend, soon joined them and took his lady from behind creating a most beautiful train. Mere feet away, my friend looked me in the eye and his thought of "Dude, this is our life!!!?" was so clear and wondrous and baffled and joyous, I could not help but laugh my first real laugh of the entire weekend. What a beautiful moment of astonishment and elation. "All acts of Love and pleasure are Her rituals," and my darling friends were worshipping in the most delightful way.

The scene played itself out and before I knew it, Abraham looked down at me with those smoldering eyes and told me to wait there. Of course I obeyed. He returned with his gloriously graceful and stunningly serene and sexy partner, Aurora. As we had all been playmates previously, I trusted my fragile state to their care. They told me to lie down and as Aurora sat, I placed my head into her lap. She took my arms and held them back, opening me for Abraham's

skill. With extreme gratitude, I surrendered. I surrendered to the experience of sensation granted me by a master.

I have to admit I can't tell you now exactly in what order Abraham used his tools of pain and pleasure. My sensual pleasure became so great that I writhed and screamed and energetically was so caught in the moment, I didn't even know about the couples fucking on each side of us or the crowd watching the scene. I had instantly released to the experience, letting my grief roll out of me in waves. As the altered state of consciousness consumed me, I felt my body literally sink into the ground, and it was as if I had melted my physical form into the earth. I didn't care if I ever returned. It felt as if I was anchored only by Aurora's arms and Abraham's lash. I only heard the drums and felt the sensation, and that grew to ecstasy so great that my entire body and soul were beyond mere orgasm.

Then, as if Abraham's ministrations had opened a gate, from out of the glowing fire behind him, came Pan. Hot and fierce, I felt the presence of the God of Desire loom over me and descend upon me. His dark primal energy pressed against me. I submitted to his wild lust in awe and gratitude. I felt Him enter me and he plowed me ferociously into the earth. As my awareness was focused on the very real and literal sensation of being deeply filled and thoroughly fucked, my soul expanded past the bounds of my very body. At that moment I was integrated into the throbbing energy of the earth, the burning force of the fire, and the union with the Divine on this most Sacred of nights.

His message was savage but real. I was no fraud. I was a worthy priestess. I was still deserving of Love. I was still beautiful and desirable and sexual.

I was fit for a God.

As the experience abated, I found myself being kissed and kissed by the Consort of our ritual team, the man holding the role of Venus' lover and divine partner for the rite. It seemed appropriate and another blessing, even if I had no recollection of how that transition took place.

The bruises on my thighs and butt and breasts and pussy lasted for well over a week. Yet I had felt no pain at all. My memory was only of Aurora's firm, loving, and relentless support, Abraham's role as beautiful and mischievous priest, and the God Himself emerging from the fire to heal my wounded heart and spirit.

These gifts are with me to this day as I continue to surrender to Venus. Her Chosen are well-used, and I continue to learn courage, strength, faith, hope, and joy in Her service. Though this blessing of grace came in an unusual way through grief and pain, it allowed me to experience the transformative power of Love.

Finding The Slow Path

By Joshua Tenpenny

I did SM for years before I was introduced to the concept of the spiritual Ordeal Path. Up until then, I just did fairly heavy recreational pain play. It wasn't a cathartic or emotional thing for me. It wasn't deeply transformative, or even particularly meaningful. I didn't have any abuse issues to work out, or phobias to face. I just liked rough sex. It was very simple.

Then I had a few experiences – entirely unrelated to SM – that gave me a much more spiritual perspective on life. At first, it didn't have any impact on my play, but one afternoon a kinky friend was demonstrating bloodletting (venipuncture) and he drew some blood from me. To my surprise, I suddenly felt uncomfortable with the whole situation. It no longer felt right for me to treat my body and blood so casually. I felt like this should be a sacred thing, or at least a deeply meaningful thing – but I was unsure about what the meaning should be. In any case, I couldn't just drop the syringe of blood into the "hazardous medical waste" bin and be done with it. Under the pretense of wanting some fresh air, I went out to the garden and with an awkward whispered prayer, I squirted the blood into the earth.

I was raised only nominally religious, and this was the very first time in my life it had ever occurred to me to modify my behavior (especially my sexual activity) for purely spiritual reasons. It wasn't that anyone had told me that certain activities were spiritually "wrong," but after coming to a spiritual perspective where all life is sacred, some things became too powerful to treat trivially any more.

Many people I knew, including my master, did SM as part of the spiritual Ordeal Path, and I asked them for help in exploring this. I tried a few things, with mixed results, and eventually ended up at a gathering where a group of people were doing hook pulls in a ritual setting. There was an opening prayer, there was drumming, there was focused intent. It seemed like the perfect setting to really connect with this aspect of spirituality, to figure out what it meant to me. While waiting my turn to have hooks pierced into my back, I began to slowly pace the room. Walking back and forth, listening to the drums, the image that came to mind was of walking a long and winding path down to the underworld. It wasn't one of the symbols the group had used in setting the ritual, but it was present for me. After the hooks were in and tied to the wall, I began to pull against them while interacting with my master. It was an intense sensation, painful, but not excruciating. I don't get an endorphin rush easily, but this did it for me; before long my head was swimming and everything seemed bright and amazing. It was ecstatic.

After a while that rush faded, and I was just standing there feeling nothing in particular. It seemed like the experience ought to "go somewhere," that there ought to be something beyond that rush. I knew what it felt like to be in the presence of the divine, to touch the deeper mysteries. This wasn't it. I experimented with intensifying the sensation by pulling more strongly against the hooks. It just hurt, nothing else. More pulling only led to more pain. The ritual seemed to be winding down by that point, so eventually I gave up and went to have the hooks removed.

Some of the other people there clearly had experienced a connection with the divine. I could see it reflected in their eyes. But I hadn't, and I didn't know why. I packed up my things and went to leave the ritual space, thinking to myself that for whatever reason, I hadn't tapped in to whatever that ritual could have connected me with. When I got to the door, I felt an overwhelming push backwards that had a faint glimmer of what I had come to associate with divine presence. I paused, and I immediately knew that the ritual had "worked." It had connected to whatever it is that turns the symbolic acts of a ritual into an experience more real than ordinary reality. And because it was "real," I needed to walk back up that winding path from the underworld that I had envisioned at the beginning of the ritual. Frustrated, but respecting the truth communicated by that push, I paced the room again. When I returned to the door, there was no further push, so I left.

That night, I prayed. I wept and I prayed. If the ritual had worked, why had there been nothing there for me? Eventually I came to the end of my crying, and a calm settled over me. With my frustration and anger and jealousy cleared out of the way, I could see that there had been nothing there for me because that is not my path.

I remembered a dear friend of mine, a very spiritual person and a heavy player in SM. For years he had been reaching further and further, trying to connect to something deeper through his masochism. The last time I had seen him, he had just done a very heavy scene that took him further into his experience of masochism than he had ever been... and yet, he felt it didn't take him "there." Like me, he had some idea what "there" looked like. He had reached it through Buddhist meditation. He said that if this scene hadn't done it, he didn't think any scene would. So he took a break from SM entirely and spent six months in a monastery. That was his path.

My own spiritual path is one of service and submission. Submitting fully to God's will is at the heart of many spiritual traditions, and while the concept resonated deeply with me, in practice I had no idea what God's will was. I could make some reasonable assumptions on clear ethical issues, but most of life is lived in the gray areas where it is interpretation of a principle that dictates action, not the abstract principle. (Does "Thou shall not kill" permit self-defense? A just war? Wearing leather?) I dearly wished for clear and unambiguous religious teachings to guide me. I flirted with Catholicism – or perhaps it is more accurate to say that I had a passionate unrequited longing for Catholicism, not just for the awe-inspiring power of their rituals?, but for the strength and certainty of their traditions. Unfortunately, Catholicism has little love for a kinky, transgendered, queer, sex-radical Pagan like me. Some people can reconcile that, but it didn't feel right to me to pick and choose among the teachings of a faith where so many of my fundamental life choices and values were considered to go against the will of God. I know myself too well for that. I'm a slippery little weasel. I knew that I would continue to pick and choose as it suited me, avoiding any discipline that would require too much of me, reinterpreting scripture to validate whatever I'd planned on doing anyway. That wasn't what I was looking for. I wanted a firm hand to guide me.

I looked into other religious traditions, but I found none that I could embrace wholeheartedly. I asked my master for guidance, but his Neo-Pagan religious community emphasizes finding your own way and being true to yourself, not following any one particular set of rules. I tried to find my own way, but I kept coming back around to a concept I learned from Christian monasticism. The first chapter of the Rule of St. Benedict criticizes monks who have never lived under the rule of an abbot: "They live... without a shepherd, within sheepfolds of their own devising, not within the Lord's. Their law is self-gratifying: what appeals to them, that they call holy; what they dislike, they regard as sinful." That rang true for me. As I attempted over the years to build a spiritual discipline for myself, this passage echoed through my mind. Eventually, I accepted that I could not meaningfully surrender my ego to a discipline that my ego had constructed. This was a sheepfold of my own devising.

Again, I talked to my master about this. He is a shaman and Pagan priest, but he had been taking a hands-off approach to my spirituality. He tends to think of spirituality as an individual matter between each person and their Gods, and he felt that in this one area of my life he had no right to interfere. However, as I submitted to him fully in all other areas of my life, it seemed appropriate at that point in our relationship for him to gradually and carefully take control in this one last area. I formally asked him to order my spiritual life, and to tell me how I ought to be following my spiritual path.

For a long while, I had assumed that the struggle to understand God's will and form one's own conclusions about spiritual matters was an essential part of spiritual development. I believed that simply following someone else's rules was an immature expression of spirituality, and that a meaningful spiritual connection transcends the need for such rules. From an intellectual and political perspective, I would still prefer to believe this. However, for me, years of philosophical inquiry did not bring me one bit closer to God. It did not make me a better person. It did not aid me in making good choices with my life. It did not provide comfort in difficult times. For some people, it does all these things, but not for me. When faced with decisions of spiritual import, I continually became mired in doubt and confusion. What is God's will in this situation? How am I to know? How can I trust I see that clearly, as confused as my mind can often be? Am I mistaking my own will, or my own fears, for the will of God? Is this obstacle a sign I am on the wrong path, or a test for me to overcome? How am I to be sure I am doing it right? How can I be anything but biased in this? The intellectual approach just doesn't go anywhere for me. It is not my path.

Submitting wholly to my master's will is so much clearer. I know exactly what he wants of me, and if I'm doing it wrong, he'll tell me unambiguously. I can't wiggle out from under a rule that challenges me by cleverly reinterpreting the rule, because he'll sit me right down and ask me, "Is that *really* what you think I meant by that?" I can't just follow the letter of the law, or look for loopholes. There is absolutely nothing to hide behind. I can't fool myself into thinking that I am better at this than I really am. I can't fool myself into thinking I am worse at this than I really am. I know exactly where I stand.

My master directs me in all ways as to how I am to live my life, but he doesn't micromanage. He sets up the goals and ideals and priorities, and I do my best to live my life according to that standard. If I need clarification or assistance, he provides it, but I am a responsible and competent adult who can manage all the normal challenges of daily life. And it is generally a very normal life, compared to what people might imagine. There is no bondage, or chastity, or punishment. He never goes out of his way to inflict any hardship on me – he says that life provides hardship enough. It is exceedingly rare that he directs me to do anything that some other reasonable person in my situation might not choose for themselves. It might not be what I would choose, but it is always a reasonable choice. There is no fear of him asking me to do something ridiculous or harmful. In fact, he makes much safer and healthier choices for me than I would be inclined to make for myself. He has my best interest at heart.

Spiritual enslavement has also given me a different perspective on my body. From what I've heard from people who walk the Ordeal Path, physical ordeals change one's relationship to the body and the flesh, usually in an empowering way. Instead of that way of winning back one's flesh through suffering and triumph, I have turned over my flesh to someone else, and I live that as a daily mindfulness. Everything about the way my body looks, how I dress it, how I care for it, what I feed it, how I do my daily yoga practice, what markings are placed on it, is a reminder that it does not belong to me. In a hook pull, one's flesh and pain can be an offering to the divine through temporary surrender, but then you get it back afterwards. My flesh is a permanent offering, and that surrender is my daily ordinary prayer. Instead of a doorway of dramatic ecstasy, this is a long, slow road of patient discipline. Of all the roads that BDSM can give us to the top of the mountain, this is the longest and most unglamorous.

The tasks set before me by my master are in part his own will, and in part his interpretation of the will of the Gods. The distinction is of utmost importance to him, but as the years pass, I find it becomes less of a relevant distinction from my perspective. If I believe that it is God's will that I serve and obey this man, which I do, then it all amounts to the same thing. I am extremely fortunate to be in service to someone who has a very clear connection to the Gods. It removes all other questions, leaving me with only the struggle to surrender and obey. And believe me, that is struggle enough for one lifetime. That is my path.

On The Other Side of the Pixels

By Alex M. Quinlan

We'd met online, Master and I, on a MUSH called Bizarre. Long before there were visual three-dimensional digital worlds, people would... just type at each other. All of the descriptions and all the emotions were brought out in words rather than the poor visual attempts one tries for these days. Lovely words, words to steal into your mind and take over from within; words to build your heat and arousal to fever pitch with only the power of imagination.

He'd caught my attention with the way he walked into the bar — all words, all description, all his body language exposed, from the flourish of the hand as he signaled a barmaid to the smile he gave as he took photographs of the girls dancing on stage. Yes, a bar in a textual world, a world devoted to kink, with people acting out their fantasies as best they could.

I was there frequently, as my husband is vanilla and not at all interested in kink, which made accessing such activities difficult despite our polyamorous natures. I'd met someone in another textual venue two years previously, and through that encounter we had reached the point of having him move in with us, as family — a milestone in my polyamorous life — and as lover and Master to me. Two years later he'd severed the relationship and moved out.

Since then I'd been sunk in "why am I bothering?" and "What am I, if I'm not partnered — how do I do something that needs a direction, a vector of energy, when there's nowhere for the energy to go?"

And so. Sitting in a textual bar, writing flirts to people I knew, writing... writing... writing my desires into the universe, in the hopes that the universe would hear and send someone back. Even if it would be only in text.

Another day, another evening of sitting in the bar, and again the elegant, mysterious, delightfully evocative, well-spoken gentleman comes in. And his eyes fall on me, and his camera comes out and he starts taking pictures. (How does he take pictures, when it's all text? By echoing back his vision of my body, what he sees as he 'clicks the shutter' — the lovely woman, the artful position, the focus of intensity he wishes to capture... all those things one tries to capture on film, in one still image that, seen out of context, never seems to match up with one's impression... one's apprehension of the real person's real presence that drew one's attention and desire to record...)

Ultimately, it was simple: he drew me to him with a single word. I followed him out, and accepted his transport to his private place. Even as we talked — about nothing, about everything except the shared fantasy-style that had us in the same virtual space — I felt myself kneeling to him in my mind before ever he expressed a desire for it.

He was the first man I knew who was unabashed in his joyful desire to serve the Goddess — not as an abstract feminine principle, but as an eager responsive woman, in all the ways a woman can be. He drew me further toward feeling the energy exchange that followed the power exchange, till despite the distance between us, I could feel his touch — feel where his fingers were before he typed it in.

The night he claimed me as his, not three weeks after we'd met — and if you haven't experienced the time-contraction of textual relationships, I cannot convince you that this was a wise move. I knelt before him in a new space, a lushly described Victorian boudoir of velvet brocade couches, deep pile rugs to kneel upon, and an altar of two candles, a plate of fruit bread, a silver chalice, and a blade. A live blade, as some might name it: in form an athame, but with an edge. It glittered in the virtual gaslight, and my skin tingled despite the distance.

It seems odd that, having this interaction be all in words, I have no memory of his words. What I do remember is his touch, his fingers over my face. Feeling my breath, the heat of my blush; finding me in the distance. I remember lying spread-eagle, him kneeling beside me. I remember the resonation of his words in my mind before ever I heard his voice.

I remember his explanation of the runes he used – Norse runes, single letters, and how they each had greater meaning. He'd found my masochism, and my libido, and took great delight in each... and so over one breast was carved "pain," and over the other was carved "necessity." And over my mons was carved "wholeness." Just enough to draw blood, vivid red in my mind. Just enough to find my Soul.

It was almost anticlimactic when he moved closer in the real world, and did the same thing, finally, with his real blade, on my real body. My skin remembered the virtual blood despite the lack of it flowing from my body. It seemed inevitable that he moved in with my husband and I, not three months from that first online meeting.

Over the months we lived together, he lived his religion by explicitly invoking the Goddess in many things, but mostly explicitly sexual things – calling up a cthonic avatar with hypnosis to lend darkness to sadism; seeking the Maiden with gleeful arousal for eager sex; celebrating the quarters and crosses with BDSM activities inside ritual space. As I found that the pagan framework of thought gave me the vocabulary to talk about my subjective experiences in ways that sounded a bit less like tripping on drugs, I felt that I didn't particularly resonate with *worshipping* anything, but there was definitely an additional... presence is the only word I have, that seemed to be watching when we did things. As I taught him the physical techniques he'd never had freedom to find for himself, to go along with the mental and emotional habits of dominance he'd long worked to attain, it seemed there was a strong sense that I was his reward for having coped with some aspects of his previous relationships.

For all that I was able to talk to people, to be with people who have a religious view of the world, I've always done it with a sense of 'that's the way they see things – doesn't mean they are right.' Accepting their subjective reality without letting it impact my own – or my own view of consensus reality. I had long ago given up the concept of "objective reality" – that's like the version of "the truth": your side, their side, and what really happened. There is no "what really happened" because every viewer brings their own bias. It was the same mental technique I'd developed when hanging out with the drug-takers – there's no sense denying their hallucinations, it's a fruitless argument. It's much more useful, not to mention interesting, to accept that this is what they see and draw them out about it. And so I did with him, accepting his word without dispute, and observing my own... impressions in the same way, even while trying to produce changes, some subtle and some gross, to see if these were reproducible: the standard for objectivity, the accepted method that defined "making sense."

All of this came to a head the day he offered to, I believe his term was "dedicate" me to the Goddess. He said he'd been watching me, that She'd been watching me, and that is was time. If I wanted it.

Something about the way he said it, the way he offered, made the offer seem as if it were something... larger. Something that had echoes, resonances in his voice and in the world at large. It wasn't quite the sense of a pure-tone bell-ringing deep inside me that had drawn me to kink in the first place, but it had much of the same momentousness. As difficult as it was to say yes, at the same time there seemed to be no way for me to say no – because as we talked about how he saw things, what would be different, it seemed I was already doing everything. Nothing would need to be changed.

Except my focus. Except my intent. Except my way of looking at the world... my objectivity within my own subjectivity.

It took me a week of talking to myself. Of considering, of thinking over the various things that had seemed to happen. In the end, after all my internal waffling, the lure of 'will it change anything?' was too strong. I gave myself to him, as I'd done in so many other ways, to do with as he willed. The fact that it scratched the same curiosity itch that had sidestepped my concerns about various other mentally dangerous and dubious experiments was merely a bonus.

He bathed me, in milk and honey, washing away, as he said, old truths, to bring in new awareness. I worked to suspend my reflexive disbelief, to be in the moment, to be open to possibility. He flogged me, slowly, leisurely, and deliciously, but without the intensity that would have made me orgasm. Over that reddened flesh he dripped wax, and it seemed it was a pattern; when he scraped it off he marked me, his athame scratching the skin without drawing blood, with what he said were the Goddess' runes. Was I reacting to the inherent dynamic between us, when my entire skin ran with gooseflesh under his blade, or was there some Power channeling through to mark me in a new way? He turned the blade and pushed the handle inside me, fucking me with it, and then said that wasn't enough of an ordeal, and slipped his fingers in, in, and in until he was fisting me, without ever using any lube. When he finally permitted me to orgasm it was admixed with such pain... I have no idea how he managed that.

More details than that I lost... there were things I never remembered, and he would just grin when something would come up that would make me wonder, or cause a reaction I didn't understand. I know he had some disturbances over our play after that. I think he was playing with hypnosis, and getting responses he did not expect. He's the last one I've let work with that, in me.

He lived with us for another four months, before his life's necessities caused him to move away. We sent him with our blessings... our spare car... and the promise to keep what he could not fit into the car, or into his new life, until he had space, and ways, and means to ask for it. He gave me a teddy bear that he'd bought a month before and slept with every night. He told me it was always meant to be mine when he left, and so he'd filled it with as much of himself as he could spare — the dreams we'd shared, the arousal we'd sparked, the joy he'd found in this safe haven.

A month, it took him, to find a place he could afford, with internet and such. A month of minimal contact, of coded messages of reassurance — 411, 777, 333 — through the pager I still paid for. Till finally there was an email, naming time, place, and task: to masturbate, for him, thinking of him. Despite that I'd done so innumerable times before, it was that time, and that place, to set the scene for both of us, to make the connection easier. To remind me of my obedience.

It was later, after dark, with no visible moon, when I went up to his room. Still his room, with most of his furniture in it. The altar we made up together, with elements of his and my choosing: Our candle, one we'd both carved runes into before he left, providing the only light; my chalice, his blade. My stones, his incense holder. My collar.

I kept the altar going — bringing in water, keeping the candle safe, touching everything to hold its energy — to hold a sense of his presence with me, and to give him the comfort of honoring the Powers through me, his property, while he lived where he had so little of himself to himself, or for himself.

And so, to attune myself to him before I did his bidding, I took my clothing off, striving to hear his voice, to feel his warmth, to touch myself in the stripping as he would touch me to undress me, to unwrap his present, to bring out his property to play with again. I dipped my fingers into the water in the chalice and touched my forehead; stroked wetness between my breasts like his tongue over my skin. Another dip of the fingers and wetness encircled my navel, trailing down to the fur at the join of my legs. I hummed an aimless tune as I moved, and only realized it when I looked around reflexively — he always hummed when he was touching the altar. I smiled... it was working. When I reached for the incense my hand landed on the one labeled "awareness."

As my humming found its own tune, I held the incense, warming it in my hands. It was awareness I sought tonight — for him, of him. Of his presence in my life despite the geographical distance; of our desire for my submission; of his immediate presence, here, now, always present with me as my Master, and present in this moment as I did what I'd been commanded.

With a small white candle I transferred flame from the pillar to the stick, and let it burn for a bit in the holder. I sat on his bed, watching the flame of the candle I held, watching the curl of smoke drift in the current of heated air rising, and thought about what I was going to be doing. Sex magic, as all of our sex, and all of our magic had been. The magic he brought into my life, a force of change for both of us.

I leaned forward toward the altar and wafted the smoke to me. I whispered aloud, "awareness," and breathed. Breathed in focus, breathed out sacred space... whether hyperventilation or something more, soon my skin was tingling, and everything had a glow around it. I stood and touched the altar, caressing the stones – my stones, so purely me – feeling their smoothness, their roughness; their individuality, their commonality.

I moved to blow the candle out, and then stopped. I've always been fascinated by flame, captured by the process of it. I could see the melted wax swirling as it was drawn up the wick. I tilted it and watched the wax bead on the edge of dripping, the liquid bulging before falling off the side. As if someone else was doing it, I held the candle over one breast and waited for the drop. I tried to hold it high, not wanting it to hurt, and then laughed at a memory of begging for more whipping. The motion of my laughter was enough and it turned into a gasp, a flinch, as the wax dripped onto me. Whimpering softly, I held the other breast up, and let one drop of wax fall onto it also. I blew the candle out quickly, knowing that if I kept going I wouldn't have the control to keep from having wax all over.

My glance fell on my collar sitting on the altar; the chain curled between chalice and stones, doubled over itself with the lock to one side. He had not said to put it on. Then again, he hadn't said not to. I touched it, and my heart pulled toward it. Taking it up, I kissed the lock, and the chain, and knelt before the altar in that small space of floor between it and the bed. I looped it around my neck, and hooked the open lock through the end-rings. I did not lock it, as I didn't have that permission. I had just my need, to feel owned. Again I breathed, deliberately, slowly. I realized the collar had been warm – my neck didn't notice the usual cool of metal as I'd put it on.

Opening my eyes again, my gaze fell on his knife – his athame. The blade so lovingly described when he'd claimed me online; that had scored my skin with his mark when he took me in the flesh; that had marked me for the Goddess.

I took it up and sat back on my heels. On each thigh, just above the knee, I scratched his mark, his initial, his rune, over and over till I could see the white line on my skin in even the dim candlelight. I drew no blood — I knew that was not permitted, despite never having spoken of it.

Suddenly dizzy, I looked up into the darkness — a tingling on my skin, a sense of heat near me. A presence? My breath caught in my throat as I tried to see, to discern who... But all I could tell was 'male.' Strong. Intense. I deliberately chose to believe it was my Master's presence, because I was not prepared to cope with it being anyone — Anyone — else. I stood, and breathed more deeply for a few moments to try to center my Self, and turned my focus to my assignment — to masturbate for my master.

I stroked the knife blade along my skin — the flat part, around my breasts. I used the edge to peel the wax from the sensitive flesh it had landed on, and the stinging of that heat was renewed. I held the knife over the large candle and watched the small bits of wax drop off into it, making of that an offering to the gods: substance returned to source. Trailing the blade around my breasts again, the flat stroked across my nipples, again. And again. Until each one got the point of the blade pushing inward, till I gasped and couldn't press any more. When my breath had slowed again I checked — no blood. Master would be displeased with blood he could not taste. I could feel the wetness inside me, the quivering melting feeling — submission and arousal and need, all the same now. I could feel the energy thrumming within me, from bottom to top, side to side, like the special effects of electricity in a B-grade movie.

The knife stroked over me, almost of its own will, tip trailing along around my body. My mind flashed, vividly, to that claiming online; to Master's intensity, to my laying at his hand, to the runes sliced into my skin: pain... necessity... wholeness.... Knife-tip trailing up my side, hard, I scratched "pain" over my right breast. Dragging the blade tip to scratch across, "joy" was writ over my left breast. Around that breast, down my side, the tip blazed pain and joy until "necessity" was scratched into the skin above my fur. Cycle completed, the knife trailed up, up my body... between my breasts, up to my neck, flat across my neck, with a feeling of the tool almost struggling to turn the edge to my flesh. Whimpering softly, I whispered, "Yours, Master," into the air so charged around me. Into the Presence that surrounded me.

The knife stroked slowly till the point was at my windpipe; paused, and started to move upward, the tip pushing from below, pushing upward, feather-soft. My head tilted back, and I felt the knife tip pushing all the way up to my chin, truly feeling like some other hand was holding it. After my head was as far back as I could put it, and the blade as far up as it could go without slicing, or passing my chin, it held for a moment as if to reinforce the surrender I'd offered. The pressure eased, then, and it trailed down, stopping between my breasts. And scratched there, over my heart, "wholeness"... Master's mark.

Shivering, I stood there – my whole body trembling, my skin alive. I stroked the blade down my body in the same motion as I stepped back and sat down on the bed. Leaning back, I pushed the hilt inside me, feeling how wet I was, how aroused, how ready for my master's attention. Turning the blade so it was flat between my thighs, and the hilt as far in as possible, I laid back and reached into the bedside toy-bag for the clothespins. I found only three – and so it was one wooden one on each nipple, holding them up, and one nasty plastic one with teeth on the tip of my right nipple. Adrift now in so many ways, I only trembled when I heard, "Yes... hurt for me," in my head. I groaned and my hand found the vibrator in the bag, turned it on unthinkingly, pushed it against my clit as my hips rocked. I heard myself say, "No. You can't come. You. Are. Denied!" and it was a male voice I heard, deeper than mine, hungry with control. I squirmed, writhed, felt the knife inside me, and suddenly felt that it was the blade inside me. Knowing, *knowing* it wasn't, and yet... and yet... hearing again, in my head, "It would turn if he wanted it to... turn and cut you, blood flowing for his pleasure." I moaned, repeating, "turn and cut... cut me, cut me." At that I could feel the flood, the wave breaking over me, and heard my own voice scream, "Master!" The answer came inside my head again, "Yes! Come for me!" and I did, crying out his name as I hit higher, came harder, my body bucking across the bed, the vibrator falling out of my hand, away from my clit.

I took the clothespins off quickly, gasping and spasming again with each one, and lay there, dizzy, mind spinning, not daring to think of anything at all. After a time the spasms subsided, and my hands were no longer shaking.

I slowly, carefully, took the knife out — finding that it was, indeed, the hilt that was inside me.

I licked it clean, then washed it, and replaced it on the altar. And then I knelt and took off my collar, kissing it as well, and replaced it on the altar. And then I picked up my clothes and teddy bear and I went downstairs to living with him at a distance again.

This was over a decade ago. The power-exchange relationship didn't survive the separation; other people, in both his local and his virtual space, had acquired a higher priority. There was a period we didn't speak, although that was because of someone else's insecurities, or so he told me at the time. Delivering his remaining belongings during that time was an adventure in social manipulation.

I, too, acquired other lovers, other kink-partners, always via the internet. And, eventually, communications between he and I opened up again. Occasionally he'd tell me about a new MUSH or other social venue, but I just stayed away, not wanting to relive the ache for him that I'd finally eased away from me.

My attendance on my altar faltered, and finally failed when I was gone for two weeks and simply got too busy to keep it up — I wasn't going in that room anymore, and I didn't have anyone to talk to about these things. My attempts to find other people to do "this stuff" all faltered on the 'that's *their* reality' idea... the skepticism that has never quite left me.

But as I moved forward in my life, I found that I could tell it would be a good relationship when I could feel their skin as my own, know when they need to laugh in scene, know in my flesh when they need a break or needed a drink...

... because all of my access to energy flow, to this aspect of spirituality, is focused through my sexuality, particularly BDSM. The luminosity I lived with him flares up in me only in scene. I called it "sharing the brain" for a while. I've referred to it as "feeding," long before I ever heard of sanguinary or power vampires, and it does indeed feed some part of me, that grows forlorn when I don't get time with someone who I connect with in this way. Some people have told me I do have some aspects of vampire about me. This ability to feel the power flowing was the primary reason that two different long distance relationship worked as long as they did. It's nothing as wild as telepathy, but it certainly seems to be a connection beyond just reading body language, as I am sometimes able to achieve this with people I've only just met.

It was nearly three years ago that I got a new-ish computer, and when he read about it in a public blog post he was all over my mailbox about a venue he'd been in for a year — a graphical one, that offered as many unlimited possibilities as one's imagination could. I'd been ignoring his praises of it like I'd ignored the rest, with the excuse that my computer wasn't supported. With the new machine, I couldn't slip out of it, and so I joined. I let him boss me around on various aspects of existence there, and after a month or so he told me that the reason he'd been so pushy about making a character there was because he thought I needed new relationships, and this was a place to find them. But not with him.

And yet, he was right. In the time I've been in the new world, I've lost the long distance dominant who had not been a part of my life in a real way for so long. I've lost him, and yet, in letting him go I have gained three other relationships. All kinky. And I can feel every one of them, feel them from a distance, feel them in my skin, feel their needs, their laughter, their desire. I can feel each of them and use my words to build their heat and arousal to fever pitch with only the power of imagination. I can feel each of them on the other side of the pixels.

In the Hum

By Sybil Holiday

When I was young, five or so, I became aware that I was part of something greater than I was. Lying spread out, face down in wet newly-mown grass, dizzy with the lush smell of chlorophyll, I realized there was a hum in the ground beneath me and a hum in the air above me and a hum in me, and they were all the same. In true child innocence I merged with it, allowing my little five-year-old identity to disappear until I was the grass and the air, until I was nothing at all but a timeless hum.

I didn't call it spiritual or a higher power then — how could I? Yet looking back through my early years, many experiences like this, sometimes when I most felt alone, supported me, infused me, and shaped me into the young woman who, in 1968, set out from New England on her own, and who has traveled far since then. These experiences were always accompanied by a hum or a vibration in my body, and so my spirituality has not ever been something outside me, because I've always been with it, with the hum. I didn't call myself spiritual nor did I recognize a higher power then, or later in life; there was simply that hum.

Fast-forward to San Francisco, in the early '80s. I am looking down at a young woman spread out, face up in my sling in my new blackroom, and she's waiting for my hand. We have a… different connection; she's clearly lesbian and butch as well, and at that time I identified as bi, and was usually attracted to what we then called "fluff" or soft butches. She's none o' that. She is eighteen, however, and I am thirty-five.

Still, each time we meet there is this distinctive spark between us, and we both feel as if we are in medieval England and she's my consort. She is very practical and does not believe in any of that "past life mumbo jumbo," so it must be something else, she says. And so we continue to flirt, she trying to figure out what the "something else" is, and I enjoying her consternation.

After a heavy petting date, we both agree we want more and set up a time for her to be in my sling. We meet and I flog her to loosen her up, and then there she is, spread wide for me. As I lube up my hands and her cunt I begin to slide into another world; the music fades from my hearing, the walls disappear from my view, and all I see is her cunt and thighs, waiting; all I hear is her voice and the sound of her cunt and my hand and the hum.

I begin slowly, yet her cunt draws me in quickly, in and yes, I am in and her cunt wants more. Sliding one hand over the other, I begin to double fuck her, double fist her, and mental snapshots appear in my mind like a transparent overlay on top of my vision. I see her clearly in the sling, a sophisticated San Francisco '80s teen leatherdyke in a chest harness and big leather boots and a great haircut, and I also see her in a cave, ungroomed, dirty, and completely naked, kneeling back on her heels with her thighs again spread wide for me, waiting.

We are in an ancient ritual together and we are not alone. Many wolves are in the cave, yet they are there to watch and protect us. Rough lumps of tallow are lit atop both her thighs, and as they burn all the way down I pierce her cunt lips open and back with crude bone needles, opening her up to herself completely, to her pain and her blood and her life. These images flicker in and out of my consciousness the entire time I fist her and I say nothing, for I know she will not welcome them. And maybe they are not meant for her, anyway.

She opens up to me more and deeper and both my hands are deep down into her and wide too and she says no and yes and no no and yes yes yes and... well, you know.

After we eat and cleanup we agree to meet again. She leaves, and I – well I wander my home, still aroused and deep in trance, deep in the hum. I am not thinking at all, I let myself be guided, and I find myself picking up an old cedar box I got from my mother. Slowly, I fill it with various small objects from various rooms: a bell with a handle, two small crystal bowls, a rose quartz crystal, a clear crystal, a small candle and holder, a very small round incense burner, a piece of charcoal, matches, a pack of Tarot cards, and a few other items.

Eventually I am standing in my entrance hall. I place the box on the table below the mirror, and light a large candle. I recognize I've just made an altar, and as I appreciate that I also realize I've already many altars all over my home; places where a candle, incense, a picture or two, and other items of meaning and love have come together: in my living room and bathroom and kitchen and even in my storage room, places of love and acknowledgment and – dare I say it – faith.

I look into the mirror and see myself in my leathers, a strong San Fran leatherwoman, and I also see that this is the first time tonight I've thought about myself at all. The earlier scene had taken on its own life; neither my teen leatherdyke nor this personality of mine had really figured into it, and it is still happening.

And now it's time for me to read something. Read something at this altar. But what? So again I wander and this time, it's not so easy.

I go from room to room to room to room, looking at books and magazines and pieces of paper, searching, searching. My body starts to ache from all the fun. It's late, and yet I must find this thing to read, dammit!

I'm done with this. Shaking off the trance like a dream with no ending, I blow out the candle and go into my bedroom. Taking off my leathers, I casually look over at my dresser. Upon it are a few books given to me that I have yet to even glance at, and _Illusions: The Adventures of The Reluctant Messiah_ by Richard Bach jumps into my vision. Oh, crap. The new age seagull guy.

Exceptionally reluctant, I pick it up and hold it unopened. I don't want to read it. I am tired, it's really late now, and the high of the evening's events has worn off. I'm no longer in a trance, the hum is gone, and this isn't fun anymore. Besides, Richard Bach? I'm done with this. I'm naked and I'm tired and I'm still horny and I'm going to bed.

But it isn't done with _me_, and very slowly, unwillingly, I open to a random page in the book.

Now, if you have read _Illusions_ you might guess the page I opened to, and if you guessed the page that is _The Messiah's Handbook, Reminders for the Advanced Soul_, you would be right. I don't get any further than those eight words and I am in tears. I don't want to do this, be this. Advanced soul? That's so not me, my life is a mess! I'm in my mid-30s already and still don't know what I'm going to do when I grow up.

And Messiah? Not me, I've always had a hard time with the whole "God" thing, remember? Reluctant? Yeah, I'll give you that.

All the fun is truly gone now and I don't want this level of awareness and responsibility, I really, really, really don't. It's not true and I'm not ready and I am naked and I want to go to sleep.

Stomping about my bedroom I continue to cry and reread the title. As I cry some more and stomp some more I find I'm stomping out of my bedroom and down the hall to the altar where I stop and, still stomping yet now more like shaking, I relight the candle.

Still slowly, yet with a bit more willingness and certainly with more intent, I ask a question: "What's all this about?", and again I open to a random page.

It says:

"You are led through your lifetime by the inner learning creature, the playful spiritual being that is your real self."

This is not new, what I am reading. I remember meeting/being the hum. So far so good.

It says:

"Don't turn away from possible futures before you're certain you don't have anything to learn from them."

This is not new either. I know what it's talking about and I don't like this, I don't want this. But I do want this. And I feel the hum. I am reluctant. I am reluctant to turn myself over to a god, to surrender that way, I always have been. I used to pray, "Dear Jesus, you know you're not the one for me but I don't know who is, so would you please give my prayer to them?"

And yet, as I read I remember the hum and I feel the hum and I hear the hum and I know I've been doing this as far back as I can remember. I've been caring and cared for as far back as I can remember, I've been with women as far back as I remember, as far back as a cave, and I'm shaking and I feel the hum and I'm so wet and I'm so alive and I look at the mirror and I see my naked body is quivering and shaking and I am in San Francisco and I am in a cave and I am I am I am crying and humming and laughing and humming humming all over and I am on my way to coming all over and then I am coming and saying Yes, Yes I will do this Yes I've always done this Yes Oh Mother Oh Goddess I belong here I remember my promise I'm coming I am your daughter I am your priestess I'm coming home Oh Goddess Yes I'm coming home.

The truth is, the hum — spirit, god/dess, the universe, creative energy, divine light — whatever you call it, is always there and it's me that comes and goes. The hum hums on and it's my job — especially when I don't want to, especially when I can't feel it or hear it — to stop and remember and trust, and to continue to learn different ways to live within the hum.

The Joy of My Service

By Domme Jaguar (Mexico)

I'm preparing candles, water, incense and rope, lots of rope, for a psycho-magic ritual I'll conduct tomorrow night.

It is for a very talented girl who wants to stop being who she is not, the one she thinks her mother condemned her to be. She is 24, but she lives again in her mother's house and has dropped school 7 times. She needs and wants to break her ties, so she can start searching for who she really is.

I will free, forget, and embrace her as she is, the day and the time of her 25th birthday. But I have to tie her first, to immobilize her, and to be cruel and insensitive to her crying, to make her suffer until she breaks herself in pain, frustration, and rage so she can rescue her own Power from her deepest vulnerability, her deepest Claiming.

I will use My sadism for a good cause: to free her and make her able to start healing. To pardon, and to transcend. And this is beautiful, and makes Me happy – along other things – of having the job of being one of the very few Mexican Pro Dommes, those very few to whom people in need can come in My country, this well-known "Macho's land."

And I mean people in diverse need. As I started to plan this ritual, I am also training a sex slave-to-be, for instance: a 26-years-old boy who have been fantasizing about being with a Goddess since childhood, who at some point lost any hope of finding a good Domme in this country. But at My hand he is now learning how to endure high octane eroticism while still being able to satisfy a woman with his full erection and his obedient worship.

This job has given Me the vision and the experience of the holiness of paradoxes such as getting pleasure from pain, freedom from ties, pride from shame, taking power from being an object of desire. The gift of personifying the Highest Sacred Feminine Power. The great joy of commanding somebody to go beyond their fears and taboo… and to lead them safely that way. The great honor of providing an older person with pleasures they have dreamed for 40, 50, 60 years in the hidden shadows of their heart.

To tell you the truth, despite My background in spiritual practices and in sex education, at the beginning I just thought that I was simply playing Domme. It was just fun that every single man at a given BDSM party wanted to receive My lashes or throw themselves at My feet. That was something like "hey, why not?" when I started to receive encouragement to become a Pro, after some 4 years as a lifestyle Domina, simply because there were nobody else in the surroundings to do this.

But things changed one day…

In My first year as a Pro Domme, a young novice came to Me traveling more than 300 km by bus to be at My feet. After that first year, in which I saw him some 4 times, he disappeared of My sight for many months. And when he finally responded to an email, I knew that he was depressed, clinically depressed, so crying for nothing even under the sun rays.

He was a good dog. He was obedient, receiving, and loved pain. I missed him during that time, and happily accepted to play with him when he asked Me to do it again. I had asked him to visit Me no matter that depression, many times, with no success on My part. He was a delicious, young dog, and finally wanted a goodbye session: he was to travel to Europe, where he had gotten a Master's scholarship with honours.

I was happy to see him again, and decided to give him a good session with most of the things he had proved to enjoy. I tied the boy to a chair, blindfolded him and sensually tortured him. I beat him with all My different floggers, alternating with rubbing furs and My own body to him, caressing and biting him until his flesh was awake and his soul went into that space where everything is right and feels so good.

I had him stand face to the wall and spanked his rounded butt with My bare hand, keeping that mixture of hardness and tenderness I truly love, and then I took him to the edge of the bed and made him bent over.

I didn't need to ask: he opened his legs and offered himself to Me, so I had to take him. But I really wanted to. His skin was lovely red and soft, and I was compelled Myself to bent over him on My side. So I hugged him and started to tease his opening with My fingers, that one by one were welcomed inside, where I found his root, and he started to growl and tremble, and speak other languages, and finally went into glowing convulsions, letting himself go beyond any worry, passing all "machista" stereotypes, and jumping beyond his own self.

I saw him shake, I saw him die, and then, I saw him become alive again.

At My touch, he became empty of everything; and then, suddenly, full as well. His root started to pulsate again at the beat of Life, and big waves of joy and life flooded his young body.

Inside and outside Me, I saw the scene and let Myself to be moved by it. He was bending over the mattress and I was over him. So sure that he could not observe My face at his back, I flood Myself as well. My own heart was overloaded by love, and my eyes watered.

Other things have happened after I saw Myself, yes, the Domme, crying in that session. I've received new pieces of that Revelation, that are still been assembled together with other parts of My background and the new disciplines I am learning.

I am still looking for meanings and may do forever, but while I prepare Myself to use all My physical force and cruelty to provoke this girl, I do know some things: that My Power transcends its erotic use, that I can work both with pain and with pleasure, that even in the simplicity of "just" challenging prejudices I am providing a Sacred Service… and that as My Top Totem, The Black Jaguar, I'm entitled to walk between Darkness and Light.

God-Sex and Consent:
Two Examples of Saying "Yes!" to Ecstasy

By P. Sufenas Virius Lupus

Three words often heard in the context of BDSM/kink practices are generally considered "essential" to the smooth running of a scene, or the larger lifestyle itself – Safe, Sane, and Consensual. These words may seem in many people's minds not to be at all in play when it comes to any sexual relationship with non-corporeal, and particularly divine, beings. Anyone who has done serious spiritual work in their life knows that spirituality isn't always safe, for a great variety of reasons, and this is often more internally the case than due to some external threat (though the latter do exist and can occur as well). For many people, "sanity" and religion of any sort are at odds with each other, incompatible, oppositional, and even oxymoronic, despite many fine religious minds over the millennia praising knowledge, reason, and the human rational soul as an elevated and important spiritual faculty. But whatever a particular person or religious group's opinions on the first two words may be, it is the third of these, consensuality, which is often thought to be the least applicable to a relationship between a human and a divinity.

To begin, let me define what I'm considering to be a divinity in this context. Anything which is non-corporeal, which has an identifiable personality and individual volition would qualify in the category of "divinity" or "divine being" as far as I'm concerned. This, of course, includes the entire world of gods from many different cultures throughout human history, but also land and nature spirits, ancestors, heroes, angels, *daimones*, one's own "higher self" or past lives, and even the spirits of individual former humans that we may have known or who lived recently. Many would argue that these latter are not "divine" in the same way as a deity is, but for the purposes of god-sex, the distinction is a minor one. The recently deceased person is still non-corporeal, volitional, and identifiable as themselves; and many divine ancestors, deified mortals, heroes, and others would have started out as simply the disembodied spirit of a particular person. Thus, there may be a difference in degree of personality, power, recognition, influence, and intelligence at work, but the basic mechanism of interacting with a human as such a being is not that different than it would be for any of the "higher" manifestations of divine presence and personality. In that respect, Kali-Ma may not be that different from Kurt Cobain for these purposes.

Too often, this disparity of power between humans and divinities leads humans to think they are quite literally powerless when it comes to divine-human interactions, and that they have no say in the matter. Mystical submission to a divine will has been heightened to the epitome of spiritual practice in the view of several dominant monotheistic religions, quite often to the exclusion of all other possibilities in such relationships. The accounts of different mystics in Christianity and other religions being "ravished by the divine" or "in rapture" are pervasive… and yet, from the viewpoint of power dynamics, what is this other than rape? It is often assumed that human-divine interactions of this sort are "okay" in a certain sense because the deity involved is the Creator, and is omnipotent, omnipresent, and omniscient (as well as whatever other superlatives are the preferred ones of the day), and that therefore humans "have no choice" in such actions and in the face of such a dissimilarity of power and even of existential level-of-being. That may be very well for Christians, Muslims, and certain other religious people, but polytheistic religions traditionally tend not to ascribe such superlatives to their deities. This does not stop many modern pagans from assuming these same ideas of divinity are intrinsic to pagan deities as well, however. The rather fearful use of "Them" in referring to deities in particular makes the gods sound as if they are an invading plague of giant ants, rather than powerful cosmic forces and personalities that fascinate, and with whom it can be beneficial for humans to deal in a variety of relationships and contexts. The mystically-inclined amongst pagans and Christians are thus, likewise, often absorbed in what amounts to a divine rape fantasy in which they want to be the one so ravished – which then brings up the question of whether this constitutes consent on the part of the humans, and fulfillment of this desire is synonymous to divine consent.

On the other end of the spectrum, there is a long-standing tradition within ceremonial magic of summoning and then binding *daimones* and forcing them through various pacts and magical formulae to submit to the magician involved, and to carry out that magician's work. This, also, is a "magical rape culture" in effect, in which the basic functioning of the system is predicated on such violent non-consensual relationships that have no regard for the *daimones* involved – many of whom are purported to be powerful commanders or sovereigns of the infernal regions in the *Goetia*. Operations of this sort do emerge in a para-Christian context, in which the individual magician is seen as doing the "work of God" and is therefore superior to these fallen beings.

But the magical traditions of the antique Mediterranean world are not that different. Greek culture was one in which tales of divine-human conception were usually stories of male gods raping female mortals (or other deities); and the common magical operations of *katadesmoi* ("binding spells") were used to bind deities and spirits into doing one's command as well as to bind other humans in order to make them carry out the will (often explicitly amorous or sexual) of the person who commissioned the spell. It is specifically this mindset amongst the ancient Greeks that made sorcery such a taboo and fraught topic, and why philosophers like Plato spoke against it, why laws were made in some places forbidding it, and why many modern pagans from a more reconstructionist methodology have what seems to be an allergy to magic, even if it is traditional to their particular polytheistic culture.

By no means am I suggesting that people should begin parading about with signs that say "No Means No!" and "No Answer To A Question Not Asked Is Not Consent!" outside of Hellenic pagan gatherings in protest of the actions of Zeus in mythology, or that there should be an organization of "People for the Ethical Treatment of *Daimones*" that demonstrates outside of occult and magical conventions (Though the image is rather amusing!). However, consideration of these issues – both ethically and theologically – is important for anyone involved in this kind of work.

Things get considerably more complicated when one is involved with god-sex outside of direct visionary experience, dreams, and other disembodied or ecstatic states. How does one do god-sex if one is not interacting with someone who is horsing a deity, or if one is not oneself in the act of horsing? The horsing process itself involves particularities of consent, but how does one gauge this otherwise when another being is interacted with on the material plane outside of the medium (quite literally!) of other humans? In my own experience, it's happened in a variety of ways. I do not usually get direct words in communication with any divine being (Outside of dreams and the occasional "multi-media" vision). I have had a very limited number of dreams that have involved sex with divine beings, but what about how this process works within waking experiences? How would one distinguish a really good wank from an erotic epiphany or theophany?

I am here contextualizing my own enumeration of a few types of these experiences with a discussion of consent because that issue, to me, was the pivotal factor in each of the following cases. Both of these sets of experiences took place for me in the last decade: the first in the summer of 2000, and the second in the late winter/early spring of 2010. They were each with different divine beings, and both experiences were unexpected, though I did have a relationship with the beings in question prior to each experience.

Incident One: Sixty-Nine With A Sword

I've often joked that the first time I read the Irish saga *Táin Bó Cúailnge* in late 1994, Cú Chulainn (the hero at the heart of the tale) grabbed a hold of my shirt collar and said, "I'm not done with you yet!" And while that is a bit of an exaggeration (though not out of character for him within the tales!), it is in a sense quite literally true. For the sixteen years since then, a day has not gone by when he's not been in my thoughts, and much of that time has been spent in academic study of him, as well as devotional activities in honor of him apart from this.

And what's not to like? Cú Chulainn was said to be the pinnacle of youthful male beauty in the stories he's in, desirable to women, and enjoying close emotional and erotic relationships with men as well. For those who enjoy a particular type of ephebic physicality, Cú Chulainn being derided constantly for his beardlessness and consequent lack of "manliness" despite his invincible battle prowess is an endearing rather than derogatory attribute. However, the visual representations of Cú Chulainn from medieval Ireland are non-existent, and very few artists of the last two centuries have turned their hands to his depiction; when they have done so, their efforts have often been vastly inaccurate, or simply unappealing to me. I worked on a drawing of him on and off from 1994 to 2002, and my results were equally fraught with difficulties. I could picture him in my mind clearly on occasion, but actually getting something more tangible and sensible (literally) through which to connect with him was mostly a losing battle. In December of 1996, on my first trip to Ireland, I found a beautiful sculptural plaque of him at the National Museum in Dublin, but it depicted him amidst his death-throes, which has been a popular theme in Irish art since about 1916. While one could honor the hero through such images quite adequately for cultic purposes, and the image was not only beautiful but erotically suggestive, nonetheless I always got the impression that drooling over this image of him with one hand on my cock was a bit inappropriate. No matter how much the death drive and the sex drive might have crossovers in certain cases, this felt like importuning someone at the wrong time, as inappropriate as a bystander propositioning a fireman about to enter a burning building.

What to do? A solution emerged quite without warning in the course of the summer months of 2000. I made the horrible discovery of eBay that summer, and not only found a number of items I'd been looking for in vain elsewhere, but also found that replicas of swords were sold by various sellers through the site. I began purchasing many of these, often without regard to cost. I eventually saw a sword that was often labeled "Celtic," which had a leaf-blade and an anthropoid hilt in the style of many Bronze and Iron Age swords recovered from Ireland and elsewhere in culturally Celtic areas of those same time periods. I was not able to find one that I could afford through an eBay seller, but a web search turned up a pagan shop that sold them for about $60. I eagerly made my purchase, and in a few days a package arrived at my house.

The sword came in a beautiful brown leather scabbard that smelled and felt fantastic, and the first time I unsheathed it – due to the placement of a metal button to fasten the sword to the scabbard – it made that "*schwing!*" sound, singing like no knife or sword I'd ever yet held in my hands, practically humming with intensity. I made it my habit over the next few weeks to never be long apart from the sword, and even began sleeping with it next to me in my bed, my hand often resting on the hilt the entire night through. This was not typical behavior for me by any stretch of the imagination. Even though I realized this atypicality in the midst of the experience, nonetheless I was moving toward what would eventually become necessary for me. I was subconsciously preparing for and becoming accustomed to a presence which I had no notion was soon to arrive in my life.

For several months, I had been practicing what I had learned via Joseph Kramer's EroSpirit educational videos, which was the art of "soloving" – evolutionary masturbation, or any number of other possible descriptions – and had been having good results over and above my own sexual particularities. I have always had a propensity for strange sexual "talents," including multiple orgasms, orgasm without ejaculation, and even ejaculation without erection. Having an open mind about these things often allowed these bodily peculiarities to emerge, and often surprise, in the midst of sexual activities of various sorts.

Lying on my bed one night with the sword, I began a soloving session. However, my mind kept drifting to Cú Chulainn. I wanted an image of him to connect with, and so I got out the sketch I had made of him, inadequate as it was. I was having some success in self-pleasuring, and then things changed. I got the strangest notion in the midst of all this: *Take out the sword.* And do... what, I wondered. I took out the sword, and noticed my hand upon the hilt. The anthropoid hilt had a large circular pommel as if it was a human head, and upturned and downturned brass "U" shapes for arms and legs, with the main shaft of the hilt itself being the body of this anthropomorphic figure. That meant that the long leaf-shaped blade, extending down as it did from between the legs, was equivalent to the sword-figure's penis. While this might have been a superlatively optimistic male phallic fantasy – and one quite at variance with what is known and can be inferred about Cú Chulainn himself from descriptions in the original Irish sources – in some sense the erotic and

death-dealing dimension implied by this bladed death-phallus made sense as an understanding of Cú Chulainn as well. Whatever his sexual prowess may have been with his own genital endowment and other physical characteristics, his proficiency in warfare and bringing about the death of his opponents was excessive… and attractive.

Now that I had the sword, and had put together the physiological implications of it (forget the symbolic ones!), I got a further message: *Use the sword.* How? The humanoid figure of the hilt was the answer. Cú Chulainn's famous spear, the *gae bolga*, killed all adversaries it was used against by penetrating their anuses and disemboweling them. This sword, in the right hands (or even the wrong hands!) could cause similarly devastating damage, and I wasn't about to try anything with the blade turned against myself. So, that left the hilt. What if the "head" of the hilt were to be used as if it were Cú Chulainn's head, and he was giving me head? What if my own "sword" were to be put against the "body" of the hilt, as if my own "head" were doing likewise to him? I held the sword's hilt against my penis, with the pommel/head between the base of my shaft and my scrotum; and instead of attempting to do any further movements, I simply vibrated my hand while I grasped both sword and penis.

The most intense and extraordinary sensations poured through me, as if I had just plugged into a divine electrical socket. I ended up having, with only a little bit more physical effort, an extremely intense orgasm with ejaculation. This was most unusual, considering that under normal circumstances, I need a great deal of friction and movement at quite rapid speeds to even approach an orgasmic state (such that use of lube, while it may prevent wear and tear, so to speak, often prevents orgasm due to lack of friction for me), and even under such conditions, it still takes quite a while to get there. Here, this divine sword sixty-nine with Cú Chulainn brought me off in a matter of a minute, but it was a minute that felt like hours. The normal bonds of time and space seemed to have been severed through the sword as well.

In the aftermath of this, I lay there for some time in an afterglow more pleasing and lengthy than any I'd actually experienced with a human lover, certainly before that time and most likely since (though I hold out great hopes for the future!). I had a difficult time processing the entire event, and had to really question if I had gone insane or something. There are several tales involving Cú Chulainn where words from him carved inside his sword's hilt speak to people in ages after his death, and in other tales, swords themselves speak of their deeds, and vouch for the heroism of their owners. I eventually understood this experience as Cú Chulainn's way of not only claiming that sword as his own implement, but of using it to connect with me physically and sexually. Strange sensualities became consensuality through that medium. And, like any good and fully-trained *fili* ("poet," but literally "seer"), a class that often used imagery of marriage and love affairs for their relations with their patrons, I have been singing Cú Chulainn's praises and lamenting his loss like a widow – the traditional trope and obligation of a patron's chief poet – ever since. I only connected with Cú Chulainn sexually through that sword on a few other occasions, and while I still have the sword itself, like many affairs in that hero's life, ours was short-lived but long in its effects. A decade of my life has passed since, which is more than a third of the lifespan of the hero, and I will still tell his tales and praise his virtues as long as I can draw breath.

Incident Two: Mediterranean Mercy Fuck

I have had a devotional relationship with Antinous, the deified lover of the Roman Emperor Hadrian, since 2002. While I was aware of his existence before that time, it wasn't until the summer of that year that I had heard he had become a god; in the books in which I had seen him referenced previously, it simply said that he had died and the Emperor's grief at his loss was excessive, and resulted in a city founded in his honor as well as statues of him cropping up all over the Empire. That key factor of these things occurring because Antinous was deified was entirely absent from the picture. I had seen and admired him, but didn't recognize his divinity until it was pointed out to me.

My cultic relationship to Antinous has been multifaceted. I have served a sacerdotal function for him in ritual on many occasions, as well as lending my considerable academic talents and knowledge to researching him, collecting and translating texts relating to him, and educating others about his *cultus*. Amidst all this, there was never any suggestion that our relationship would be anything more than these things. I had encountered him in visions and dreams, and innovated a modern version of his Mysteries, but a sexual relationship

was beyond the boundaries with him. Some of our interactions had been physical and even sensual in these visionary states, but not sexual. I had an experience in 2009 of Antinous "coming to live" inside my body for a period, and I can still sometimes feel that, and am reeling with the implications of what that could mean. I have been praying a hymn for many years now that invites Antinous to come and build his temple in one's heart, but for him to suddenly show up and set up shop in my solar plexus was unexpected, but not unwelcome.

In the later part of 2009, I was speaking with two gentlemen who were self-confessed "psychic voyeurs," and they asked me to describe what my relationship with Antinous was like. I struggled for words, and said that I sometimes feel like I'm a publicity agent or advertising contractor for him, and while I spoke about this, both of the fellows were riveted in their attention, and described this particular relationship (from their viewpoint) as energetically different and quite distinct from any they had encountered previously amongst the esoterically inclined and god-bothered. While there was an erotic and flirtatious element to the entire mix, it was not at the forefront, at least at that period. This was an intriguing set of observations for me to hear.

In early 2010, I was living alone in an unfamiliar city for a short-term job, and was often quite isolated and without spiritual community for extended periods. During this time, I consecrated my living space to Antinous, with the four walls of the room as the four sides of his Obelisk from Rome. When I would commute back and forth to work each day on the bus, I would listen to some music on my iPod that I overlaid with a mantra to Antinous and Hadrian, and sometimes I would end up doing up to two hours of this practice every day due to the length of my travel. Over the coming months, a variety of interesting and quite wonderful experiences took place within that space at home. It was at the beginning of a series of revelations that the following took place.

I had found a book, in the library at the university where I was working, that was in French. It had some photographs of various statues of Antinous that were familiar to me, but the photos were better and from different angles than I had seen previously. The front cover of the book had a photo of one of the most beautiful and complete, original nude statues of Antinous, the Farnese Antinous now in Naples. On the back cover, it had a picture of the same statue, only from the back. I joked that it was the "Antino-ass" photo – and what an ass it is! I located a copy of this book for purchase in Belgium, and eagerly ordered it. Once I had my copy, I would often carry it around with me as a portable, flat, and yet nearly life-like icon of Antinous. I would look at it admiringly quite often. After having it for a short while, one night I felt in the mood for some soloving, but something was "different." I couldn't keep my eyes off the book. As a trained academic, an intellectual, and a bibliophile though, something seemed wrong about using a book just for its cover and not being able to read very much of it. There were internal ideas and hidden guilts that I had not yet confronted.

I didn't want to just use an image of one of my principal deities for instrumental purposes, particularly since I consider images of Antinous potent icons that not only connect his human devotees to him, but through which he is also able to connect to and experience us. In a *cultus* that is so blessed and fortunate to have as many diverse and beautiful images of its divinity as ours happens to be, this idolatrous (in the positive sense!) dimension to our cultus' devotional activities seems natural and obvious. I have always held that prayer and ritual to Antinous of any kind should take place in the presence of a representation of him, no matter what it happens to be – a postcard, a photograph, a coin, a statue or bust, or even an image on a computer screen. It is through the eyes and ears of his statues and his representations that Antinous is able to look upon his worshippers. Even with that being the case, and this entire religious endeavor being one that is body-positive, sex-positive, and explicitly and unapologetically queer, the idea of wanking before one's gods still wasn't sitting right with me. Just using an image to get off, and making that a part of one's spirituality, seemed more like objectification, and to be missing an important mark for me.

But that night was different. At a certain point, it no longer felt as if I was alone in the room. The photo took on a new semblance to me, as if Antinous was smiling where he had not been before, and that he invited me to pleasure myself, and by doing so to give him pleasure. I did it, reveling in the invitation and the permission that this gave me, to be as fully and as filthily myself, in that brief series of moments of sexual self-satisfaction. The feeling of hopelessness and languishing in celibacy, of all the rejections I'd experienced recently and in the past, of the sexual exile I had been in despite advocacy and visibility work on many sexual issues, and of embarrassment that I had to "resort" to these masturbatory acts, and that I even had the audacity and hubris to try and justify them and to make them "sacred" (as if they were not inherently sacred already – it was not realizing that in which lay the hubris!), went away. For that short period of time, it felt as though Antinous was giving me some physical appreciation for all of my work; and like many a good friend with benefits, he was throwing me a divine mercy fuck because he could see that I really needed it! I am not his god-slave or his lover, I am not bound to him in devoted servitude; I'm equally as able to criticize him and contradict him, as anyone who is a friend and an equal could do. His power is far greater than mine, but my ability to do things for him and on his behalf is far more important in the present world in which I am living.

When I have been lucky enough to find someone to whom I am attracted, and who is interested enough in me to engage in a relationship, a session of sex, or even just a bit of fetish play, consent of the expectable sorts has always been obtained. As someone who is rather shy and introverted, it can be difficult enough to walk up to someone and say, "Hello, would you like to talk for a moment?" In the years before FetLife, it has been even more difficult to say, "Hey, I'm into flogging and I hope you are too!" or, "I can't tell you in words how much black PVC *turns me on*." Yet, on some occasions, I've been fortunate enough to find someone with common interests or at least a mutual attraction strong enough that they'll entertain possibilities in pursuit of that attraction.

No matter how liberal they have seemed, however, or how much they say they care or that they support what I am interested in, there has always been something missing. I have seen it in their eyes, while I am in the throes of pleasure, that something is bothering them. I am turned on by a bit of roughness, and they are disgusted at me. I get excited over a certain type of visual stimulation, and they are uncomfortable with it. They are using their hands and other implements to make me gasp for air and enter a state of physical ecstasy, and they're not happy to be along for that ride. No matter how much they have given their consent to the actions or to the relationship generally, the most essential consent has been left out of the situation. This is the consent in which one person allows the other to be what they really are, allows them the freedom to be as they most desire to be, and the other person accepts their being so. Overlooking, ignoring, or not even realizing the essentiality of this type of consent is something that I am very aware of now, through my interactions with lovers who care, my encounters with god-sex, and my own journey into self. I know that there are other people out there who can give both kinds of consent, and can enjoy what pleasures I can afford them, as well as what pleasure I take in their doing likewise for me. I can't wait to find more people like that, now that I am more aware of how important the need for this deeper and more important type of consent is.

In these experiences of god-sex, that consent, and that allowance by the divine beings involved, represented a turning point in my own sexual and spiritual development. My own boundaries were not pushed in these encounters, but were instead deeply and profoundly respected as the encounters were fully explored. I was able to be fully myself within those boundaries, and to fill the entire container in which I was at those times. For these reasons alone, much less the thousands of others which would potentially cause a person to want to have a devoted relationship with these divine figures, I cannot see my relationship to them ceasing at any point in the near or far future. Whether through the unconditionally loving and accepting gaze at me through one of their icons, or through the physical embodiment of a weapon of war becoming an implement of eroticism, Antinous and Cú Chulainn have both touched me sexually, and have added a further dimension to my spirituality and my subsequent religious insight through having done so. Their own affirmations of my ecstasies ended up being an affirmation of my relationships with them, and with life more widely.

Gaining the consent of others — whether human or divine — in our erotic and spiritual lives is essential; but there must likewise be an important consenting within ourselves to bring everything we have and that we are to the encounter and to our spiritual actions consciously, honestly, and without shame or fear. This is the ultimate "YES!" to life to which, with any luck, all spiritual pursuits and all expressions of love that humans can experience should lead.

Another Dead Nigger

By Mollena Williams

Not over... haven't you had enough blood sweat flesh hate pain sickness despair you feasting hyena hunger on me and so I say yes to your appetite insatiable. Un. Suffer. Able... unable. I am not able I am not willing I. Please just let this be over. I truly can't take any more go any further endure one. More. Moment. Of this fleshless wickedness. Of this depraved evil. I'm sorry, I am so sorry... I'm just not strong enough and I tried I tried so hard. I wanted to survive to be strong to resist to triumph over evil but today today now right now even the darkness overcasts absorbs and silently inhales this little light of mine I'm gonna let it shine this little light of mine I'm gonna let it shine let it shine let it shine sweet Jesus sweet Jesus it hurts why won't he just do it already do it let me go move on move past this earthly coil this goodly frame because I'm tired so... tired and alone and past comfort God I know I have sinned and come short of your glory but please just... make it stop I'm done I'm lost I'm afraid I'm going to put myself in Your hands please... please...

I've walked edges as a path for the entirety of my current spin on this earth. Walked between multiple worlds, Venn diagrams defining my boundaries between poverty and wealth, obscurity and fame, brilliance and ignorance.

A poor kid from the Johnson Projects who also made money performing and acting in film, theater, and television from childhood. A kid who lived in East Harlem but attended one of the most exclusive schools in the U.S. A child who knew both the squalor and poverty of Manhattan and of Marrakesh. A world traveler by the age of 6 who, nonetheless, was Venn-ed out of the spheres of her neighborhood because she "Talked like a white girl." A little black kid who found acceptance among the white people whose privilege erected invisibly solid barriers between me, a provided pauper and Them, who couldn't even know this divide.

What made me special, and set me apart, was also dangerous. I questioned. I asked. I felt everything too deeply. And when I asked questions that baffled adults, and their responses were puzzlement, amusement or, worst of all, displeasure, I learned pretty fast how to backpedal and keep my freakish nature to myself.

I first felt the word "Nigger" when I was about 4. I had been playing in the 86th Street sand park with another little girl, under the watchful eye of my Mother. Apparently, my playmate's Mother wasn't as watchful because, after a while of building castles and pushing tiny doppelgangers of heavy machinery around and about to raze our creations as soon as they took shape, my new friend's Mother came striding over with a rather startling energy, pulled her daughter away behind her, leaving her piles of toys behind. I looked up, surprised, and a moment later my friend came back crying and started gathering her things. I was upset because she was upset, but also because she had some pretty wonderful toys. I asked her where she was going. She looked at me, crying and said, "My Mommy said I'm not allowed to play with niggers," and she gathered up as much as she could and started back to her Mother.

I had no idea what that meant. But I was certain it was not Good. Something in my stomach felt abruptly, wrenching horrified, and I scrambled backwards leaving tiny troughs of sand behind me as I stumbled to my knees, then feet, running over to my Mother who had been watching this exchange with some concern from where she sat talking to some other black women sitting on the benches around the sandbox. Most of these women were nannies, watching over their pink-cheeked charges alongside the occasional parent. When I got to her side, I relayed to her what my new friend had said and my Mother, who was not someone who moved through the world aggressively, shifted her energy in a way I'd never seen before. Shooting off of the bench into a rigid stride, she called over her shoulder for me to stay where I was. I watched, wide eyed, as my usually placid and passive Mother strode over to the sandbox, where my crying playmate was gathering the last of her toys under the eye of her own Mother. I watched, but couldn't hear, as my Mother confronted this other woman who stood, stock still and seemingly stunned. My Mom then picked up my toys, turned on her heel and strode back to me, her face hard and beautiful. I thought I might have been in trouble somehow, but she took my hand gently, shook the sand off of my toys, calmly took her leave of the other ladies on the bench, and lead me out of the park.

A few blocks later, I worked up the nerve to look up at my Mom. Her face was still hard, but I sensed she wasn't angry at me, so I ventured to ask the question that had detonated in my head when I first heard that new word.

"Mommy. What does it mean, when she said she wasn't allowed to play with niggers? Am I a nigger? Is that bad?"

Mom kept walking but slowed a bit, and she took a few deep breaths. She looked down at me, and I couldn't read her expression.

"Mo, it is a really bad word. People use it to hurt us, to hurt black people. It is a hateful word for black people. Your friend didn't know how terrible it was. But her Mother knows, and she shouldn't let her child use hateful words."

I thought about this. Even though I hadn't known what the word was, it felt bad when I heard it. I didn't like it, at all.

"I don't like that. I don't like being called that." I started to cry again, and my Mother let me cry.

"I know, Mo."

At some point, I'd escaped my tormentor and was crying and screaming and crawling across the cold cement floor of the dungeon. I didn't know where I was going but I knew I had to get away. I hadn't gotten very far when I was caught by the shoulders by two more people and hauled to my feet. Disoriented, I struggled at first just to stand, then to resist the people who, though vaguely familiar, were distorted by my panic and tears to unrecognizable, fiendish obstacles to my freedom. Even as I tried to gather my thoughts the unrelenting tormentor was back in front of me, nodding in approval to the ones holding me against my will. My tongue tumbled treacherously and bit the inside of my mouth, tasting the coldsaltmetal of blood trickling across my parched tongue and I tried to focus. He was asking me the same question he'd been asking me for hours... ? Minutes? I can't tell... and I still didn't have an answer for him. The relentless questions, the beating, the pain, the casual observers on the periphery of my vision, the stream of epithets that blistered my brain as the whip striped my skin all served to push and shove and bludgeon me into a place where the reality of now was blending with. Something. Else.

The hands that held me squeezed tighter and I struggled against them until I realized this was a pointless thing, that there wasn't anything I could do, and maybe if I just stood down, I would be OK. They'll stop beating me if I stop resisting... I reasoned... so I stopped, slid to my knees and let the impossible weight of my head take me almost to the floor. Curling away from my tormentor, shaking and waiting in my cowed position only earned me a kick to the thighs and buttocks, a hand wrapped in my hair, hauling me back upwards where a series of slaps to the face spun be further out into a dark glassy nothingness.

"Y're gonna tell me what you saw, gal, or it'll only be worse for ya."

I shook my head because I couldn't imagine worse and I had no answer and because it was dawning on me that the fevered, fetid smile on his face wasn't one that carried a message of mercy. It was clear to me that my answering this question wouldn't stop the pain. He didn't care about the answer. He only wanted to hurt me. Another shake to the head as my scalp prickled painfully and my barking coughing sobs resounded anew against the bare walls and floors of this cavernous space. He threw me back to the floor, a boot on my throat and my hands scrabbling to relieve the pressure I was sure was going to crush my life away at any moment. I willed my fingers to fight, I tried to order my left hand underneath me, to rise up and push this motherfucker off of me, to get away, but my parched mouth, cold of words, soundless plead for mercy. Hot tears

ran from my eyes into my ears, momentarily distracting me from the pressure of foot on throat but only momentarily because the incremental increase of pressure was inspiring me to fight harder. There was a dark blurry moment, the wings of a murder of crows balefully careening across my vision and inner space as I whirled away from the pain and confusion to a dark calm place. If I can't get away out there I can escape inside. You cannot reach me here, and while this was true, I couldn't stay in my safe space for too long and it was shrinking. I was truly afraid. Afraid because I did not have the information that this man insisted I had, and afraid because I was sure he was capable of pulling me apart, and he seemed to crave my destruction.

And the susurration of another truth coiled around the base of my throat... I, too, craved it.

In 1977 was sitting with my Mother and watching *Roots* as it unfolded in all of its serialized glory. This was an amazing event, and I was glad to see the stories of people from whom I'd descended portrayed on television. And as a child actor, *Roots* was a bonanza for me: several commercials in which I appeared were running throughout the time-slot. They knew millions of Black Americans were glued to their televisions, and we'd just stated to emerge as a marketable demographic. My difficulty came when I began thinking, objectively, about slavery. I wondered if, possibly, just maybe, it wouldn't be so bad if your master was... nice. And maybe he gave you an OK bed to sleep in, and some decent food. And if he was handsome, then that would be kind of neat, too! I started to wonder who I might like to have as my master, if I had one. I mean, maybe Chuck Connors wasn't someone I wanted as MY master, but Captain Kirk... yeah, that would be great! I thought about how I could ask my Mom about whether or not there were ever masters who were nice to their slaves. It made sense to me that there had to be.

"Mommy?"

"Yes?"

"Were all slave owners bad?"

"What?"

"Were there nice people who owned slaves, who were nice to them?"

"... Oh! I suppose there were people who weren't evil who owned slaves, but that doesn't make it OK!"

"Well, would it be OK if they were nice to you, and didn't beat you, and didn't sell your children, and gave you enough food?"

"No, Mo, it isn't ever OK."

I, of course, couldn't let this go. My Mom was at first puzzled, then increasingly baffled, by my line of questioning. And so, as it became more awkward, of course I dropped it. It was clear to me I was asking questions that didn't even have any business being asked. I felt horrible for even doubting the unilateral evil of slavery. I'd certainly read about the history of slavery in the Americas and around the world. Being raised in a house that phased from casually religious to fervently Protestant to devoted soldiers in the Salvation Army, I was also raised to believe that we all had sinned and fallen short of the glory of God, and that no sin was too great but that being washed in the blood of the Lamb could cleanse our eternal souls. So you can imagine my thought process as I watched a program where some of God's whiter children degraded, debased, and dehumanized some of God's darker children. Obviously, there had to be some reason that it was allowed to happen! But it was also obvious that this question was too complex for even my "Gifted" little brains to process. I figured this was yet another "Grownup Thing" that would become clear to me on my 18th birthday.

When it came down to the day of That Scene, it was unexpected for me, and I was whisked away from a rather strange and disjointed conversation at the food table at a local dungeon off into the world of this scene: and this world wasn't at all comfortable.

Though the basics of this racially-motivated take-down scene had been pre-negotiated,

the "When" had been left up to my friend. One of those "Surprise me!" things. This made for an extended mind-fuck, because any time I saw him at an event I wondered if this would be the day that the scene went down. I was on edge in the dungeon for a couple of months. And you can imagine how delightful it is for a sadist to put a submissive into skittering prey mindset just by walking into the dungeon!

But the twist was this: I had never done a scene that incorporated interrogation before. I did not expect that added layer, and I was not prepared. I had rarely done a scene of this intensity and duration, or that involved the complicity of bystanders. I hadn't been fully prepared to play in this way on that night, as was part of the challenge of a "Surprise" scene. And the elements combined to form a tincture that loosened my tenuous grip on "reality" as the scene progressed. All of these elements were tossed into the furnace of my own self, seething wild, ego, soul, and mind, and the resultant slag burned away the Me I thought I knew and left... left a Me I didn't ever expect to face.

I might have admired the efficiency of his movement (lean down buck knife click sick clack) drawing the knife into place grip firm blade against my belly sluicing aside the sweat of fear and exhaustion that trickled there. I might have admired it but that I was mortally terrified. My feet, barely touching the damp and cold cement and my hands, numb and clasping in a mute upcast prayer above my head, tied as they were to a hook above my head which pulled my shoulders painfully tight. My eyes were swollen shut from crying, throat swollen and raw from screaming, heart thudding with trip hammer speed and force and I hitched in a sobbing breath... and another and another... as the knife scraped its way up my belly, the tip intermittently alerting me to the fact that this knife meant business, and the business was not good.

In a flash the knife was against my throat, and my head was brutally yanked to one side, and I was face-to-face with my tormentor, his otherwise jovial face twisted into a flat smile, blue eyes impossibly empty, amused, hair matted to his sweaty forehead.

"Now gal, you gonna tell me what I want to know or am I gonna cut open that lyin' throat of yours?" he drawled, and though I wanted to scream... again... that I had no fucking idea what he wanted me to tell him, I was beyond responding. I just hung there limply, crying. Grabbing the nape of my neck and yanking on the hair, he twisted my head so that I looked back over my shoulder, forced me to look at the crowd gathered a few yards away.

"You see that? None of those people, not one, is gonna help you. You been kicking and screaming and no one has helped you yet, have they? Couple of 'em even helped drag your black ass back when you thought you were getting away."

As I peered through eyes heavy with tears and vision dimmed by panic, I saw that what he said was true. I could make out a crowd of people, lingering, their interest levels seeming to swing between mildly interested, to fascinated, to focused, but no one moved to help. And it was true that, hours back, when I'd been knocked down and dragged to the feet of this motherfucker, not only had no one helped me, several had helped him to restrain me, letting him beat the hell out of me, all the while insisting I had information he was gonna get, by God, or he'd call the rest of the Night Riders in and they could take turns with me.

A cold truth coiled around the base of my spine, sibilant certainty that was, strangely, a relief. "He's going to kill me," I thought, "and I just hope he makes it fast because I can't take any more. Please God, if you are listening, make it fast. Merciful." And I wasn't even afraid anymore. The knife had dragged its cruel intention back down my ribcage and flank, and now pressed between my legs, the tip pricking into me, and I wondered how much longer it would take to bleed out if he started there. He slapped my face again, my head wedged into my shoulder didn't even move.
"Yeah. Another dead nigger. No one will give a shit. No one."

And I believed it. Even as I pleaded for mercy, I knew he was right. No white person would help me, and even if I were to escape again, or again and again and again, there wasn't anywhere safe for me. Nowhere. And he would slice, seaming me and leaving me to bleed out twisting in the wind alone, crying, moon rising over my sightless eyes as they all went home to safety warmth love life happiness and the arrogance of breath leaving another dead nigger behind.

When I had fantasized, as a kid, about being Harriet Tubman or leading a slave uprising, I at first thought, *"Well, of COURSE I would be brave and strong!"* and I never doubted my capacity to withstand any amount of pain, of pressure, of damage, in order to triumph over evil. Anything less was simply not acceptable.

After the scene was abruptly terminated, perforce, by the imminent closing of the dungeon, I was in no position to speak to anyone. No aftercare could ever "bring me back." I desperately wanted to be left alone. As I lay, face down and deboned by rage, fury, and shame, one thought kept slamming into my face as I tried to bob and weave the hammering blows of the truth. And the truth was? After that beating, that pressure, that abuse, I had NOT been brave. I did NOT endure. I gave up.

I gave up.

And not only did I give up; I was begging to be defeated. I WANTED to die. Death had become preferable to me to enduring any more pain, than one more stroke from the whip, than the toxic aural effluent of epithets covering me in spiritual slime that threatened to suffocate my soul.

"So, it IS true," my shattered consciousness stuttered, "you really DO believe you're worthless, that you are expendable, that you are the same dead or alive." I stared into a place in myself that I never expected even existed. The entropic, destructive self-consumer. The event horizon of the me that craved light, love, and life that brims into the singularity of the me that craves darkness, dissolution, destruction. It screamed, it howled, and it was OUT now and wasn't going anywhere...

"How can I live with THAT?" I shook with a very real, palpable fear. How can I walk with a shadow self that is solely dedicated to my demise?

I wanted to make sense of something that was beyond sense and logic. I wanted to blame someone. And there were plenty of people to blame here. My scene partner, for not seeing how far gone I was. The dungeon monitors, for not stopping what was obviously an out-of-control situation. My friends, for watching a scene that spiraled too far. And myself. For not taking care of me.

And that last one was the toughest one.

Once my rage died down, I was able to forgive everyone... except myself. My

safety is, ultimately, my responsibility. And I failed myself, I thought, by not safewording, for not "tapping out" when I first became viscerally terrified, because weren't we supposed to do that whole SSC thing? Safe, Sane, and Consensual? How sane is it to play when you're disassociated? And how consensual can it be when one of the people in the scene has little grip on reality? And I had some new, hard truths that had been birthed in this crucible:

I couldn't safeword.

I craved destruction.

I had a submissive core so profound I could neither see nor feel its Stygian depths.

The last thing I wanted was to be that person. Untrustworthy, unstable, unable to take care of herself and play responsibly.

Part of the aftermath of that scene was the second-guessing done by so many people who had witnessed it. I found it deeply troubling that I could be so lost, so far gone in my own hell right in the hands of people who loved me, and yet, somehow, have walked beyond solace.

For years, I pulled apart, analyzed, dissected, replayed, and sourced this scene and its rather substantial aftermath. And the aftermath was far-reaching. The fact that I'd not been sufficiently provided with the "information" that my evil, racist tormentor was ostensibly trying to extricate from me was criticized. My inability to safeword out was taken to task. My reputation as an "Edge-Player" was cemented.

And I was afraid of myself.

And I hated myself.

As scathing and searing a word as that is, it is the only one that encompasses that self-destruction run riot. I hated that I was **weak**, that I had **lost**, that I had believed a mind's lie, that I had stopped fighting. I retreated, howling, from the "Me" that wanted to roll over and die. Like a litter of rats attacking a runt, I tore about the part of me I assessed as pitiable and not worthy of existing. I had no room for weakness, I had to be strong strong strong because to be weak was to be despised and cast out.

I spent years pulling apart, analyzing, dissecting, replaying, and sourcing the root of my self-hatred. And the corrosiveness moved with a quickness into the very foundations of my Self. It poured into spaces I never knew existed. It masqueraded as masochism. It pulled on the sheep's clothing of submission. It pulled strings that painfully stretched me into precarious positions that left my heart in danger, and my soul exposed. This was a double-edged sword, because there was a heart-wisdom to this process. I wasn't afraid to tell this story. I moved past shame to a frank curiosity about how I had managed to get myself into, out of, and through that process, that trial by fire. But alone, to myself, I whispered the siren singsong of hatred. I put a brave face on this "Lesson" that I refused to admit was a failing. And I believed that. But the angry, vengeful part of me avulsed that moist-eyed weakness again and again, tearing at a wound that wasn't ever allowed to heal, reminding me constantly of how terrible was my weakness.

Like any true story, this one took on its own life, grew legs, opened its eyes, and told itself. I was able to see it as something with its own life, and something that was more a rite of passage in which I participated rather than a defining moment of systemic collapse.

But still? I tuned my eyes from the weakness. From the pain, from the Failure. I let my bullying Self harm something as precious, as beautiful, as my weakness.

Precious? Weakness?

Yes. I say it is precious, and I call it by its name.

My weakness is precious.

It is precious because it walks side by side with vulnerability; it is precious because it served as the baseline for my strength. It is counter measure, and that by which strength may be measured. After years of wrapping this "weakness" up in the swaddling clothes of failure, I have to reveal it for all it is.

It is Human.

The desire to jump when you peer over the edge of a cliff or off the side of a bridge is human. We are curious creatures, and information about the point beyond death, beyond madness, is very scarce. No wonder we crave it. No wonder I push myself, again and again, to that edge, to that brink.

It is who I am.

Hatred and fear row oars in the same boat. And how terrible it is to ride those rapids driven by these fearsome co-pilots.

And I spent years... years... hating myself for being human. Abusing, haranguing, shrieking, and debasing something that simply made me "Me."

Though I had forgiven my scene partner, years ago, for his missteps, despite my capacity to forgive the bystanders, and every other passive participant in that difficult scene, I had missed one key player.

I had never forgiven myself. I had neglected to accept the part of me that was weak. Instead, I judged. I had not embraced my own human frailties. Instead, I endeavored to hide them. Rather than being at peace with the depth of my submission, part of me pathologized it, even as I spoke words to thousands of people encouraging *THEM* to find peace with *THEIR* submission.

I had betrayed myself, and I was filed with regret.

In my flailing to try and reconcile this devious dichotomy, I revealed my revelation to a dominant I trust with this sort of thing. I was startled to feel the overwhelming sense of loss and guilt I'd felt at the full frontal body slam of realizing how poorly I had treated myself, and how I'd shortchanged my own humanity.

"Hindsight is 20/20," he replied. "Forgive and be gentle with yourself."

Forgiveness.

Yeah, OK.

Sometimes the truth is too fucking simple because it is so obvious.

I offer my forgiveness to myself. As I feel and replay these memories, this frustration, pain, these many years of fearing my own power, my own weakness, and how intertwined they are, I offer the soft hand and open heart of forgiveness. I release the debt of self-hatred; I lay my hands on the battle wounds born of these internal struggles. I see that my strength is only as deep as my weakness and that they are facets to the jewel that is my soul.

I embrace the rejoined Me, my Self, my beauty, my pain, and my pleasure. I see the wealth in the gloriousness of suffering and overcoming pain. And I see, too, I must embrace that sometimes, part of being Me is being overcome by the suffering and the pain. This is my birthright as a Human.

And I know I am worthy.

Prism Living

By Kyndyl

Kyndyl is, to the outside, a 37-year-old male. Inside Kyndyl there is a group of people: men, women, children. They are different races, backgrounds, and ages. They work together to create the life that others see as one person. Sometimes it works out better than others. All of us serve the Morrigan as Priests, Priestesses, or in other roles determined by Her. This is the accounting of the oaths we took.

Our spiritual path is eclectic; crossing between Celtic reconstruction Wicca, Asatru, and shamanic traditions. We have felt a Calling to work with the Morrigan for several years. We denied it and ran from it. We wanted to serve Brighid or Flidas; Goddesses of healing or who are connected with animals. The only images we had of the Morrigan was the "washer at the ford" or "battle crow." We had had enough of battle after the life we have lived between us, and didn't want to serve a Goddess who only wanted blood and war. What we didn't realize before was that life was conflict, and death had to occur to make room for healing.

This year has been one of lots of internal exploration and getting back in touch with my spiritual path. I have been Called by the Morrigan for several years.

Most of the past several years I have run from this Calling, or perhaps it was only sometimes that I tried to run from it. Trying to ignore a Call like that is like trying to ignore the sun in the Sahara, and about as dangerous.

We decided that it was time to stop running. We stopped running from my feelings of being in the wrong shell. We stopped running from the issues and training of my past, and the dreams we had for our future. We decided that it was time to stop running from this also.

With the help of friends, we've begun to see a pattern to the things we have experienced, and to help make sense of our feelings. We have found raven feathers and were constantly being gifted with art connected with Her. The gifts came in so many forms, from photographs, to paintings, statues and to stories. We are constantly "finding" depictions of Goddesses that at first seem threatening, but then you see that they're holding children or defending others.

We've been being more faithful to our practices and our relationship with and connection to the Morrigan has grown. There has been a sense that things are rolling towards a large change. Tonight, we pretty much decided that it was time to take the brakes off, for lack of a better term. We decided that we were ready to face the Calling and make our first oaths.

We cleaned our room up, laid out our restraints and collars (without the locks, at least for now), showered, used our sandalwood soap, and stepped into our Altar room. Our Altar is laid out according to the Wiccan tradition we were trained in. We laid out a white blanket with black Celtic knot work on the floor to kneel on. The Altar is a small table covered with a sarong, with moons and suns in white. A dragon-shaped incense holder for East/Air. A small statue of a phoenix for South/Fire. A small pottery cauldron in the West/Water. A clear crystal point for North/Earth. A wooden altar paten in the center (inscribed with a pentacle, circled with different types of feathers for our tribal name). A statue of the Morrigan sits in the North. Antlers with feathers I've collected sit on both sides of the statue.

We knelt before the Altar for a long time contemplating what we were about

to do would mean. Would... could we, as a household (who never agreed on much), agree to serve a Goddess? A Goddess as multi-faceted as we are. One that we are just learning about, just as we are still learning about ourselves.

Could we face Her with all our doubts and concerns? *Yes*

Could we answer Her truthfully when she asked for our Service? *Yes*

Could we, who hated being out of control, surrender that control to Her? *Yes*

Were we prepared to face whatever She might ask of us? *Yes*

It would mean that we gave up running. It means that we accepted Her Call and Her Plans for our lives. Would we accept the changes taking this oath, this responsibility, would mean? Would we sacrifice all that we are, for a chance to glimpse what we may be? To embody the changes She wanted whatever those changes and challenges would be?

Acutely aware of everything the actions meant, we put on the restraints.
Left leg,
Right leg,
Left wrist,
Right wrist
... and finally, Collar.

We walked into our room and knelt before the Altar. Darius was in front, in control of the body. He lit the candles and cast a circle. Calling the elements and Guardians of the Directions. He knelt on the blanket, before the Altar. He closed his eyes and meditated on the Morrigan and all that we knew of Her. He reached for that spark outside of us that we connected with Her. He asked for Her attention and She joined us in the circle.

He spoke to Her, explaining that we wanted to serve a Goddess of healing. She lifted his head, looking into his eyes with Her star-filled ones and said, "What healing can there be without destruction to make room for it?"

He explained our fears, that we were unworthy and scared. That we were unworthy of serving a Goddess. Who would want a broken old piece of junk like us, when they could have anyone? She grabbed us by the back of the hair, pulling us up to our knees. Ice flowed through and around us. She said, "I will determine who is and isn't worthy of my Calling. You have endured much, and will endure more. Broken, is not for you to say. I choose all of you to serve me. The ways according to your skills. Why do you continue to deny what your souls tell you is true?" She released the back of our head and we collapsed on the blanket.

The Morrigan smiled. She told us that she wanted us because of the pain we'd suffered, and that we would find healing in Her Service. She wanted us to help those who had experienced what we had survived. She wanted a wounded Warrior to guide others to healing that She could provide. That no, She wasn't a shiny, happy Goddess, but our souls haven't known that kind of love, so we couldn't express it to those who needed it. We could and have experienced healing after transformation and change through darkness.

He sat back on his heels, and began the slow rhythmic breathing that we used to enter Her Realm. As our body slowed down, our souls journeyed to Her realm. Once there, We were kneeling on cold, rocky ground. In the center of a circle of stones. The stones hard on our knees, the wind blowing through us. Even though it was May here, it felt like Winter there. She was standing above us. She was dressed in a dark red robe, with a leather bodice with a wolf's head on it. We could sense, more than see, the raven wings behind Her. The raven resting on Her shoulder peered at us, and peered through us.

He asked Her what She required of us. She replied that she wanted to speak to us as individuals. He bowed and She caressed our head and She called each of us forward.

One by one She talked with each soul.... She spoke to the girls, and offered Her collar to them. She answered their questions, calmed their fears, and got their agreement to serve Her. She talked to the children, offered them small gifts of knowledge, hope, and healing. She spoke to the men, and negotiated their own forms of Service to Her.

She caressed our face and touched our third eye area. She called Darius out front, and said that from now on he'd be known as Morgwen's Hound, and not MorgwensRaven. She ran Her fingers over our restraints and Collar. They changed color from the black they were here to a deep blood red. She said She needed everyone's agreement before She accepted our Service and Oath.

At the end of that time, she slowly ran Her hands from our head down to our heart, touching our chest, both male and female forms. She ran both hands down our thighs and around our privates. Her touch was ice, followed by heat. The restraints and collar melded to our spirit form so we'd never be without them. As we knelt there before Her, She ran Her claws along our lower back. Cutting Her Mark there and telling us it would be cut into our body at the next step of our Oaths.

She told us it was time to return to our world. She began singing, no human language we recognized. As the song continued, we slowly felt a heaviness and found ourselves back in our body. The circle intact, and our back burning where Her Mark was. Our throat crying from the love and acceptance She had shown all of us.

We rested in the circle for a long time. Not wanting to, not being able to part from a place of such Power and Love. We lay there thanking Her and slowly began moving. What began as stretching transformed into a dance of thanksgiving. We slowly took down the circle and slept. As we moved towards slumber, we hoped we would be ready for a life much different than it had been a few hours ago.

Our life has drastically changed since that May night. We have new views on many things we took for granted before. We have new self-confidence. We no longer accept being put down or told we can't do something because we're plural. Six months ago we would have never written this, or even thought about submitting it for publication. Part of everyday, no matter how hectic, is spent in communication with Her. If we don't, we feel like a machine without a battery. We are much more careful about what we say and do. She has made it very clear that as Her Servants, Everything we say or do reflects on Her. We are never without a mark of Her Ownership. During the day it's usually a chain and dog tag. We sleep in Her Collar every night.

Our kink lives have done a complete 180 degree change since that night. We have ended all relationships where we were the dominant partner, or had them taken away from us. We have started a new period of training as a submissive/slave. We are being trained physically, mentally, emotionally, and spiritually starting from square one. All by Her insistence and Direction.

Probably the biggest change is that we are more public about our lives, both in and out of the lifestyle. Working in the hopes that others can see that living as we do isn't a disability; it's just a different way of living.

And in Her name, we are living.

Balls, Hooks and Fists:
Universal Transportation

By Cléo Dubois

Have you ever danced to live drumming with steel hooks piercing your upper chest, balls sewn onto your arms and back, and found yourself traveling to an inner place where transformation and healing occurs? Did you know that people in Southern India and Sri Lanka have been doing this ritual for thousands of years? This ancient means of universal transportation was brought to our culture a little more than thirty years ago by my life partner, Fakir. I was honored to be first to try it with him.

Just out in the San Francisco Leather Scene, I would not miss a single Society of Janus meeting. Janus was the only West Coast organization where kinky folks met to share ideas and techniques. In December 1981 the cover of their newsletter called *Growing Pains* featured a man decked out like a Christmas tree, with shiny balls sewn on his torso. Looking at objects pierced onto his flesh, I wondered how it felt. Why did he do such things?

Like all "newbies," this was a period of great discovery and joyous partying for me. My bisexual boyfriend Mark invited me to come with him to a Saturday night of unabashed pleasure at the San Francisco Catacombs (sometimes called "Temple of the Butt Hole"). Yes, you had to be invited by someone

already welcomed in this very private Club. It was the community playground
of fisters and SM comrades. Fred, the owner, let me into the party with a big
smile, checked my hands for the proper manicure, and handed me a nail file!
Later that night, he flogged me to the disco version of Handel's *Hallelujah
Chorus*. I was in heaven!

Joyous and primal energy filled the room. Leather chaps, grease, groans of
pleasure, and sexy disco did mix well! There was something very raw, hot, and
yet intimate about that kind of man-to-man sex. I liked the energy; it did not
frighten me. From one of the many leather slings a young man called, "Hey
Lady, you have little hands. Want to fist me?" "Oh, you've never done it
before? No problem, I'll tell you how." And he did exactly that.

There I shared big sexual energies with these leathermen who became my "fuck
buddies." A particular kind of love emanated from our romps in the slings. I
returned again and again. I was valued for my small hands and welcomed for
my obvious enjoyment. One night, surrounded by gay men witnessing my
orgasms at the hand of a gifted lover, I found a powerful reclaiming experience,
an ecstatic coming home to myself that my family of origin would surely label
hell! In these focused and kinky sex rituals I, a multiple rape survivor, started
healing.

I am eternally grateful that some of these leathermen became my mentors.
There were guys, however, who did not like a woman's presence. After several
months Fred asked me not to come to the Catacombs on Saturday nights.
Mark and I asked if we could host mixed gender parties on Fridays. He said
yes and agreed to share his guest list with us. I called each man on the list
inviting all to come play, "pretty please." Thus our "Down and Dirty" parties
were born. The burgeoning mixed San Francisco community enthusiastically
embraced them.

What we didn't know was that a plague was lurking just around the corner.
Within a few years, countless of these vibrant sexual explorers died in their
prime. Mark, too, became affected. The editor of *Growing Pains*, Mark was
a friend of Fakir, the esoteric pierced human Christmas tree. Together they
edited that ground-breaking newsletter for Janus, widening the parameters of

consensual, sexual, sensual SM play.

By 1987, the death of so many of our comrades and Mark's impending decline led me to approach Fakir about doing a body ritual. This time I would be the pierced one, the devotee. I asked Fakir to suture balls on my skin like I saw on that old newsletter's cover. It was not to be a Christian ceremony, and yet our roots are our roots! On a hot August weekend we went to a friend's secluded land in northern California where I could hold my grieving ritual.

The three of us prepared my "stations of the cross," meaningful for the good Catholic girl I used to be. We drove two rows of wooden stakes in the ground, creating a path where my dance was to take place. On my right I attached to each stake the name or photo of a dear departed. On the other side I did the same for those we were afraid we were going to lose to AIDS.

Fakir threaded monofilament through each needle he pierced me with and attached a rubber ball, seventeen in all on my chest and upper back! My body prayer was dancing hard, shaking the balls, running, building up as much sensation as I could to release my pain, fear, and feelings of helplessness in the face of AIDS. I screamed goodbye to the departed and sent my love to those on the verge of their last journey. Mark beat the drum and Fakir encouraged my trance state and saw to the safety of it all. I lost all sense of local reality and zoomed into an altered state. Later, as night fell, Mark fisted me back into my body, a powerful and familiar grounding rite.

That was my first ball dance. Mark passed in 1988. A year later we lost Cynthia Slater, the founder of Janus, a brilliant community visionary. Two years later I tied the knot with Fakir.

Body-based rituals are always about your inner landscape and personal myth. No two are the same. You might "trance in" or "trance out." Several years later, with balls hanging on our skin, I recall bouncing on a little wooden bridge over a creek in a remote California retreat with my dear friend Steven. We faced each other jumping on creaking planks and became so very much bigger energetically. It was a different kind of love we were making, laughing and shining as brightly as the sun on our skin.

Many dances followed, as other folks wanted to have their own experience: some wishing to shed light on their fear of dying and release some of their grief, others seeking ecstatic trance. Fakir, piercer and shaman, facilitated many Ball Dances in the Wicca and Faerie circles. He also brought these rites as part of shamanic workshops in California, Texas, and Europe. Seekers and artists everywhere saw the link between Body Art and Body Rites.

In January 1995, we traveled to Penang, Malaysia to attend Thaipusam, the sacred Hindu piercing festival Fakir had wanted to witness since he read of it in *National Geographic* fifty years prior. He decided we would go to Penang rather than Kuala Lampur's huge affair, which attracted too many tourists.

In Penang on a hot humid afternoon I entered a little temple and was "taken" by Kali, overwhelmed by her fiery energy and yet knowing it as my own. Philosophically I have always been interested in what Archetypes run through us. To feel it directly and so suddenly was really awesome. The Kali priest approach me, blessed me with a red kumkum mark on my forehead. I was entranced. He told us the community ritual piercing would take place in the parking lot of the Hindu soccer field.

That morning I didn't wake up early enough to witness the women getting pierced. They had already made their way to the road leading to Murugan's Temple. It was now the men's turn. Encircled by their entire families, little hooks and cheeks spears were inserted directly into their skin. Only holy ashes were used for skin preparation and no sharp needles were used for the piercings! The energy was incredible. We joined the procession, witnessing the many tandem devotees pulling on their hooks, mouths silenced by the Shiva spears. There were stations of altars all along the road leading to the Waterfall temple (not unlike my first ball dance). Each station was decorated with gaudy images, garlands of mylar, and plastic flowers. The pungent aroma of sweet incense filled the air. Loud music and drumming added to the joyous atmosphere. Torture Festival or celebration? Sound familiar? We felt at home!

Fakir, who had already hung suspended by hooks in his chest during "The Great Wyoming Sundance of 1982" (documented in the film *Dances Sacred and Profane*), felt compelled to share this magic with others once we had returned to the United States. At first, three of our friends were willing to go for it.

The Hook Pull combined with a Ball Dance quickly became part of our annual Summer Gatherings. In August 2009, tethered to an olive tree, sweet tears rolling down my cheeks, gently rocked by my lover, I energetically journeyed to the Middle East, somewhere in a place that was not a place in a time that was not a time. I had a strong flash of a previous embodiment as a sex slave. This last summer, hooked to a California oak in a beautiful meadow, my scared inner child burst out singing in French, a song full of courage and hope. That magical moment gave her a confidence that furthers her integration with who I am now.

For several years now we have rejoiced in bringing these rituals to leather conferences, teaching others how to facilitate them. Pulling on hooks is topping and bottoming to yourself and stepping out of your own way. How hard you pull against your hooks is up to you, whether you hook your cord to a tree, a stationary piece of dungeon equipment, or your partner's outstretched hand.

How precious it is to be in a safe place where you can roar like a wild cat, sob a river full of tears, travel through time, and open up to Love as shared energy. This is what brings us insights, ecstatic trancing, and healing.

That Penang Temple blessing continues to infuse my work. This last decade I stepped into my Ka-See-Ka shoes. This is a Mandan Indian term for experienced guide, "one who knows the way." It is a true honor to encourage someone to pull harder, go further, and embrace their larger Self. As you put tension on your piercings and pass that resilient edge of resistance, you see your core self, you see YOU, embodied Spirit and how much capacity you really have for pleasure and empowerment. Just the other side of the same coin, you know!

And it doesn't even have to be balls and hooks! It never ceases to delight me that the simple practice of pulling on cords attached to nineteen gauge needles, while gazing into your partner's eyes with full attention, takes so many on a journey of true intimacy, like Sarah and Sam.

They booked three hours of private, guided play in my dungeon. She wanted to feel her feminine power more. He wanted more depth in his surrender. They both wanted more heat in their play. They had done some tantra work. They knew how to breathe and connect. I taught her how to tie him up, flog him without fear of damaging him. All of a sudden it hit me: connect them with needles and have them pull on each other's cords. They rocked back and forth and she leaned back, arching her body. He took a wide stance and held the tension for her, feeling the pull on his own heart chakra. She dropped to her knees, wide open, threw her head back, cunt reaching up to the sky. Her breath grew deeper and faster and wave after wave of full body orgasms sent her flying.

Flesh to Spirit, embrace your self and soar! Grieve, heal, forgive, rejoice, create your heartfelt rituals to let something go and bring something in, taking your time, giving yourself space to just be!

Aesthetics, vulnerability, protection, grace, guidance, leap of faith, suspension of reality, pain, catharsis, and ecstatic joy; that is the Magic of Ritual SM.

In leather pride, with heart,

Cléo Dubois

For more about the Catacombs and early ball dances, the formation of the leather community read *Leatherfolk: Radical Sex, People, Politics, and Practice,* by Mark Thompson at www.markthompsongayspirit.com

For more on body rituals, Spirit + Flesh energy hook pulls in San Francisco and Fakir's work visit www.fakir.org

The Pain Was Not Just Mine

By Lady Jazelle

He took a step back from me and I felt His eyes sear into my body. His chest rose with pride and enlarged slightly while a smile crept across His face. Then His eyes rested on me as I slowly took in air, a tremble running through my body with the exhalation, my arms rising slowly to get into place. He had spent months preparing my body, mind, and soul for this. Now it was time.

He circled around me, watching my body quiver. "Take the pain," He growled and paused for a moment, letting the words hang in the air. "Take My pain," His voice sounding as though He were a predator about to catch His prey. His fingers carefully wrapped around the implement and He stepped into place.

My mind flooded with the journey that led me to this moment as His voice resounded in my ears and made every fiber of my body tingle with aniticipation and pleasure. When He signaled for me to rise into place the room became suddenly smaller and I quietly questioned if I could handle this. "Breathe," I reminded myself as the butterflies in my stomach rose and I felt dizzy, the calmness of His movements around me causing my mind to center and as my hands slowly opened wide.

My mind danced on memories of my life. It started with the memory of when I was lost inside my own life. As my mind's eye glazed over my life of trying to be what everyone said I should be and feeling empty, He reminded me of my place by softly lifting my chin and seeing my soul, whispering to me,"Take the pain, Take My pain."

A memory flashed as He slowly let go and I corrected my stance, and I saw how alone I once was. I had been trying to be what society said I should be and failing because inside I was dying and crying out for help. I knew I was supposed to be successful, and yet here I was in life, unemployed, unhappy, and feeling lost while life did not make sense. I had grown up knowing I had a place, knowing I was loved, and knowing that I was designed for a purpose. My parents not only taught this to me but showed it time and time again. They brought me to church and set me around people that believed in me. Yes, they all set expectations, they taught me what they believed and lived out, and somehow I could not live up to it. I lost myself through the expectations of what I was supposed to be, as compared to what really happens in life.

Society told me I was to become a "good Christian that lives the life," a good daughter, a good student, a good mother, a lady and on and on. There was never a question of what I wanted or needed as this was the way life was to be. There were promises in scripture that we lived out and in what the authorities around me said would happen, and it was expected of me to do these things. I tried to live up to it all. Yet I never understood why life in all its ways never seemed to work out for me and I was never good enough. As I grew promises were broken and I began to question, and as I continued in life all of my realtionships failed. I was the outcast in society, and I began to question if what I had grown up to believe was even true. I was supposed to be this dynamic leader, woman, and churchgoer, and the reality was I felt that I could not live up to it all and I could not be perfect. I did not feel I could live up to what it meant to be a good Christian, a perfect Christian.

My sense of self began to diminish until I was as lost as I had been as a child. As a child it was easier to believe somehow that the idealism was possible: that I could be the best. I went to church every Sunday morning and night and Wednesday with my family, and my family lived out what was taught there.

My parents not only went to church but lived out the beliefs in front of me and tried to show me the way. I was loved and knew that God loved me. too. There was never a doubt about that love or where I would be in that love. I did believe. It was ingrained in me. Yet, through the years I became broken. Broken by the fact I was not perfect, broken by promises of others that were unjustified, and broken by what seemed to be the inability to achieve what the church deemed the goal to be. The anger within me rose and came out through self-sabatoge. I was at a place where nothing made sense and I knew I was broken. Only now, there was nothing to believe in and I became empty.

As He started His prowling around me for the first time, my mind went immediately to the start of this journey. It seemed as though it was just yesterday that I was about to take my first step into His world. He began to ask questions, and through our discussions I began to understand that I felt everything I believed was not possible for me. He started slowly walking down my path, and when it seemed to go off course, He was able to show me an explaination and a way to get back on the right track. He talked to my soul by showing what I had learned, what I had believed was real. In the midst of my confusion and unbelief He showed me the way to go and gave me hope that I was not lost. He had a path and if I was to walk it I would have to use those things I had learned growing up: That discipline and faith *were* real and that through those I could attain perfection. I would have to believe. I would have to give of myself in ways I did not yet understand. When I questioned this He would simply rise and He would guide me to the floor in a kneeling position. He would explain that on my knees would be where I would find strength just as I had learned with God.

When He paused for a moment, His eyes enveloped mine as if to say, "Follow the way." He started the second prowl around me, each step deliberate, each step resounding with meaning. The vibration of His steps built up and I suddenly felt small. He reminded me without words that while I may be small, He was there for me. Just as God was there for me and had a direction for me, so did He. He was able to guide me into a life if I just followed His direction. As I followed His rules and followed His direction I became more

complete within myself. Every step, each moment bringing me closer to Him, and to my God.

He completed the second circle, He stepped closer to me, and He carefully started the third. My breath quickened as I knew within me that He would demand my surrender to what He wanted. By His actions He showed my heart that when I surrendered, I was cleansed. My surrender was what made me at peace within myself. He wanted me to know that only when I would surrender as I did to God that I would be fulfilled. He wanted my strength, He wanted my obedience, and He wanted my surrender. I closed my eyes as I was gathering what He wanted, and I needed to give that to Him.

The sound of His voice jerked me back into the moment as I opened my eyes and He and His words centered me. "Take My pain!" Then almost sharper, "Take the pain." Those words spoken brought a realm of emotions throughout my body. He had taught me to accept pain – to allow the pain to go through me as a cleansing act. He taught me that through the pain I had strength. I followed His ways and I surrendered. He started slowly and built me up, giving me stamina and endurance for it. He brought my past relationships into sharp focus – past relationships with rules and things in the way of me being open. I realized that with Him I was not in my past relationships; I was with Him, and I felt the capacity to be open, honest, and available blossom within me. My journey was not complete, but it was starting with me fully present, and I began to think about today.

It seemed that this weekend was going to be different although I was not aware of why. He had told me we were going to the party, and that while there I would learn more about my relationship with Him and God. He had me meditating on strength, following the way, and surrender, and how through that I was complete. He had me consider how I needed and desired to be closer to God. So all week, I had been preparing, both physically by packing and mentally through thought and prayer. There was anticipation of the party, if nothing else because I never wanted to disappoint in my behavior, and I was deeply curious to know how He would have me learn about these connections.

That day I awoke a bit before the alarm. It had been hard to sleep, but I smiled as I turned off the alarm without waking Him. The morning ritual was the same as it had been for months: I went in and started the coffee, turned on His computer, padded down the hall with a nod after inspecting things in the bathroom. The time to wake him came all too soon, and I went to the side of the bed, the warmth of the carpet greeting my knees as I begged for Him to arise for the day. As the morning disappeared I found myself fidgeting a bit more and tried to slow down to not mess up on the chores that he had assigned me – at least not on this day. During this time He drank His coffee, read the morning news on the computer and His email; I found it almost impossible to be still on the floor next to Him. Then the world rushed by, the vehicle got packed, and we were on our way.

I finally noticed that the day was a perfect spring day, and as we got closer to the party it seemed like I had to concentrate ever more. I looked over to Him, trying to calm myself down and relax, and I realized how strong He was. It was almost a panic that set in the closer we came to the venue, and I wanted to beg Him to turn around, and tell Him that we did not need to go the party. He seemed to almost smirk as I looked to Him for strength, knowing as He always did how nervous I was. He soon began to talk to me, reminding me that I was exactly where I needed to be.

The quieter I got the more He knew I was panicking about what would happen. He drew me out of my shell of panic by asking little questions that always were so perfectly timed. Questions like, "What are you thinking?" and "What is your purpose?" that brought me back to the present each time I struggled with why I felt this way. Why did I feel this way, I asked myself. Why? Because He wants this.

In what seemed like a flash (although it had been a two hour drive), He was pulling up to the party. As we stepped up to the door, I held my breath and lowered my eyes out of respect. The door opened, as handshakes and hugs were given to Him and He introduced me to the Host. I am not sure, but it seemed like the Host was 6 feet tall and almost scowled at me. Just as He instructed I begged for enterance to the party and bit my lower lip when the Host waited a moment to grant it. It was then that the Host smiled and told me that sometimes we have to accept that people will not accept us in the moment but will warm up to us.

As I stepped inside, I quietly removed my shoes and went to His side. I must have seemed like a child, almost clinging to Him and being very scared that in some way I would mess up and would disappoint Him. There was lots of laughter and small talk, music playing loudly, the bustle of people getting food and drinks from the kitchen. Although I didn't know anyone there it did not take long to feel at home. When I finally peered from behind Him, I noticed that many other people were sitting at the feet of others, and I was not the only one. He picked a chair and had me sit to His right on the floor. After a few moments He leaned down and told me to "begin." I rose quietly from the floor and went to the next room where we had laid our bags, retrieved the necessary items for what he was asking of me, and went to the kitchen.

While in the kitchen I was asked who I was since I was not known and I quietly spoke back and got to know the people there while I continued getting what I needed. When I returned to Him, He smiled softly and sat back as I started to roll up His pants from the hem. Carefully I untied His shoes as a slient smile came across my face and I removed them slowly. I then removed His socks and put the washcloth in the warm water. As I washed His feet there was such an intimacy and calmnes between us that I wanted the moment to last, I leaned down and kissed His feet. As I put on His new socks and the shoes I removed from the bag, I felt His hand upon the back of my neck going up towards my hairline. He tugged my hair and it seemed to both settle and cause my mind to go into a flurry of thoughts. He leaned down and seemed to give me strength through His look, and I felt such a serinity in that moment that there was nothing better than being here with Him. He slowly let go and it was then I realized that many were watching closely as I cleaned and put things away as He directed.

As the night proceeded, I had many conversations. I was able to relax a bit and I felt like I had really calmed down. He then looked at me and said, "It's time." I froze for a moment. I wanted to tell Him I was not ready and that surely we could do this another time. As I swallowed my tears back, realizing that this was to be done in front of everyone at the party, I quietly said, "Yes

Sir." I waited for His instruction as I felt that even the walls were closing in on me. I was sure that everyone could hear my heart beat as He pulled out the music and set it in the player. With a simple hand gesture He commanded me to rise and then remove my clothing. I felt every emotion in the space as He pointed to the place He wanted me in the center of the room. My mind was going a million miles a minute and then His words came to me: "Take the pain. Take My pain."

The sound of His voice was still vibrating in my ears as He stepped back from me. I drew a breath in, raised my arms up to my sides and opened my hands, palms facing towards the wall. A chill of expectation ran throughout my body as I moved into place. The first impact struck my body, sending a wave of pain through me, the nine braids shifting my body ever so slightly. Gasping for air, I filled my lungs and corrected my position, a small breath escaping from my body. My thoughts rushed around me to so many things, and then when my body registered the pain they all stopped. I had to focus and accept the pain He was giving me, and I concentrated on the strength He was gifting me. The pain settled into my body, and I wanted to drop to my knees and beg for it to stop. I knew I must not allow the pain to control my thoughts and accept what I need.

As I steadied for the second lash it came quickly and I exhaled. The pain overwhelmed every thought. I imagined the pain flowing through my body, washing me new.

As the next strike jolted I told myself, "three – breathe," and again adjusted my body slightly from the impact.
"Four – breathe out. Accept."

As the strikes came, my alabaster skin became a rose color, then a deeper hue. Soon the only feeling was the pain. It seemed to pour into me from everywhere, and the emotion from the room rushed in to me from everyone. As I began to feel the emotions my face became stained with tears. It was then that I heard the words He spoke, "Take the pain." I knew I had to take this pain to become the vessel for cleansing it, and I slowly began to steady my mind with each strike He gave me. They came over and over until the pain would pass through me. The only sound I could hear was each thud, and with that the emotion, at first overwhelming then slowly leaving me until nothing was left to hurt. It was at that moment I felt alone and my mind settled in on the knowledge I had heard so many times from my childhood of Jesus calling out in pain. I felt the fear, I wanted to call out, I wanted to not take any more, and then there was a sudden strength. I was to bear the pain of others to become more like Christ. I then heard the words resound in my mind again: "Take My pain." This wasn't just any pain, I was taking His pain and my heart settled to be the pain bearer He needed. I wondered if this is what Christ felt as He took the pain, and in that moment a humblance struck me, a realization that this was more than the pain, but was a mirror of the relationship I had with God.

It seemed to never end. The strikes seemed to be ripping out my flesh, and soon I began to cry out with each pound, my mind screaming although my voice seemed to have left me. "I don't need this. Why are You doing this? Can't You see I hurt? That's enough!" The emotions pouring into my mind, my body shaking, through the tears I looked up as if to say I'm done, and then I heard a small voice just quietly say, "Take the pain. Take My pain." In that moment, in that blow against my skin that was hot from the multiple lashes, I found a new strength and it grew. Although my body yeared for it to stop and deep within I groaned from pain, I remembered that He was there for me and that I was following His direction and I was strong and it was as through pain I knew this. The lashes kept coming, and I felt that they were going to rip me apart.

"Take the pain. Take My pain." It became a mantra within my mind. Suddenly it was only Him and myself in a safe place; the pain was cleansing me. As it washed through every pore of my body, I felt a sense of renewal and strength. Finally my body began to quiver with pain, I was sure that He was never going to stop and I cried out to Him through the pain.

It was then the clock behind us began to chime, "dong, dong," and I counted each one as the hour struck midnight. I then heard His voice as a sweet whisper: "Two more to thirty-nine." As the last two stikes came I felt all my strength leaving my body, and the pain began to overwhelm all of my senses.

Taking a breath in and weeping with the pain, I felt Him walk up to me. He took a moment looking at me with such devotion and took a breath in, and with a quiet wisper in a melodic tone, "It's Easter, my little one." He took a step back.

It was then I realized that He had put me on a small "hill." It was then I realized that the pain was not just mine. I was taking the pain. I was cleansed. As small trickle of blood rolled down my back, the welts began to turn colors. Here I was standing with my arms out and feet together. I was the cross.

Care and Feeding of Predators: How to Play with a Therian and Not Be Eaten Alive

By C.A. Sizemore

Meet the Beasts

So you want to play with a Predator? I am not talking about jumping the fence at your local zoo and petting the kitties on the other side, or about a person who role-plays the part of a pony, puppy, or other animal. I will touch on role-play shortly, and the former is a really painful way to die. I find that wild animals almost never respect safewords and running away screaming "RED" will at best amuse them.

I am talking about Therianthropes, or Therians for short. Folks like me. Therianthropy is from the Greek words *theri*, meaning animal, and *anthrop*, meaning human; literally animal-humans. Those who chose to use this term believe that while we may have human bodies, at least some portion if not all of our soul is that of a non-human. OtherKin is a term that is sometimes used; I don't use it because too often it is used to discriminate against some members of our small subculture.

The term was adopted by the community in the 90s; sources vary as to its first citation. The term was used back in 1915 to describe a spiritual belief in animal transformation, and at least one source raises the possibility the term may have been used in the 16th Century in criminal trials of suspected werewolves. But that information, and the discussion of where Therians come from, will not help you learn how to play with folks like me. Instead I am going to talk about what to do if you or your partner suspects or knows outright that they are a Therian. Whether you want to play with that aspect of your partner for just a single scene or incorporate it into your relationship dynamic, this knowledge will hopefully make that experience a more enjoyable one. I have learned these lessons by trial and error, by asking around and by figuring out what happened when things went right and when they went wrong. Hopefully you can learn from my mistakes; that way you can make your own.

Being a Therian differs from animal role-play, although I know of Therians who role-play as their animals. For a non-Therian, animal role-play is a form of invoking or calling down the role onto oneself; be that the Mother Goddess, Fenrir the great wolf, or Fluffy the fuzzy kitty, these are from outside of one's self; roles they play for an evening, for a scene. When a Therian engages in animal role-play as an animal, they feel drawn to would-be evoking or calling up from within themselves.

Among those who claim the term Therian as their identity, there are many differences, not just in the species of animal we feel the most drawn to, but also in Origin, Manifestation, and Reason we believe this admittedly strange idea. For myself, I believe that my soul is that of something similar to a Gryphon. Meanwhile, my wife feels that she is sharing her body with the soul of an extinct North American Lion. Others I have talked with feel that they are a collection of facets from multiple beings residing in one human body.

My wife and I are not unusual in the Therian community, being drawn to animals we have little or no way of seeing on TV let alone in a zoo or the wild. Dragons, gryphons, even elves and trolls are part of our community along with the lions and tigers and bears, oh my!

The most common question I have heard boils down to how a person can tell if they or their loved one is a Therian. Therianthropy in not an infection or a curse, it cannot be passed along like some form of demented white elephant.

Being a Therian is a lot like being a Dominant, submissive or switch; the only person that can truly decide if you are or are not is you. Being a Therian is something you are, and just as being heterosexual, homosexual, bisexual, or asexual, it is not a choice. I have heard more than one Therian express a kinship with people affected by gender dysphoria; instead of being bodied in that of a different sex than their soul, many Therians feel they are a different species then Human, and this two-legged form does not match their internal identity.

Communicating with Predators

Open, honest communication outside of the bedroom, dungeon, and play space is vitally important. I have found that you need to be able to fully express your wants, needs and desires; if we do not, then it is unfair to ourselves and our partners to expect those desires to be met. This goes double for emotional and psychological landmines; expecting your partner to know that the scent of catnip makes the cat inside your head want to smash things without telling him or her is a recipe for a bad scene.

Verbal communication is such a human trait that many Therians lose it as their non-human aspect manifests. Instead of using words we may mew, bark, whinny, or chirp. This can be difficult if your partner is trying to safeword but all that is coming out is a mew or growl.

My friend Lee told me a story about once being deep in horse-space, and his partner was riding him. At one point horse-Lee tried to buck his partner off. His partner held on tighter thinking that horse-Lee was being playful. Unfortunately, his partner did not understand horse-speech, and could not tell that Lee was bucking because he was in pain. His partner had forgotten that they were wearing spurs, and by the time they caught on Lee was covered in cuts.

Playing with someone who is so deeply inhuman at their core can lead to some interesting conversations. Some of the conversations I have had with dragons, for example, or my wife with me as a gryphon, have led each of us to ponder our own nature and what we ourselves are drawn to in our lives. A lion thinks differently at its core than a human, and thus setting up communication systems with them requires knowing what that sort of beast needs at their core.

We have started building up a safe word process not for her but me, so that I can call a pause in a scene where she has dropped into cat-space. I am investigating some Neural Linguistic techniques to train both my wife and her feline aspect to switch places as needed, but this is a long term process.

Part of communication is also a question of ethics; if we are playing with someone who is an animal at their core, how do we know when they are consenting to an act? Can a horse consent to being gentled? Can a dog consent to being brought to heel? These questions are out of place inside of a standard BDSM relationship, however, inside of a relationship with a Therian partner these questions are relevant and important. How do you obtain the consent of a partner's animalistic side?

For myself, I feel that you need to know how your partner sees themselves. For those like myself who do not feel a separation between their human and non-human portions of their soul, I feel that I am able to give and withdraw my consent easily. However, in cases like my wife where she feels that her body is inhabited by two separate and distinct individuals, obtaining consent from both takes a bit longer. From my experience, almost all of the Therians are in communication with their other-selves; my wife describes this not as verbal communication but as impressions and images. I would think that it would be the same for individuals who feel they are made up out of a collection of facets; although I have not had the opportunity to discuss this matter in depth with someone who feels this way. With both of these of Therian types I feel that if they are in communication with their otherside or sides, then they can consent to actions. On the other hand, if your partner or you do not feel that you can communicate with your facets then you cannot consent to any acts.

Preparation and Safety

For my wife, being in cat-space is a process of evoking her feline aspect. We start this by giving her a place where it is safe for the cat to come out and play, normally the bedroom or the house empty of other people – although the cat does not express herself only in those safe venues. There is nothing quite like being at a sushi buffet and realizing that the reason your partner has gone quite is because she is not in the driver's seat of her own body! Endless fish makes for a very happy cat, and a very challenged wallet.

One of the things I have found that a person needs to look at when selecting a location to evoke a partner's Animalistic nature is the environment. Not long ago we decided to try playing in public at an intimate party in the local dungeon. The spot we chose was an area we had not used before enclosed on three sides with metal pillars supporting the loft above us. It seemed like a lovely enclosed area, but those pillars were a problem – they made the cat feel trapped. This lead to a very emotional, rough scene for her feline aspect; it took weeks of coaxing to get the cat to feel safe coming out fully again. Among the lessons we learned that night was that her feline aspect is afraid of being trapped in a cage. This helped us rule out cages and jail cell-type environments for us to play in.

We have discussed playing again in public, but have not done so, yet. In planning for this next public-play session, we have discussed when and where, including bringing the DMs and Guardians up to speed before we start playing. We are still talking and have not yet chosen a location.

Another lesson we learned was that her feline aspect while, exceedingly playful, is still a cat and does not know what to make of canines, especially bio-canines. I was downstairs while my wife and metamour were in their bed cuddling. Our pit bull, never one to be left out of a cuddle pile, joined them. Eventually, the cat had enough cuddling and wanted to play. The cat and dog wrestled for a bit then the cat bit the dog's ear. The dog snapped at her (no blood, no foul). My metamour broke them up and we got everyone calmed down. The lesson learned was that cats and dogs get along like, well, cats and dogs. Needless to say, the cat and dog don't wrestle anymore; instead, when she feels that need we provide her a human subject for her to play with.

The three most important things you and your partners can bring to this exploration are Attention, Will, and Humor. Attention is crucial; if you are not listening to what you partner's animalistic soul is telling you, you both can be harmed. Will is nearly as important, making the mental shift that your partner is a Kangaroo or a Dragon under their skin. A sense of Humor is the most important thing. Without a sense of humor you will be lost when the most amazing things happen; when a stranger's four-year-old calls your perfectly normal-acting partner a kitty or your teenage son comes out to you as a werewolf.

The main role for a Therian's partner is to ensure their safety and that of others around you. If your partner is in danger of hurting herself or others, then you need to get in the way and stop them. A Top or Dom who is not willing to take the wrath of their partner's more animalistic aspect should not be in that position.

Playing with Your Predator

So you have your partner's animalistic aspect comfortable enough with you to come out and play. You have a 230-pound terrier chewing on his squeaky toy in the middle of your living room floor... now what? How do you play with him? You could train your partner in Obedience and Agility skills; teach him to be displayed like the bio-dogs in dog shows. Watching these events on TV, observing or attending a canine training class will give you plenty of ideas. You can also just play a game of fetch. The same idea goes for most animal-souled Therians: all animals play, some rougher than others. Although horse and dog-souled partners will be more likely to enjoy these types of interactions than cat, bear, or other animal-souled partners. Keep their beast nature in mind when devising activities, or consider asking them when they have verbal communication capacities what their inner beast is longing to do.

As far as supplies go, playing with a Therian can be fairly cheap or outrageously expensive. A collar from the pet store and a squeaky toy can help your partner drop into puppyspace, add in a pair of gloves with padded knuckles and knee pads from a hardware store and you can play all day. A curry brush and a rope from the tack store can help your partner's inner-pony come out and frolic long before you need to invest the money and time in building out their human-pony kit.

The only thing I personally would be hesitant to do is the standard BDSM play; floggers, bondage, and pain/pleasure interactions are not appropriate for most animal-souled partners. I would be more willing to try these with a dragon, elf, ent or other sapien-souled partners, because of their capacity for clearer communication mid-scene. But you never know. I've met more than one bio-cat who loved a good spanking, a dog or two who relaxed during their time in a crate.

Headspace and Phantom Limbs

Headspace can be a tricky subject when dealing with Therians. Unlike subspace where your partner checks out and no one is running the controls, a horse-souled Therian will be in horse headspace. They will react to the world as a horse would. Needless to say, this can lead to physical danger and possible injury, not only to your partner but to innocent bystanders.

Of the Therians I have talked to, some feel that they go into a headspace when their non-human aspect is drawn out, losing control of themselves to the other. My wife describes that she feels that she takes a back seat to the "Cat." I do not seem to shift; I am always in gryphon headspace. Many Therians only manifest as a feeling of being ursine, feline, or whatever animal they feel drawn to. My wife tells me that the cat misses her teeth and claws; she also feels her ears are in the wrong place.

Others Therians like myself feel what is described as phantom limbs; my wings are the most prominent portion of this. I am always aware of them behind my shoulders. The relative size and presence of my wings tends shift throughout the day, but I never truly loose them. However, my tail, talons, beak, and crest tend to come and go.

Phantom limbs are a strange idea; having limbs that you can feel and sometimes see and that most people cannot. Sometimes I feel my tail, something similar to that of a canine's tipped with feathers. The most common and disturbing sensation is people passing through my wings. When I can feel my tail, I try to keep it up and away from others' feet. I feel my wings bump into the real world objects: car seats, doorways, even clothes.

I have heard Therians speak of having wings or other phantom limbs bound, and this is an intriguing concept to me. I have rarely been bound and to date no partner has tried to bind my wings. I do have a feeling of dissociation or a cognitive dissonance when I am tied on my back or when my back is being flogged; if I don't keep them out of the way I can feel the falls pass through my wings before impacting my back. I can see how these sensations can be put to good uses, being able to pull on a tail or astral predicament bondage.

Aftercare

Aftercare can be a tricky matter when dealing with people coming out of a non-human headspace. It is a good idea to have the standard items available: water, a blanket, some kind of good carbs, and protein. My wife tends to crash hard after playing in feline headspace, preferring to curl up and go to sleep. I tend to think about the aftercare needs about cats in general when I play with her – for example, when an average cat has had a busy day chasing things and running about, it would make sense that she wants to curl up and go to sleep. Why would my wife in her "cat-space" be any different?

For some of us, our aftercare needs can go beyond the normal needs because of how a shift went and what happened during the session. If you are off in horse headspace, you may not feel a calf cramp developing, or recognize an impending sugar crash. If we are not in a normal headspace, it is important that a Top or other partner watches out for these sorts of concerns. Sometimes you or your partner may not come all the way back from an animalistic headspace, or not want to come back at all. If you or your partner is prone to this, setting up reasons to come back, tools to ground you back into your human skin, or developing other systems can be incredibly important.

Sometimes after a long scene or an extended time in other headspace, you can paradoxically struggle with self-doubt and questions about the reality of your experience. I consider this to be part of aftercare; when you need a reality check. It can be useful to have a partner who went on the journey with you, someone who is a touchstone, and can confirm with you what happened.

As I have come to grips with the strange idea that my soul is not that of a human, the realization has forced me to think about not only my needs and desires but those of my partners. What do I want from the world, my partners, myself, and what am I able to give myself, my partners, and the world? When I began this journey, I was collared to my late Lady, a kinky but closeted heterosexual and monogamous woman, who passed a few years ago. In the years since I first heard the word Therian, I have taken more than a few steps in my personal journey. I have come to know that I am a poly bisexual kinky-Therian. One that is blessed to have a wife, metamour, and girlfriend who know me for who and what I am. A predator, a lover, and a friend.

How I Found My Way Back to Kink Magic

By Taylor Ellwood

The day I got my copy of *Kink Magic* in the mail was an ironic day. On that day my ex-wife and co-author Lupa and I came to the realization that we were having some trouble connecting with each other as kinky partners, and in our marriage in general. We eventually got divorced, but what I am going to tell you about is how I found my way back to kink, and back to kink magic. Still, that realization was an important one, because we not only realized that we didn't have much in common when it came to fulfilling our respective kinks, but I realized that I didn't even know what I truly liked. Actually, I did know to some degree, but I was afraid of admitting it to myself or really going after it. We'll chalk it up under ignorance... but believe me, ignorance wasn't bliss.

A Year of Love

Shortly before the time I realized that there was a distinct lack of kinky compatibility with my partner, I also started a year-long ritual to the element of Love. Each year I pick an element to dedicate myself to. The element I choose (or sometimes it chooses me) is usually one I need to do a lot of work with. The purpose of the elemental working is to bring that aspect of my life into balance. Love was certainly no exception, as I had a very unbalanced relationship with it. I didn't know how to love myself or anyone else. I had no appreciation of the person I was with, so much as I was concerned with trying to fill some unfathomable void within me. I felt that if I worked with Love I could come to a better understanding of it and its place in my life.

When I work with an elemental energy, I usually do so through an intermediary, an entity or deity that represents that element. I invoke the elemental energy into me for a year, and during that year I work with the entity or deity that is an embodiment of the element, but also a guide to it. The deity that chose to work with me for the year of Love was Babalon, the sacred whore. And she chose to manifest to me as a dominatrix, energetically collaring me and teaching me a lot about love, myself, and the relationships I tended to get into.

In fact, what Babalon really taught me about was my illusions about love. Over the course of a year she ruthlessly stripped away everything I thought I knew about love or myself. She objectified me, even as she showed me how I had objectified others. Every experience I had, every humiliation, every crack of the spiritual whip and snap of the spiritual flogger showed me that I was a weak person, enslaved to what I feared the most and wasn't willing to face. She grabbed my hair and forced my face to look into myself and see the emptiness that I was always trying to run away from, always trying to fill up... even as it was devouring me inch by inch every day.

Babalon taught me a lot about my kink. She embodied, as a dominatrix, everything I really wanted in a kinky partner. I wanted someone who could master me, who could be my match as a partner, and yet be able to also show her ability to dominate me, whenever she needed to. But Babalon also taught me that until I could master myself, no one else would ever be able to master me. She showed me that just as I had always looked to other people to fill up my emptiness, I'd also looked to them to also be able to somehow tame my impulses and desires. However, the only person who could help me come to peace with my emptiness and also master my desires and impulses was and is: me. Once I made peace with my desires and my emptiness, then I would master myself, and with that self-control in hand I could offer myself to another in submission that was genuine.

In our final working, as the element of Love concluded, Babalon took me into herself and showed me that the next element, the next year, would involve working with the very element of Emptiness I had run so far from. If I thought the element of Love was hard, the element of Emptiness made it seem like a cake walk.

A Year of Emptiness

My last act of dedication to Babalon was an act of sex magic. As we fucked, she took my essence – physical, energetic, and spiritual – into her, into her womb. An interesting aspect about Babalon is that she'll take on all comers and give them pleasure, but they all have to pay her price. Usually that price is experiencing the abyss, and my emptiness working was that abyss.

As she took me into her, I met my next spirit guide for the year of Emptiness. For lack of better word this entity was my Holy Guardian Angel (HGA). Truth to tell, he'd been with me in one form or another since my first near-death experience at the age of 7, so I wasn't surprised he was also with me during my year of Emptiness work. He didn't act like Babalon. He didn't dominate me, but rather he encouraged me, reminding me go at my own pace and not to push too fast. Wise advice when working with Emptiness. And it was to the Emptiness that I submitted myself, letting it fully into my life, where I could come to terms with it.

My year of Emptiness working was really my year of coming to grips with my desires and how much they controlled me, in part because of how much I repressed them. Babalon had told me I needed to master myself and that self-mastery really involved coming to grips with all of my desires and all my wounds. I'd spent my life using my desires to escape from my emptiness, but as a result I didn't really know what I wanted, or why I wanted it. Did I want something or someone because of appreciation and interest, or just to fill myself up? My working with emptiness forced me to realize that I mainly wanted something or someone in order to fill myself up. I didn't know how to be involved with someone just for him/herself, and I didn't even really know if my interest in BDSM just wasn't for extreme experiences that could help me escape the feeling of emptiness that pervaded my life.

When you face that kind of self-doubt about your desires, it makes you realized how constructed everything is within your life. During the year of Emptiness, nothing I did or indulged in satisfied me. When I tried to play at a dungeon or at home, I didn't really felt connected to what I did. Everything was meaningless. Some might call it depression, but the truth is it was the Emptiness itself filling my life, showing me the one great truth I had always run from: there will always be emptiness in my life and nothing can fill that emptiness up. I could either keep fighting and running from that fact, or I could accept it as part of my life and come to peace with it.

Because of that very realization, I was also able to realize that kink wasn't just about filling something up for me. I genuinely wanted to live a kinky life, and in fact I wanted to live a 24/7 dynamic where I was a full time slave to my partner. The night before I finished the Emptiness working, Babalon came to visit me and I told her what I had realized, and she told me to enjoy the present moment and experiences I had, and when the time was right someone would come into my life, someone who could fulfill that for me. When I ended the Emptiness ritual, I felt reborn, my slate wiped clean and ready to start my life from a much more conscious place.

Aftermath

I wasn't surprised a few months later when my ex-wife asked for a divorce. We'd both been unhappy for a while with each other, and she'd found a partner who better fulfilled her own kink needs. We also still loved each other enough to want to be friends, but realized staying in a marriage would eventually cause one or both of us to hate the other. While I was sad, I also was able to let go and we parted ways.

A month after she told me she wanted divorce, I met my current partner. We didn't actually hook up at the event we met at, but we did get to know each long distance for a while, and the more I learned, the more I realized there was a fit. Eventually we started dating and I found out that she'd always wanted someone to dominate, and that best of all her style of domination fit my style of submission and slavery. She was also a magic practitioner, so it wasn't hard for us to take that next step into kink magic.

To most other people we appear as equals. There's no obvious sign that she's in control. You have to know what to look for. When I am with her, I know my place in her life, and in our shared spirituality. She is the master, who directs our combined sexual energy for our mutual goals, while I am the slave, who uses Taoist breathing techniques to circulate the energy and gradually build it up so that she then can direct it. This dynamic is applied with the kink play we do as well, for even when I top her, still I am giving her my energy and she is directing it, sculpting it, creating with it the pathways toward manifestation.

I found my way back to kink and kink magic by going through a journey of realization and submitting myself to Babalon and to the emptiness within me. Through that journey I came to know what I really wanted for myself, in my life, my love, and also my desires. Instead of trying to fill myself up, I now know that kink is something I desire to experience for appreciation of the experience and the intimacy it provides. I also know that same intimacy is integral to my spiritual life, and so I embrace it as sacred kink, a means of opening the door to the heart of the universe, where potential can start the journey to become reality.

A Long-Awaited Ordeal, That Wasn't

By Nanodot

Imagine a cheerful nerd-girl, aged 35, sequestered at home with a little family for 15 years. I was deeply isolated by my own introversion and my husband's. We had no friends, and I could rarely convince my husband to leave the house to do something fun. We were poly, but our other relationships were online and mostly served to give us both fantasy worlds where we could escape from each other. I am autistic, and I felt that my interactions with other people were automatically doomed to failure, and I didn't want the pain of rejection anymore. I had given up for a long time.

Finally, starving for human contact and feeling like I was boring and socially worthless, I took the courage to live for myself. I started to claw my way out of my isolated shell by immersing myself in the *Rocky Horror Picture Show* crowd. I had been going to *Rocky Horror* occasionally for many years, because I felt accepted and at home there. This time, to escape a stagnant self and a stagnant home, I got much more involved. I started going regularly, meeting people, and doing some costuming for the players. Through *Rocky Horror* I met Interesting People. One of the Interesting People I met was into BDSM in a big way, and he showed me around the local BDSM community.

I was fascinated by BDSM and body modification, entranced by the power, beauty, and self-expression. The words "submissive masochist" gave me a new anchoring place and new definitions to describe who I already was. Rapidly, I embraced change to let go of my feelings of being boring and unworthy of the unique people I wanted to be with. I forced myself to go to events and introduce myself to people. I made awesome outfits that matched my inside self and wore them on the outside. I went to raves and house parties. I confronted my fears of interacting with people and being rejected.

I lived on the weekends, and spent the weekdays as a wife, mother, and career woman. In only a few months, I found that I was being myself out in the fetish world, while I wore a mask of normalcy at home. My main concern was balancing my worlds well enough to keep the kids happy, and I accomplished that. However, my relationship with my husband continued to slip further away because he had no interest in joining me where I was real.

I ended up one Saturday at a flesh hook suspension party. I immersed myself in the powerful energy of people who were fearless.

There was a beautiful girl there, who struck me to the heart. Young, willowy, with long black hair and a peaceful expression, she had calligraphic tattoos that I had to stop staring at. She had never been hooked or suspended before, and she had to go to work in two hours. She took two hooks in her back without a flinch. With that peaceful expression still on her face, she was raised into the air and flew. Her energy was beautiful, and I craved to be so self-assured, fearless, and peaceful.

I knew then that this ordeal was in my future. I imagined hook suspension to be an apex of pain and endurance, based on what I had seen in the media, so the people flying in front of me seemed like superheroes. I knew that when I could do that, I would be who I wanted to be. I also knew that I wasn't ready yet.

For almost two years, I ravenously explored myself as a submissive masochist, woman, and human being. I got divorced. Having the kids half the time gave me more time to explore my world, and made me a better mother as well. I had several M/s relationships that brought me great joy and pain. I bottomed to kind Sadists and learned my physical and emotional limits – which kept stretching for a long time. I learned that my deep capacity for love is the only thing that separates me from the lizards. Most importantly, I made friends.

Two years after starting my journey, I was a new, strong, reasonably fearless woman who did not wear many masks at all. I wore some masks for my parents, and for work, of course. Even around my kids, I was myself in a vanilla way. I was still looking forward to doing a hook suspension because I still felt like an untested newbie. I felt ready to transcend my self-limitations, and I knew that hooks would be my defining moment.

I expected an agonizing physical ordeal that would make me proud of who I had become.

There aren't many opportunities for hook suspensions even in my big city. Several months after I felt ready, an opportunity arrived to get hooked at The Dance of Souls at the Southwest Leather Conference. The Dance of Souls is a hook-pull and ball dance of several hundred people, driven by endorphins, natural opiates, pheromones, and tribal drums. For financial reasons, I got my ticket at the last possible moment, when a reservation was unexpectedly cancelled.

With almost no physical or psychological preparation, I got in line to be hooked.

The line to get hooked was very long, filled with mostly-naked people in various states of tension, exultation, reverence, and terror. I chatted with my Witness and swayed to the steady drum music, deeply amazed to be there at last. I was wearing a sarong and a tank top, I think. People who had already been hooked wandered onto the dance floor, with glazed triumphant eyes. The drums were hypnotizing everyone.

I reached the end of the line in a focused, lightly powerful headspace. I wasn't very nervous, just curious. At the assembly line piercing lanes, I was assigned to a piercer who looked like a biker high from a long ride. Straddling a hotel banquet chair, shirt off, I gave my back to him. I felt strangely predatory. He cooed his appreciation of my freckles. First the small burn, then the big burn, as the hook followed the needle through a pinch of my back by my shoulder blade. One side, then the other. The piercing hurt less than a dragon-tail's snap. I was quiet and still for it, feeling my power rise up with each sting.

By the time I stood up, I was high as a kite on my own power and the endorphin rush. The physical ordeal I had expected had been a rather minor thing! The real ordeal had been the journey of changing myself into someone who would be here, doing this, in the first place.

Since I had already passed my own test by getting hooked, the rest of the experience was a bonus round. A friend tied a rope to my hooks, looping from one hook to the other. I paced out onto the floor with my loop of rope in my hands like a soft live snake. With careful amused curiosity, I gently pulled on the rope. I was rewarded with a quite pleasurable hot, stinging pain. I could actually feel my body adapting and flooding with pain killers, adrenaline, and other goodies. By tugging on the rope loop, I intentionally built up my endorphins and relaxed into the sensations. For perhaps 30 minutes, I just lightly danced to the drums as I pulled my own reins.

After a while I hooked myself to the support structure in the center of the hall, so that my rope was attached to a beam just above my head, and I was facing away from the frame. The dancers attached to the structure were all very intent and pulling powerfully on their hooks. I danced there with my hooks until I became joyful. I became deeply aware of the tethered arcs I could move in while attached, and I danced with them. Swinging, swaying, and experimenting with how much of my weight I could give to the hooks, I flew inward and outward at the same time.

When I could not feel any more pain, I unhooked from the structure. I flipped the loop up over my shoulders so it was in front of me again, and I danced with it, pulling it, tying my wrists with it. I barely felt the hooks now. Once I had weaved through the crowd to a space beside the drums, I stayed there the rest of the time as the drum beats made my bones thrum. I had lost all self-consciousness. Topless with my sarong slowly slipping down my hips, I stomped and danced with violent elation.

Sometimes I was awash in grief. My Master was not there to Witness me,

and I felt abandoned. I reached out to my Witness, who was my sister-slave, but she was closed to me. In this state I could feel that she was closed, and I grieved for it.

At one point I was more joyfully aware than I have ever been, profoundly aware that I am a mother. At another point I felt connected to the earth like I was solid, indestructible, made of the Earth's mantle. Mostly I was in a timeless joy, one with the drums. I danced for two and a half hours without ever stopping.

Around me, 200 other people were making their own ecstatic journeys. I could feel their energy; feel the supernova we made together. I could have gone on dancing to those living drums and unsheathed souls for hours more, but I had to get home to my children by 7 p.m. My Witness drew me out when it was time to go.

I had proved upon my body that all my silly little fears are just silly little fears; and danced my body the way my soul dances; and felt the joy of 200 friends in the same state of freedom. I would never be the same. I had proven my strength, to me, and I was proud.

Removing the hooks was painless and simple. I exited the dance hall floating and purposeful, acute as a predator. Changing clothes in the bathroom was surreal. Driving home was a shocking change of state – not a good idea. Snuggling the kids and putting them to bed, I collapsed at last.

It took the hook-punctures about three weeks to fully heal, and there were no complications. Psychological healing was a different matter.

I had instantly felt like a new person. I was someone who wanted to do THAT and followed through and did it. I was someone who had taken two hooks with serenity. I was someone who made her dreams happen. I was someone more fearless. I had done what the beautiful girl had done.

I had worn hooks. More importantly, I had gone to the hook-pull and sat down in that chair.

I felt wiser, stronger, calmer, and much more self-assured; but also like I was changing daily. I definitely felt that I was no longer a "newbie". My bullshit-tolerance (tact, patience, whatever) was critically low. My FetLife.com profile now seemed naive and silly, so I erased it. This upset my Master and sister-slave, who felt that I should keep up a public front that everything was always just dandy. Several huge arguments ensued about whether I owed my mates a false public face of normalcy. I did not feel willing to wear a mask for their social comfort after I had worked so hard to take it off. Once again, my people did not want to join me where I was real.

I settled peacefully into my new growth after maybe three roller-coaster months. My relationships survived the immediate aftermath, but eventually failed in part due to my new self-determination. Partly, they failed because of my new, wiser view of them.

For almost a year, my hooks sat in a little Tupperware dish on my desk, where I could see them. The current custom, or fad, or fashion, is to take your hooks and weld them together in the shape of a heart and make a pendant out of them. Several times I got them out to plan how to do this, but I would just end up putting them back on the shelf.

I finally realized that their Sharpness was central and inseparable to their meaning to me. Any alteration to blunt their points would be a wrongness. So, I strung them on a black bead necklace, hanging down with the sharp points pointed toward the center. They do form the shape of a heart as they hang there over my heart. They sometimes catch on my clothes as I move, and they are a hazard to huggers. If my hooks make me bleed again, it's okay.

The necklace is a talisman and a happy warning. When I am wearing my hooks, I am myself, I am unmasked.

Dancing the Dark Divine:
Ecstatic Masturbation
in the Worship of Lilith

By Galeogirl

I feel like I was born to identify with Lilith. I have always been sexually precocious, a born hedonist. I quietly defied my family's humiliations and harsh punishments – their attempts to quell my youthful masturbatory adventures – learning to cleverly hide my explorations from their disapproving eyes. When I would touch my body, I felt an ecstasy that lifted me up heart, mind, and soul. I could not believe that anything that would transport me so wholly to such an exalted state could be sinful or evil. I saw my secret pleasure as my right and my gift, no one was going to tarnish it or take it from me. I knew that they were wrong.

Lilith first made herself known to me by name when I was eight years old and my grandmother handed me our family's bible of femininity, Glorea Lavonne's *Guide to Beauty, Charm, and Poise.* I was left with instructions to read it from cover to cover and memorize its contents. Amidst the endless instructions on etiquette and dress, there was a section on feminine personality types. When I came to the description of the Voluptuous Type, with its restrained praise of Lilith's independence and seductive charm, I remember shivering with pleasure and excitement. Having not been raised in a Judeo-Christian household, I didn't then know who Lilith was, but I knew what I wanted to be when I grew up – a powerful, sexy woman.

My next encounter with Lilith was in my teen years, when I found one of the few occult books in my hometown library. While leafing through the practically unread tome, I found a painting of a silvery woman in a transparent shift drifting toward a sleeping man. Her expression reminded me of a cat about to toy with its prey, and then I saw the name "Lilith" in the caption I knew that I had to take the book home for further reading. By this time, while still a virgin, I had become a quite sophisticated practitioner of the solitary sexual arts and I spent hours in my room reading those few paragraphs about Lilith, staring at that painting while I ground my cunt against the heel of my foot and climaxed until I reached unprecedented levels of bliss.

Before that night, I had felt so trapped by the moral restraints of my small, religious community. I didn't fit in. I couldn't be a good girl by their definitions because even though I hadn't had sex with anyone else, I knew that I would like it. But now I felt free. I didn't have to fit their definitions; I could be something else, the human version of a succubus, feeding shamelessly off of my own abundant erotic energies.

Since those glorious weeks when I had my first real knowledge of who and what Lilith was – the succubus fully in her sexual power – Lilith became my idealization of my own budding eroticism, my antidote to a girlhood rife with messages of female inferiority and sexual repression. Meditating on Lilith raised my sensuality from profanity to divinity.

The call to worship can come to me at any time. I can be sitting at my desk at work, on the train, at a restaurant when I feel the first signs of my Goddess-ridden arousal bubbling beneath the surface. My heart beats a little faster. My belly feels heavy and tight. My breasts ache, nipples hardening. My cunt feels both too empty and too full, my g-spot and clit throbbing slowly at first, then with increasing insistence as the hunger grows. My skin gets exquisitely sensitive. My senses are flung wide open, everything is just a bit more vivid – smells, flavors, colors, textures. I want to fuck. I want to feed. It takes all of my self-control to stay outwardly calm and get through my day so that I can come home and ecstatically indulge in my adoration of the strong sexual female, the hungry succubus – Lilith.

Once I am alone, I follow my instincts instead of ritual. Lilith is earthy, a cum-as-you-are goddess. Tonight I stood before the mirror with candles flickering on my altar and stripped off my clothes, admiring my generous curves. I drank in the sweet, musky scent of myself, licking small tastes of salt off of my hands and arms. I gently stroked my soft skin. I swayed and undulated to soft, slow music, moving my hips in serpentine curves as my hands drifted down my body to my hard nipples, teasing myself with feather-light fingers. My swaying hips lured my fingers lower, down over my belly, down to the soft, silky fur that hides my slippery core. Touching. Caressing. Bringing my wet fingers to my face to taste and smell my sweet, luscious juices, smearing them over my lips. I danced for myself. I danced for the goddess within me. I danced my desire for lovers past and present, for lovers to be. I danced for my hungers and longings. I danced for every crush I've ever had.

Deep within my dance, my knees started to bend and I sank to the floor in front of my altar. I felt my surrender to Lilith coming over me. I transformed from personification of my goddess to her supplicant, my hands spread in welcome, my thighs parted, open, head thrown back in the early throes of the coming ecstasy. I reached out my hand, finding the small box of clips and clamps that sits nearby. Black, toothed, miniature hair clips, seven counted out into my palm. Six clips attached my inner labia to my outer labia, spreading my pussy open wide, teeth digging into my soft, wet cunt lips. Delicious pain. I stroked my erect clit as I ever so slowly eased the seventh clamp down over the shaft, savoring the sharp bite of small plastic teeth on engorged flesh.

Again my hand reached out to the larger toy box, pulling out my favorite, sparkly blue silicone cock. So wet, I straddled the dildo, easing myself down onto its length, filling my pussy with it. The pleasure of insistent pressure on my g-spot mingled with the pain of my clamped outer cunt brought me quickly to the edge of climax, my breath coming in short pants. I turned my mind to my sexual power, to my lovers, to my goddess; thoughts and energy coalesced on the waves of my breath, filling me with a warm sweetness that tasted like burned sugar melting on my tongue. Erotic energy given form within my mind, so clear and lovely; steeped in a vivid waking dream over which I have complete control, this is where I do my work. I heal and hope and pray. I cast blessings and benedictions for lovers and strangers and our aching world. I send my energy, born in love, born in lust, out to the universe. At some point far beyond the polite bounds of clock-kept time, I writhe, I cum, growling and moaning, hot juices streaming from deep within my body, flooding my thighs and the floor beneath me.

I am Lilith in this moment. I am hungry succubus. I am seductress. I am defiant, strong, sexual woman. I look in the mirror, my body still shaking with climax and I am myself and yet not myself. I am radiant with power. I am female eroticism made flesh. I look younger, softer, and somehow more feminine. The sexual vampire in her satiation. Tomorrow I will go out into the world to seed the dreams of others with sensuality unabashed and unashamed.

A Master's Love for His slave

By Master Malik

There are things in life which feel just right even in times of chaos and turmoil. There are presences in our lives which give us strength and resolve even when we do not realize. There are blessings that abound which keep us on course and straight even when we think that we are going astray. In multitudes of these uplifting and life-sustaining factors, there is one which always stands out when I analyze my journey and struggles.

It was seven years ago, when heaven sent me a gift without my realization at the time. A gift which has never lost its sparkle or newness. All I had done was kiss her hand and greet her. I close my eyes and I can live those moments with clarity, a smile writ across my face.

At that time, I promised myself never to fall in love again. I promised myself never to get too close to anybody. I promised myself to continue my journey, which was pretty much without any particular direction. I promised myself to live like a nomad of centuries past and reap the bounties of nature and life. So many promises.

And then, taken completely unexpected, I found myself saying the dreaded words of love and my heart felt a contentment and peace. I realized that I had always loved her. We talked about shibari and many other exotic-sounding names concerning bondage, and we had forgotten that the bondage of love is the strongest of all. The threads and rope and chains of this bondage are invisible and leave the deepest rope burn of any rope in the universe. And this burn feels so delicious. It leaves me with a bigger high than the highs of endorphin or adrenaline, than the myriad of other feel-good chemicals our brains produce.

But nobody can live on love alone. Life is tough and unforgiving. It demands real efforts, sacrifices, adjustments, compromises, and results. Life is never a straightforward road. It has its ups and downs, mountains and valleys, rivers and deserts, rain and sunshine, and so on and so forth. Heaven sent me the one who is by my side during all of this and more. Together we climb those mountains and valleys, trudge rivers and deserts alike, bear witness to the rain and sun, tethered together by the bonds of that simple word. Love.

I hold her in my arms and my world is complete. I look into her eyes and I drown in them and become alive. I caress her body and the vibrations and warmth she generates energize me. She is the keeper of my heart. She is the depository of my spirit. She is the caretaker of my soul.

She has given me her tears. She has sung the songs of her sobs. She has allowed me to feel her trembling. She has shared with me her darkest secrets and fears. She has seen into my shadows and not shirked away. She let me see her soul through her blood, the most precious in the universe.

Indeed she is my rock, my lover, my slave, my partner, my friend, my confidante and my life.

Managing Psychic Waste:
Transcendence through Humiliation

By Eve Minax

You say I hold the key and perhaps I do.
I hang people for a living.
Listening to their stories of respectability and convention.
I cleanse their darkest psyches and make them feel whole again.
I help them orgasm too.
I struggle to know what I already know
and die a little death every day.

Watch me take handfuls of red leaf lettuce, carrot scraps, coffee grounds, and other sundry waste I have recently discarded, and see how gingerly I place them into my submissive's mouth while gently cajoling, "chew" and "swallow." His eyes are wide open, bulging a bit, horrified and amazed at his ability to eat my garbage in an erotically-charged fashion. I feel myself gagging internally without stopping, even hesitating, as I cram in more and more remnants of last night's dinner, this morning's breakfast, and perhaps a well-placed treat or two.

My subject is suspended in midair, rocking gently back and forth as I thrust my pelvis into his groin. I push deeper, my hand on the throat before me, my hips between legs spread wide. His erection is enormous and I am not even touching his cock, not physically at least. Just as I feel the energy expanding well beyond the four walls, I begin vomiting on the body that was once a high-powered corporate lawyer. My subject explodes wildly: vomit, cum, sweat shooting through the air, cascading into a cavalcade of erotic ecstasy and primal bliss. For a moment, both of us are transported to the space of being and nothingness, at once together, and then no more. Afterwards, his glow is radiant and shiny, all the dark clouds peeled away. I am pleased then, knowing that the sensation will endure; even if he doesn't realize it, he feels it. That is why he came to see me in the first place. It's why I know he will return.

I am a Psychic Waste Manager. I help people reduce, reuse, and recycle the psychic waste that accumulates with our "modern condition." This is my calling. It is part of a spiritual quest that brought me to this path over ten years ago. I simply wanted to "do" what I do well in this world, to have it matter in a way that would make my life meaningful, and to help others along the way. I knew I would teach, but academia stifled my creativity and my libido (well, except masturbating between the stacks at the library). I never aspired to be a "Dominatrix" per se, but I knew from the dawn of my BDSM explorations that this calling was bigger, deeper, and more powerful than any mainstream view could represent it.

The stereotypical view of the Dominatrix – the carefree catsuit-clad vixen about to unleash her sadism on any victims, willing or not – is completely mythological, and it ignores the authentic pathos involved. The complexity, the aching, and the rawness of my work astounds me at times. It is simply beautiful to strip away the conditioned self, allowing the primal sexual self to be revealed, if only for a moment. Given the heavy psychic work involved for both practitioner and recipient, the result is nothing less than a stunning achievement. It requires an energetic exchange with another(s) to reveal the primal force, a universal force, not individuated. This is not a journey that can be conducted alone. Removing conditioning, social mores, and internalized voices of ancestors strips away a significant part of the self simultaneously, thus it is work best undertaken with assistance. Psychic Waste Management is what I do best, yet I am only a catalyst, a conduit for reconditioning, an outlet for repressed energy.

Focused intention is everything in the arts of healing and magic. You can strip away someone's ego, but if you do without clarity of vision, you could not only ruin a good scene, you could also defragment a soul. Every day in life our souls are battered. Each time we confront bosses, kids, partners, and strangers, we run the risk of losing bits of our selves. Worse still, we run the risk of forming too-solid ideas of what the self is, what our identity is. We risk thinking that we can actually explain away our desires and fears with logic and reason. The Psychic Waste Manager must peel away the extraneous layers of self to reveal a gleaming core, must tear down in order to rebuild.

Humiliation peels back the layers of civility. If you keep rubbing, keep digging, keep searching through the muck and grime of "what should be," you will find the rawness underneath. That rawness is where you find the goodness, the meat. It's all there, mixed in together in the shadow, in the dark places we aren't supposed to look. So perhaps I am a bit of an excavator also, a trash picker, if you will. I pick out the extraneous matter, the layers of conventionality and civility, and give you back your id.

This crucial work of excavation is not easily understood by society at large. Can you imagine trying to explain how shooting your wad into the air while eating a woman's garbage as she vomits on you is transcendent and worthy of discourse? Who would listen to this without judging you as a deviant (which surely you are), or fearing that you may sully their little world of comfort and respectability? Better yet, how do you explain what you do when this is what you do, every day of your life, whether it's with a client, a loved one, or an acquaintance who really needs a sexual psychic cleanse?

Psychic Waste Management encompasses a spectrum of psychological responses that help the Manager reuse what the recipient already has, clean it up, and return it to them renewed. It begins with embarrassment, progresses to humiliation, and reaches it crescendo with degradation. It can be physical or verbal and often both. It is subjective, contingent, and incredibly powerful, compelling. The act of being embarrassed flushes our face and consequently genitalia. It can be exciting and lead to turn on but is not necessarily humiliation in and of itself. Embarrassment occurs usually when bringing attention to something about the person – which is why objectification is so useful in embarrassment play. For example, if I wish to embarrass someone just enough to start the turn on I might say, "Ooh, look how tight your pants are" or if more familiar, "I bet you suck great cock." I'm simply making an observation, perhaps an assertion, but I am not excavating a deeper part of their sense of self or their identity.

Humiliation rips away what is superfluous in some ways, but is also necessary for survival in other ways (clothes are not necessary in temperate climate, but mandated by social mores). It generally requires tapping into the sense of self, utilizing observation to begin the process perhaps, but also bumping up against a deeper truth: "Oh, look at the way you suck my cock. You are a positively perfect cocksucker!" This example also bumps up against a more, a cultural appropriateness, a should or should not. Generally speaking, no one is supposed to be proud or pleased to be a good cocksucker. They're not even supposed to say the word! No matter what, humiliation, when done effectively, always gives back. It becomes a battery that fuels everyone charging it.

Degradation tramples something that an individual holds near and dear to their hearts, a core value, or something that the person is particularly proud of, especially if it feels intrinsic to their being. For example intelligence; saying, "you are stupid" to a person whose intellect is of high value could challenge their self-identity in a non-erotic way (this is where nuance and subtlety matter; it could also be really hot!). Conversely, if the person actually embodies, or at least feels as though they carry said traits negatively (eg. you are fat), then you could perpetuate low self-esteem. Degradation stomps on the worthiness of the subject. Saying, "You're the worst cock sucker I've ever met" to a person with an incredibly challenging gag reflex potentially supports their notions of lack of worth for not being able to perform oral sex well. Of course, if it's an amazing porn star with deep-throating capabilities, it may be a huge turn on to be critiqued on their cock sucking skills. No two acts of degradation can be identical because no two identities or sets of core values are constructed in identical manners.

Of course, I use embarrassment and even a little degradation from time to time, but humiliation is my main tool for psychic excavation. What looks like simple spitting, face slapping, whipping, or condemnation to most should be done with a certain understanding between the parties. It's an unspoken rule that it's not what you do, it's how you do it. If I slap your face repeatedly with pure contempt or indifference, I am not there with you; I am merely performing a function. If, however, I slap your face hard and repeatedly while staring directly in your eyes, periodically having you open your mouth for an opulent pearl of spit from my mouth and telling you all the things I'm going to do to you if you do not swallow (or if you do, depending on the person), together we can transform a rather dry pornographic act into a deeper more meaningful exchange.

I like to say that the sacred and profane are flip sides to the same coin, and they both shield the primal self. Working towards that self through either side of the coin gives me pleasure. I love making bottoms squirm – begging, fearful, and desperate. Scraping away all their gender codifications and turning them into the little sex kittens they crave to be turns me on to no end. Imagine now with me a large, hairy, masculine construction worker dressed in fishnet stockings, super high patent leather heels, ruffled crotchless panties, butt plug in his ass, 9" dildo between his heavily rouged lips, being beaten with a whip and told what an incredible slut he is. I love watching his gestures transform into the sultry slut he knows he is. As I stroke my cock telling him how he's gonna take it, and all my friends too, I relish the discarding of societal contempt. I hold this experience for both of us. I can transcend the marginalization and societal ignorance and he can transcend heteronormative socialization to become the best slut he can.

Cleaning up psychic waste post scene reduces the excess baggage that's not necessary for the recipient to flow more easily through life. It means less work for you, your recipient, and all the people they come into contact with later: it's the maintenance after the fact. If I have excavated your matter, flung it around, then given it back – regardless of how shiny your spirit is after – there will be a mess to clean up. People have come to me telling stories of being cut, urethrally dilated, and marked unwillingly in the hands of those who did not understand the delicacy of their work. Traumatized, the subjects often don't return for years, and the excavations can be challenging. Developing trust slowly and carefully can help manifest the scene. Physical follow-up and psychological follow-up are each valuable ways to clean up. Physical follow-up, like moderating their temperature, offering water, a hot shower, a hug, or all of the above, is basic. Psychological follow-up requires checking in on their psychic space – not hand-holding them through their every emotion (that's what a talk therapist is for), but making sure they feel cared for. No one readjusts with the same rhythm or cadence. Simply put, follow-up helps keep the scene clean. Note the word "clean," not "sterile." Nothing is sterile in this world, just ask a surgeon.

Having someone dress up like a dog, crawl around on all fours, and bark can be an embarrassment to some, humiliation to others, and downright degrading to the rest. That is why it's imperative to know your subject, listen to them carefully, keep those boundaries in mind while playing, and clean up your mess. Messes occur in lives, but we have the power, as Psychic Waste Management technicians, to leave the world that much more orderly after we do what needs to be done. And don't expect transcendence. Every time I excavate, whether the person be familiar or not, I leave the scene open to fall where it may. Ideally, some level of transcendence is reached – if only through laughter and catharsis – but to predict that transcendent state is almost like speculating on nirvana. We can never know for sure. The best we can be is present to the possibility. I would add, however, that being fully present and noting those little twitches, embarrassments, fluttering of eyelashes, can make a simple action into a magical space. It can illuminate and enlarge the world so much that everything and nothing has meaning anymore. The universal primal can take over and a microcosm becomes a macrocosm.

Honestly, I think that most clients do not even realize what happens to them when, nor do I think they should. That's my job. Must you know every tool and skill in how your recycle system works? I remember when I used to rent a workspace from a friend of mine. She would sometimes sit outside, waiting for my text to reenter. Oftentimes, she would know before the text came that the session was over because she would see a person departing from the space, glowing, grinning, and walking with much more pep in their step. She still marvels and tells people who will listen about the radiance of the clientele. The experience of having sexual psychic waste excavated, reduced, and recycled, given back all shiny and loved makes another person's trash this person's treasure.

Service Topping as a Spiritual Practice

By Lady Elsa

"Breathe," I whisper in her ear as she whimpers quietly, almost silently. "We're almost there. You can do this." Her breasts bristle with two dozen clothespins, and I know they are throbbing – and that it's not enough. I place my hand carefully on her breastbone, and press her back against the cross.

Smiling, I brush the damp wisps of hair away from her face. I see the flicker of doubt in her eyes. She fears that this may be the end, that I think she's gone far enough. She isn't sure she can trust me not to stop, not to take pity on her, not to be moved by her cries. Her eyes plead with me, a silent prayer I have prayed myself in her place. 'Please don't stop.'

"We're not stopping," I whisper to her. Her eyes widen with surprise that I heard her thoughts. "We won't stop until we get there." Staring deep into those eyes, my fingers find one of the clothespins and begin to twist it – slowly, the scraping of unpainted wood across skin a subtle counterpoint to the flashing blaze of the twisting pain. Her whimper turns into a full-throated woman's wail, pushing out the pain as she throws her head back, the adrenaline hits the blood, and she finds her voice. As the clip pops off in my hand, my own adrenaline builds with hers, my voice soars with hers, singing out, "Yes, push it out, here we go. That was 24. Count them down with me, here comes 23…"

Love and fear. That's all there is, in the end. Everything boils down to one or the other.

Love is God. God is the river that my bottoms and I navigate together, sometimes floating slow and lazy, but more often sailing breathless down the rapids, paddling like crazy. God is the journey down the river, and the boat we are riding in, and the water that envelops and drenches us both.

Fear is the Other. It is the obstacle, the barrier we move through, the rocks that batter and bruise us as we pass them on the way. Our fears are our signposts, our mile markers that help us measure who we are becoming along the way.

Tell me your concept of God, and I will tell you who you aspire to be. Tell me what frightens you, and I will tell you what prevents you from reaching that goal. Turn your love and your fear over to me for a while, and I will ride with you down your river. Together we'll avoid the rocks – or smash into them, hurt, and by doing so move past. Together we'll hammer at the barriers, making holes in them that let the water rush on through. For that short expanse, you won't be alone in the journey. I'll be with you. I am a service top.

My concept? God is *all of us.* So when I serve anyone, I serve God. (Jesus tried to tell us that, by the way.) And I, too, am God. Not in the largest sense of the word – an all-powerful being with a personality – but in the same way that a drop of water can call itself Water as legitimately as an ocean can.

The Old Testament God has always puzzled me. A jealous God. An angry God. A God that wants worship. A God who punishes and takes revenge. In people, all those things belie weakness and lack, so how could they be positive attributes in God? The God of my imaginings, the perfect God, needs nothing, cannot be harmed, cannot be offended, and because of that perfection, is constantly and completely available to "be" love. To shower everyone and everything with blessing after blessing, without expecting or demanding anything in return. To be endlessly and joyfully creative, always experimenting, always building, always growing. *That* God is the one to whom I willingly offer my life as a tool. Because serving that God enables me to be who I aspire to be.

Does my version of God really exist? I believe so. Does it *matter* if my God exists? Not really. The totem of my belief enables me to live my life in the way I consider "best." That said, however, I have as much evidence for it as anyone else does for theirs. I have my internal compass, which is being run by some greater force, and which leads me more directly and more frequently to opportunities to serve as time goes by. That's probably the strongest evidence there is.

Popular BDSM lore paints tops as hungry predator sadists who gleefully inflict pain on helpless bottoms for their own gratification. There are plenty of tops who genuinely feel that way – and God bless them, because there's certainly a demand for their services. That's not me, though. I could never relate to that image, probably because I didn't relate to that jealous Old Testament God who needed to be worshipped. It's just not my "home archetype." What does compel and seduce me about topping is *creativity*, which to me is very God-like. Topping provides an opportunity for creative leadership. It feels like making art to me, taking the raw materials of the situation, the tools, and the people, and creating an outcome that takes our breath away.

When I was first learning the physical arts involved in topping, I loved the creativity for its own sake. I just wanted to make the art. While it was God-like in the sense of God being a creative force, I didn't experience anything explicitly spiritual. It was more like a kid building a city with Legos. I'd pick my bottoms like a child would pick a toy to play with. Which one was an interesting canvas? Which one would give me a chance to try new things? Which one had good energy, or pretty curves, or an infectious laugh? The other half of it – the spiritual service part – didn't come into my life until later.

The "service" aspect crept up on me slowly, popping suggestions into my head, tossing unlikely people into my path that needed my skills. The more I listened to those suggestions, the faster they began coming, and louder I began hearing them. As I obeyed those directives, I was led into experiences that I had no frame of reference for, but that gave me opportunities to use my topping skills to be of real benefit to people. Combining the creativity of topping with the spiritual high of serving God? I was hooked.

Here's how it works. I show up, and try not to have any expectations. Sometimes I don't get any instructions, and I go about my own business of having fun. But more often than not anymore, I get "the nudge," if I'm looking for it. Sometimes it's someone asking me directly to scene with them. Sometimes it's to sit in a certain place and wait, or just to be present. It's not even always kink-related. Sometimes it's just about being Person Elsa, rather than Lady Elsa.

"Speed Tricking" was the workshop, and everyone, it seemed, was there to hook up. Kris and I were there to find a bottom to play with — a yummy, pain-slutty bottom boi we could share. I'm very specific in my tastes, when left to my own desires: I like butches. Butch tops, butch bottoms, butch switches... anything else is just not as tasty.

There weren't many bois to begin with in the workshop, and luck of the draw said that we probably wouldn't get a chance to talk to any of them. Five minute session after session, I chatted perfunctorily with one femme bottom after another. I began to get frustrated, and to wonder if it was even worth staying. Nobody was matching up with what I was hungry for.

Then I felt it. The poke in the ribs that reminded me that I'm in service. The gentle reproach that maybe this particular day is not ABOUT me. That maybe it's about being present for the people I'm supposed to be serving. And that those people can come in any type of packaging. So I took a deep breath and let it out, said "Yes," and waited for him or her to appear. It didn't take long. It was actually Kris who found her and pointed her out to me. A middle-aged femme, naturally shy, but hunger was making her bold, like a deer in winter. Lovely wide open dark eyes that radiated kindness. "We can do her some good," he said, and I knew he was right.

I have always felt a strong pull toward service. Being a "good deed doer" gives me the opportunity to demonstrate my highest self, which for me is the ultimate form of spiritual practice. At first, though, I wasn't sure how spiritual service was supposed to play itself out in my kink life.

My first significant BDSM relationship was with someone who self-identified as a master, with whom I shared some common values and spiritual beliefs. It was primarily a romantic relationship of equals, and I bristled at traditional definitions like "slave" or "submissive." Yet I often felt strongly called to be of service to him, in my own rather dominant way. It didn't feel like ownership to me. It felt like I was being "loaned out" to him, for a limited period of time,

by my *real* owner, whom I eventually identified as God. And in time, that loan period did expire, and the relationship ended, and I was left to figure out what it all meant, to be owned by God.

Owned by God? That sounded crazy, and grandiose, and just plain odd. Especially when nobody else around me had any idea what I meant by that. But over time, I began to encounter people who identified as masters, dominants, and tops but saw themselves primarily as servants to their deities. What a relief that was, to hear it articulated by others! Most of their deities are nothing like mine, but that's beside the point. The call we feel to serve is not for an earthly master, but for God as we understand him or her.

One of the recent lessons I've been given is that my call to serve as a top is not just about being of service to random people who come into my life. I'm also called to be a responsible keeper of others. In other words, I'm called not only to be a service top, but also a service dominant.

Dominance, like topping, is not usually about my own preferences. When I'm doing it right (that is, in alignment with who I want to be), "being the dom" often feels more like serving as a teacher, preacher, or wilderness guide. I may be in charge of the situation, but only in order to execute God's agenda: more love, less fear. (Oh, don't get me wrong; I enjoy having my shoulders massaged and luggage carried as much as anyone. The little perks of dominance are wonderful. *But they're not what it's ultimately about.*)

About a year ago, I was given the most awesome gift – my very own butch boi. I've wanted my own boi for so long, and waited patiently for years, putting it constantly out there in every prayer… and then suddenly, he was here, and was everything I had asked for and more. Each time we meet, he kneels and greets me with "I'm at your service, M'Lady." The sound of that always makes me smile. His service to me is a gift from God, a reward for services rendered, and a reminder of what's expected in the future.

At my service. I wonder if what God feels when I offer my service is anything like what I feel when I hear those words. Energized and excited at the possibilities. Full of love and eager to shower every blessing on him. I'm grateful that I've been given that tiny glimpse of God's experience — or that God is perhaps experiencing it along with me, through me. Most of all, it makes me want to renew my own commitment to serve.

Boi Kris is also a gift in another way. He's a switch, in nearly every sense of the word. He can top; he can bottom. He can dominate; he can submit. His chameleon-like ability to adapt is in itself an amazing service, challenging and expanding my understanding of the roles we play, for one another and for others. When I'm weary and need a break, he steps up and takes over as the leader for a while so I can rest. Leading… following… it's all service to him, and all part of his service to me.

And I think that's the most important lesson I've learned so far. That ultimately it's not about working at being a service top… or a service bottom… or a service *anything*. It's about *being of service*. The roles don't matter to God. They're as incidental to him as whether our children play hopscotch or tag on a sunny day is to us. They're all part of the fabric of All That Is. We all serve someone or something, either directly or through another person's guidance. We all have that small voice, that nudge, which points us in the right direction, toward more love and less fear. It's all made out of God, and it is all service.

The last hard stroke of the rubber flogger broke the dam inside him. I sat on the floor and held him as he sobbed great huge tears, all the pent-up sadness in him carried away in the rushing flood. 'Which was the real me?' I mused as we rocked back and forth together on the floor. 'The precise, dispassionate torturer who left the purple slashes across his back, or the gentle mother who holds him now? And which was the real him — the angry beast hurling invectives at me and struggling with his bonds a few minutes earlier, or the small child rocking and healing in my arms?' Maybe both, and maybe neither. It doesn't matter. In serving him, I served myself. In taking what I had to give, he found his release. Who's to say what aspects of God we embody when we do this work? It's enough that we leave the scene knowing that we have moved in the right direction, a little or a lot, toward love and away from fear.

Dancing Into Darkness, Dancing Into Light

By Lee Harrington

The whispered voice has slowed its insistency. The voice that whispered *let the tales be told* seems to be happy for now, or at least it is no longer ravenous.

Thirty-three tales. Thirty-three journeys of men, women, and genderqueer explorers. Some have just begun their long, slow, ascent to the mountain top, while others have been doing this for over 40 years… but both still have so much to share.

These are slices of life, of love, of passion, of faith. These are but one dance, of a lifetime of dances.

But I can hear it again in the darkness. *Let the tales be told.* I can hear it again in the light. *Let the tales be told.* That voice who resides in the heart of the earth, whose heartbeat cries out for our power to shine, who knows our greatness… it will not sleep. Because this is only one collection. Because these are only thirty-three dances.

So I pass the voice on to you. I pass on the call, *let the tales be told.* I pass it on to you, dear reader, because it is your turn to dance. I cannot tell you whether yours will be a long slow climb, or a revelation that rocks your world wrapped in tears or laughter. Perhaps you have already tasted God on your tongue as it caressed along a lover's flesh, or you have seen in the silence of your bondage scene your own mortality reflected back. I do not know whether you have been here before, or whether this has been your first glimpse into your own possibility.

No two dances are the same. Your tale will not be the same tale as told in these pages. And yet, oh and yet. And yet the tales will be told. Your tales, my tales, the tales of the world. Because we are the keepers of the dreams, we are the weavers of the tapestry. We are Star Goddesses birthing the world every time we cum. We are Sons of God bearing the pain of the world on our shoulders so that others might be washed of sin. We are howling monsters in the night who know the beauty in destruction. We are beings of love who shine out, in our examples, for all the world to be inspired to greatness.

Sacred Kink is everywhere. Spirit is everywhere. Desire is everywhere. And here, in the Spirit of Desire, I call to you. I call out this prayer. Live your life fully. Live it from a place of authenticity, whatever your authenticity it is. And then, when you have danced, even if you choose to only whisper it into the shadows, whisper it into the light... *Let the tales be told.*

Acknowledgements

This project would not have been possible without the amazing support and hard work of a large number of individuals. An anthology is, by its definition, a collaborative effort, but this piece, touching on such deep and profoundly personal topics, is truly a group effort of the heart.

To my authors: you have blown me away. Working through hospitalizations, family crises, and challenges of faith, you have reminded me that the work is worth it. Whether you made my week by getting contracts in far before deadline, or were willing to talk out differences of literary opinion over phone calls, or had the courage to ask former lovers for permission to list their names, or simply had the gumption to lay it all out for the world to see, thank you. Thank you for your courage, your dedication, and your vision.

Thank you to the authors, who could not, for whatever reason, be part of this project. Many more folks submitted than were chosen, and in a few cases, chosen authors had to back out. Your willingness to bare your souls to me and open up about why your tales needed to stay out of print once they had been penned reminded me of my own quest for personal authenticity and the balance of what is right for public viewing, and what should never be touched by the neon light of analysis.

To my editors: wow! Rob Z at SmutCraft.com yet again came through with beautiful interior and exterior layout work, while JoSelle Vanderhooft (joselle-vanderhooft.com) stepped in as copyeditor and provided insight and a detail-oriented eye that was invaluable. Brent Dill, my comrade in arms for writing and more, and Aiden Fyre, my Boy of much brilliance and delight, who both listened to me vent out options, read favorite passages, decide on orders of appearance, and provided a lot of sanity and stability.

Circle23.com: yet again your photography has done its job of invoking energy and emotion into the work I do. Freya (FunWithFreya.com) and J were delightful models to work with, and the rope, provided by TwistedMonk.com, was perfect for binding two people together for the work... evocative of a few of the stories shared in this collection. It was fantastic to rig you both, and to have Circle23 capture the moment.

To all my readers, fans, friends, and students who pushed me on: thank you. Your love notes over Twitter, your excitement about this anthology on FetLife.com and Facebook, your hugs in the flesh helped keep me enthusiastic on the days I thought the project would never be done. Would never see the light of day. Well, here it is, bringing the richness of shadow into the light and the glimmer of light into the shadow. The sex into the spirit, the spirit into the sex.

And finally, thank you to my own Patron, Mama Bear, in whose name I do this holy work of bringing stories and ideas into the minds of others. Thank you to the deities, spirits, and aspects of the divine that charged the work of so many of the authors in these pages. Thank you for the spark of God within those who inspired our writings, to the fallen spiritual and sexual warriors who came before without whose sacrifices this work could not have been possible. Thank you all, every one, thank you.

Biographies

Alex M. Quinlan

Alex M. Quinlan lives on the East Coast of the United States with as many spouses, pets, and children as are consenting at any given time. They all spend too much time on the internet, but not necessarily the World Wide Web. Alex has used a variant of this for years of sex-writing, deliberately avoiding any mention of gender – just for the mischief of it. Today, however, she'll add that she's been poly since age 10; she's still with the man she married in 1988, and had two children with; Coyote, Eris, and Murphy will likely continue to 'help' her as they have for longer than she cares to think about; she's dismayed she called herself het in front of her girlfriend; she hopes that she continues to enjoy all the myriad types of kink – especially new ones! – as she continues past 'middle age'; and that she intends to never, ever, grow up.

Alexandra Entendre

Born into an Armenian family with strict, ethnic, conservative values, most of Alexandra's summers were spent in the village in Lebanon that her parents grew up in. By the age of 13, Alexandra came to the realization that she was transgendered, and over the next six years struggled with self-acceptance and the decision to begin transitioning. She graduated college during her nineteenth year with a double major in mathematics and economics. Now twenty, Alexandra forges her way through the unknown, championing one calamity after another as she passes through life.

C.A. Sizemore

C.A. Sizemore tries to write fiction daily and read as much as he can. He lives with his wife and her other husband, two dogs, and two turtles and a tortoise. When not riding his motorcycle or out on a date with his girlfriend, he helps his partners run the *Kinky and Geeky in Arizona* group on FetLife.com, and plans the semi-quarterly parties. C.A. Sizemore can be found on Twitter, Facebook and FetLife as CASizemore.

Cléo Dubois

Cléo Dubois is a BDSM Educator, ritualist, and creator of the Academy of S/M Arts. A versatile sadomasochist, she came out in the San Francisco Leather Scene in the early '80s. She made two educational docu-films, *The Pain Game* and *Tie Me Up*, and continues to present at local and national leather events. She is proud to offer with Eve Minax and Selina Raven Erotic Dominance Weekend Intensives, now in their 10th year. A couple's course has been added to the intimate weekend Intensives they offer.

Cléo has been published in many anthologies, starting with *Different Loving*, by Brame and Jacobs in 1993. She wrote a monthly column on alt.com for 3 years and a yearlong series, *Cleo in her own Words*, on Ms. Gloria Brame's blog. For video clips, interviews, information on initiations, private coaching for couples and newcomers to the scene and Intensives, please visit www.sm-arts.com.

Crystal Gem

Crystal Gem, a visual artist, has recently discovered a new palette in the written word. A steady stream of erotic poetry became unleashed after she was introduced to the wonderful world of kink. She continues to paint and a collection of her poetry entitled *Something Fierce* is available at Lulu.com

D. Christopher Dryer

Christopher serves his communities as a researcher and educator, studying intentional ordeals, spiritual intelligence, queer theory, and research methods. Currently at the California Institute of Integral Studies, he also has been a faculty member and department chair at the Institute of Transpersonal Psychology. He has published his research in journals and conferences such as the *Journal of Personality & Social Psychology*, the American Psychological Association, the European Transpersonal Association, and Pantheacon. He created the Ordeal Pathwalkers Forum and is a Member of the Divine Rhythm Society.

Domme Jaguar (Mexico)

Domme Jaguar has been an explorer for a long time, in art, sex, politics, and spirituality; bisexuality, swinger, polyamory, Universal Tao, Tantra, Kundalini... She is a certified sex educator, dancer, and professional media maker. After some years as a lifestyler in Mexico City she went Professional in 2007. At the beginning, it was just playing, and she somehow just wanted to be a sensual, glamorous, and caring Mistress, to deny the "mainstream" views about what a Dominatrix is. But now, having embraced Her Top Totem, The Black Jaguar, she is On a Journey Between Darkness and Light. Today Domme Jaguar accepts this Power as a Blessing, understanding that her job is to safely take other people beyond their frontiers, their taboo, their fears, and the roles they are required to play, into a journey of Erotic Alchemy where shame, pain and cruelty are transmuted into pride, pleasure, and enlightenment. Her Calling is to be one of the very few who can do this in the well-known "macho" land that Mexico is. To know more about Domme Jaguar and her work please visit www.dommejaguar.com.

Eve Minax

Renowned kink presenter and pleasure artist Eve Minax (www.mistressminax.com) delights in proliferating carnal knowledge with a spiritual edge. She is a lifestyle and professional Domina, Clown, and Psychic who also acts as the Lead Staff Instructor for the Cléo Dubois Academy of SM Arts (www.sm-arts.com). Minax presents at numerous BDSM, Kink, Queer, Spiritual, and general lay events, organizations, and private parties around the globe.

She is the former coordinator for CineKink:Chicago, and the West Coast Coordinator for the Leather Archives and Museum, LA&M, Roadshow. She writes a regular column for Carnal Nation called *Welcome to My Parlor*, works often with www.SeriousBondage.com, and has been pioneering a new genre of pairing kinky sex scenes with cuisine: Sexcipies. Minax maintains a loving and extended leather family throughout the world.

Galeogirl

Award-winning Destructo-Bot Galeogirl has been sent to Earth to prepare the planet for the coming invasion of the Rat People, or as they will soon be referred to, The Mighty Rat Lords. Her skills include telepathy, pyrokinesis, horseback riding, dance, and the ability to make sharp stabbing weapons from most of her body parts. In addition to sharing the words of The Mighty Rat Lords, she also enjoys crocheting, watching movies, plotting the downfall of every major government on Earth, and vegetarian cooking. To help her in her preparations, she recruits creatures from all across the animal kingdom, although primarily those with more than two eyes, "So they can see the infidels," she says. With lightning-fast reflexes and venom the toxicity of which has never actually been lab tested, all of her projects tend to succeed. "It's all about luck, perseverance, and attrition," she says. "Especially attrition."

Jaki Grier

Jaki is a genderfluid Black American Leather feminist with a passion for alternative sexuality and getting off. Jaki has begun a one-person campaign to promote "yo" as a gender neutral option because it is fun and original. Yo has always been interested in writing for the underdogs. This passion has led to minority studies in many flavors which ultimately lead to the BDSM/Leather Community. Through Leather, yo discovered the connections between sex and soul which have become a large part of Jaki's personal spiritual path.

Jaki has several relationships, central being with the guardian Orisha Oya. With a supportive husband Shawn, and a submissive puppy Momo, yo has a safe space to continue to grow in the ways of sacred kink. Jaki is a volunteer for the Carter Johnson Library (www.leatherlibrary.org) and The Next Generation, Baltimore (www.tngbaltimore.com). On rare occasions, Jaki has been known to sleep.

Joshua Tenpenny
Joshua is Raven's Boy, a wholly owned subsidiary of the vast enterprise that is Raven Kaldera. He is a professional massage therapist, Shiatsu practitioner, and yoga teacher. He is polymorphously perverse, and finds spiritual fulfillment through any kind of worthy service.

Kaye Buckley
Kaye Buckley entered the SM Community as part of a triad in 1975. Together they created the first women's San Francisco SM support group, *Cardea*. Pro-player, belly dancer, and performance artist, her explorations took her to Japan where she lived and worked for two and a half years and met her Matron Saint, *Benzaiten*, Goddess of love, art, prosperity, and sex workers. Returning to SF, she created four play spaces, two of which were based on a Japanese theme. Due to an Ellis Act eviction, she lost her live/work space of 23 years, and has relocated to the East Bay where she contemplates whether creating another private and pro-play space would be wisdom or folly. She currently does sado-erotic phone counseling, educating and guiding others on their journeys. In transition, she continues to write, considers learning hypnosis at HCH, and drums for ritual events. For more info, please visit her website at: www.sacredflames69.com.

Kyndyl
Kyndyl lives in the Northeastern United States. Currently exploring the lifestyle and pagan communities in their new location, he has degrees in religious studies and psychology.

Lady Elsa
Lady Elsa is a poly femme leatherdyke with a passion for making heart and spirit connections via BDSM. She is very active in the Indianapolis area

community, where she co-founded and leads Andromeda, a kink group for women and transfolk, and has held various offices in National Leather Association Indianapolis.

Lady Elsa's primary spiritual influence has been Neale Donald Walsch, author of *Conversations with God: An Uncommon Dialogue*. In her 10+ years of participating in a study group for Walsch's books, she has transitioned from a liberal mainline Protestant to an avid devotee of New Thought spirituality. She aspires to become a positive force in bringing love-based spirituality to the BDSM community, and to help others integrate their sexuality and kink with their spiritual callings.

Lady Jazelle

Lady Jazelle (aka heather) has been an active member of the lifestyle for over a decade. her passion can be seen through the grace, loyalty, protocol positions and service of many forms that she provides. she has presented for such educational sexuality gatherings as Beat Me In St. Louis, Spanksgiving, Eros Bound, and for various BDSM clubs. Through her experiences, heather passionately shares the world of power exchange and relationship dynamics with others.

layla tromble

layla tromble is a writer of fiction, non-fiction, and poetry. She is a strong, opinionated, outspoken, queer, submissive who is proudly owned by her Lady. Her spiritual path has been a winding one and has arrived at an eclectic mix of the physical, natural, and supernatural. She believes firmly that the closest we humans get to touching the divine within ourselves is at the moments of true vulnerability with another person. She is passionate about sex-positivity, kink, polyamory, and revolutionary kissing. She resides in the Pacific Northwest with her large and varied chosen family and is working on her first novel.

Lee Harrington

Lee Harrington is a passionate spiritual and erotic educator, gender radical, eclectic artist, and published author and editor on human sexuality and spiritual experience. He is a nice guy with a disarmingly down to earth approach to the fact that we are each beautifully complex ecosystems, and we deserve to examine the human experience from that lens. Lee has been traveling the globe (from Seattle to Sydney, Berlin to Boston), teaching and talking about sexuality, psychology, faith, desire, and more since 1995, and has no intention to stop any time soon. Along the way he has been a brainy academic, a female adult film performer, a world class sexual explorer, an outspoken philosopher, and an award-winning author and artist. Check out the trouble he has been getting into, as well as his many books, audio classes, videos, and more over at www.PassionAndSoul.com.

Margo Eve

Margo Eve is a passionate lifestyle kink and energetic explorer, long term sexuality geek, and holds multiple degrees in Communication... but prefers to put them down and do other things on occasion. When not engrossed in gender and sexuality debates, unraveling the nature of human experience (social, psychological, spiritual, and otherwise), adventuring with her partner/ husband, or reading a good book, she is either dancing (with or without fire), experimenting with makeup, or thinking up something devious to do to others. Margo has also been known to give out hugs on a regular basis.

Master Dennis

Master Dennis has been a member of APEX (Arizona Power Exchange) since 1997, of MAsT AZ, and been a part of the Butchmann's Experience for many years. He founded the 'Dom Roundtable' at APEX in 1998. A contributing writer to Leather and Roses as "Dragon~Lord" (www.leathernroses.com), Master Dennis has been a speaker/presenter of lifestyle topics from the basics to the extremes for such organizations as APEX, AZ-TNG (Phoenix), SHIBARI (Las Vegas), Desert Dominion (Tucson), Rio Grande Leather (New Mexico), GLLA (Indianapolis), SDL (San Diego), and Leather Spirit, Lair and Threshold in Los Angeles. In addition he has also presented at the 2005 and 2006 AZ Fetish Balls Phoenix, and the Tucson Fetish Ball in 2004. He has also served as a requested guest lecturer helping to demystify the BDSM lifestyle at various colleges for their sociology and psychology classes over the past

9 years, and has been a judge or head judge for many M/s or leather events across the country. He is the proud Master to Mistress Bonnie, Slave Kia, and Slave Tiffany.

Master Malik

As a student of life, Leather and BDSM, Master Malik is always eager to share his views, thoughts, and ideas with any willing people who give him some of their time to listen. He has been part of organized BDSM/Leather lifestyle since early part of 1999 when he joined Tulsa Dungeon Society in Tulsa, OK.

Significant similarities between Leather and Sufism have helped Master Malik to continue his journey on the path of mastery and slavery with his precious slave Cathy. This is not a lifestyle for them anymore but life itself. Master Malik is an avid practitioner of old fashion SM and strongly believes in a powerful connection between SM and spiritual realm. He also believes with passion about "Acceptance," "Tolerance," and "Diversity" of our larger tribe.

Master Malik is proud to serve as Southwest Master 2008. He is also co-owner of Xpressions, and Alternative Lifestyle Food Pantry in Tulsa, OK.

Michelle Belanger

Michelle Belanger is an author, lecturer, and television personality who is also openly bisexual, kinky, and intersexed. She is best known for her work within the modern vampire community. Her 2004 book, *The Psychic Energy Codex*, pioneered the concept of psychic vampires as people, not predators. The founder of the magickal society House Kheperu (www.Kheperu.org), she also works on A&E's *Paranormal State*. For more information visit www.michellebelanger.com.

Mollena Williams

Mollena (Mo) Williams, "Delicate, Trembling Flower of Submission" ©, is a NYC-born and raised writer, actress, BDSM Educator, fat fetish model, and Executive Pervert. She is extremely honored, humbled, and proud to be

International Ms. Leather 2010. She is also thrilled to have been named Ms. San Francisco Leather 2009 after that contest's decade-long slumber. Active in the Leather and BDSM communities since 1996, she speaks at Leather events across the U.S., Europe, and Canada on many BDSM, Leather and kinkcentric topics. A founding member of Crowded Fire Theater Company (www.crowdedfire.org), she blogs on The Perverted Negress: www.mollena. com. Mo is also author of the *The Toybag Guide: Taboo Play* and of the essay *BDSM and Playing with Race* which appears in the *Best Sex Writing 2010*.

Nanodot

Nanodot is a scientific shell over a being of passionate love. After a 15-year vanilla marriage, Nanodot sought out the kink community to feed her need for acceptance, growth, and violent sex. A masochistic pain-slut and slave-heart, Nanodot serves her local community by maintaining a public calendar of a wide variety of kink events.

Otterdancing

Otterdancing is a polyamorous bisexual witch. She has lived the poly lifestyle for 16 years, has embraced her bisexuality for 18 and began practicing pagan spirituality two decades ago. A priestess in her home community, Otterdancing is also on staff with three different mystery school/festival events where she is most often called upon to perform ritual, lead workshops, or offer rites of passage ceremonies. Introduced to kink two years ago within a sacred spirituality context, she has found it to be cathartic and transformative. Otterdancing is also a 49-year-old married high school teacher with four kids, proving that the universe has a lot of space for a sense of humor and joy.

P. Sufenas Virius Lupus

P. Sufenas Virius Lupus is a founding member of the Ekklesía Antínoou (a queer, Graeco-Roman-Egyptian syncretist reconstructionist polytheist religious group dedicated to Antinous, the deified lover of the Roman Emperor Hadrian and other related gods and divine figures), a contributing member of Neos Alexandria, and a Celtic Reconstructionist pagan. You can find Lupus' work published in the *Bibliotheca Alexandrina* volumes dedicated to Hekate, Isis, Serapis, and Artemis, with upcoming writings and poems in the devotionals to Zeus, Pan, and the Dioskouroi. Lupus has published a book of poems, *The Phillupic Hymns* (2008), and also has poems printed in the Scarlet Imprint anthology *Datura: An Anthology of Esoteric Poesis* (2010). You can find Lupus' blog, Aedicula Antinoi, at http://aediculaantinoi.wordpress.com/.

Raven Kaldera

Raven Kaldera is a queer FTM transgendered intersexual shaman. He is the author of too many books to list here, including *Dark Moon Rising: Pagan BDSM and the Ordeal Path* and *Dear Raven and Joshua: Questions and Answers About Master/Slave Relationships*. He and his slaveboy Joshua have been teaching and presenting workshops regularly for 6 years, bringing BDSM to the Neo-Pagan, Sex/Spirituality, transgender, and other communities. His hub website is www.ravenkaldera.org, and his spiritual BDSM website is www.paganbdsm.org. 'Tis an ill wind that blows no minds.

Sassafras Lowrey

Sassafras Lowrey is an international award-winning author, artist, and storyteller. Ze is a genderqueer-identified high femme Daddy's boy with a complicated gender history. Sassafras is the editor of the *Kicked Out* anthology which brought together the voices of current and former homeless LGBTQ youth, and hir stories have been published in numerous anthologies. Ze teaches storytelling workshops at colleges, conferences, and community centers across the country. To learn more about Sassafras and her work, visit www.PoMoFreakshow.com.

Scratch Hunter

Scratch Hunter is a Utah native, and while that doesn't make him a Ute by blood or birthright, he's still proud to be a "Ute," graduated from the University of Utah with a bachelor's degree in Film Studies. Scratch is fascinated by the human condition, its narratives, and the archetypes that each of us explore (whether you admit it or not). He is a producer, writer, and provocateur slinging rhetorical arrows at anything that moves – so watch your tail. *Prrr* =^_^ ~

Shuphrique

Shuphrique is a long-time perv femme who loves to scare subs with needles. A natural female, she is a fan of all kinds of extreme play and a big believer in laughter in scene play. Product of the anti-femme years of women's lib, she adores being a girl, especially when it involves the wearing of corsets and heels. She loves to make long-haired men and short-haired bois cry.

Sybil Holiday

Sybil Holiday, co-author with William A. Henkin, Ph. D. of *Consensual Sadomasochism: How To Talk About & Do It Safely*, has been active in San Francisco's Leather Communities since 1980, and in 1984 was a founding member of The Outcasts, San Francisco's second woman-to woman educational and social organization. She has presented on the physical, psychological, and spiritual aspects of BDSM at organizations, conferences, and universities nationwide, and on radio and television. Sybil – as M. Cybelle – was a professional domina specializing in energy-based SM, Tantric surrender and service, and age and gender explorations from 1983 to 2005.

Sybil holds certifications in clinical hypnotherapy, sex education, and energy work, and is an ordained and initiated priestess/spiritual counselor. Since 1997, the majority of her clients have seen her regarding BDSM & relationship education/counseling, archetypes, personas, the inner family, phobias, energy work, and spirituality. Sybil maintains her private practice in San Francisco. For more, please visit www.sybilholiday.com.

Taylor Ellwood

Taylor Ellwood is the co-author of *Kink Magic* and solo author of other books on magic such as *Inner Alchemy* and *Space/Time Magic*. Taylor is currently working on *Inner Alchemy 2*. When he isn't working on his new book, Taylor is experimenting with magic and kink. For more information, please visit www.magicalexperiments.com.

Xochiquetzal Duti

Xochiquetzal Duti (or Astrid or Chuck or Lina or whatever you want to call her) plies her trade in Southern California, although a move up north is in her near future. She lists herself by the following qualities: bi-poly-pagan-kinky-geek-biofemale-genderqueer. She tries not to say that too fast for others to catch. As a pagan, she trained and priestessed in the Treebridge tradition, an eclectic, syncretic, smorgasboard of spirituality and protective magic practitioners. She brought in the pre-Colombian branch of the tradition when they rode in on her during her dedication. As a kinky person, she identifies as a Service Switch: whether top, bottom, or outside both of these purviews, she serves. Her working name identifies her as belonging to her psychopomp mother and her Tantric initiate name which means, She Who is Ambassador. Yes, she is in on the joke. Priestess of Xochiquetzal, Odin, The Morrigan, and Kali, she knows what it means to hurt and grovel and beg for more.